ESSAYS ON PREMILLENNIALISM

A Modern Affirmation of an Ancient Doctrine

Essays on Premillennialism

K. Neill Foster
David E. Fessenden

Editors

CHRISTIAN PUBLICATIONS, INC.
CAMP HILL, PENNSYLVANIA

CHRISTIAN PUBLICATIONS, INC.
3825 Hartzdale Drive, Camp Hill, PA 17011
www.christianpublications.com

Faithful, biblical publishing since 1883

Essays on Premillennialism
ISBN: 0-87509-964-5
© 2002 by Christian Publications, Inc.
All rights reserved
Printed in the United States of America

02   03   04   05   06   5   4   3   2   1

Contents

Editors' Preface

The unprecedented popularity of the Left Behind series of novels has brought the issues of eschatology and the return of Christ to the forefront of popular thinking. Many in the pew and the pulpit are asking if these novels are an accurate portrayal of biblical prophecy or a tragic misunderstanding of the teachings of Scripture. Ironically, some today are coming to the latter conclusion. These novels have come on the scene at a time when premillennialism, the theological position upon which the Left Behind series is based, is under attack.

Some of the questions we find ourselves asking involve the historical roots of this doctrine. Is premillennialism merely a recent and unprecedented innovation, as some amillennialists claim, or are its roots deeper in church history than is commonly supposed? What led to its more recent rise to prominence?

We are concerned about how the premillennial position influences our belief and practice today. Does the rejection of the premillennial view necessarily lead to the erosion of other traditionally evangelical doctrines?

One issue of current praxis which appears to be affected by one's eschatological paradigm is the question of whether evangelism should take priority over social ethics. Amillennialists and postmillennialists tend to approach social work with much the same fervor that premillennialists approach evangelism, and for much the same reason: they believe they are ushering in the millennial kingdom. Are postmillennialists neglecting the Great Commission in a misguided attempt to bring the kingdom of heaven to earth? Are premillennialists neglecting the responsibility to show love to their neighbor by their strong missionary focus? Michael Tymchak has pointed out admirably that we may have created a false dichotomy.[1] The Great Commission tells us not merely to evangelize, but to "make disciples"—people who will live out *all* that Christ has commanded, including "a cup of water in Jesus' name."

And finally, our re-examination of premillennialism naturally leads to questions about the days to come. What is the believer's role in the such events as the Rapture, the Tribulation and the Millennium? How does belief in these events impact such things as our focus on world missions?

This collection of essays seeks to answer these and other inquiries surrounding this important doctrine (note the Historical/Current/Future division in the table of contents). These authors seek to establish premillennialism's venerable historical foundations, its current viability and its hope for the future. In the process, they address the implications of the amillennial and postmillennial positions. For example, premillennialists have historically been, and currently are, leaders in worldwide evangelism; does the rejection of this belief lead to a flagging of missionary passion?

It must be admitted that there is one kind of premillennialism that militates somewhat against the missionary mandate. Dispensational premillennialism, which is traced back to Darbyism in the current era, suggests that Israel will finish the missionary mandate during the tribulation days. That dispensational view, while generally missionary in perspective, tends to erode missionary passion in one respect: it says someone else will finish the task. Strict dispensationalists, in contrast to historic premillennialists, have also shown a tendency toward vigorous argument over the interpretation of prophetic details, which can further distract from the priority of worldwide evangelism.

These essays, for the most part—though not all—are written by historical premillennialists; you will find that as a group these authors believe that the King is coming and that the missionary mandate must be relentlessly pursued.

It is our hope that this volume may serve all our fellowship and the larger Christian Church as a much-needed voice in the current eschatological debate.

K. Neill Foster
David E. Fessenden

Endnote

1. Michael Tymchak, "Ethics and the Coming King," available online at http://online.cbccts.ca/alliancestudies/ahtreadings/ahtr_s1423.html.

Historical Considerations

Premillennialism
and the Early Church

• Paul L. King •

Many great Christians have taken varying views of the place of the millennium in the second coming of Christ. Augustine espoused an amillennial viewpoint. Jonathan Edwards was a postmillennialist. A.B. Simpson became a premillennialist. These are all interpretations from godly men. How are we to know what is right?

It is the thesis of this writer that the beliefs of earliest church fathers, though not infallible, are closest to the beliefs of the first-century apostolic church. The farther one becomes removed historically from the original church, the greater the likelihood that the message has been watered-down, faded, distorted, readjusted. This is the phenomenon of historical drift. If the earliest fathers were amillennial or postmillennial, that is most likely the understanding of the primitive church. If the earliest fathers were premillennial, the strongest likelihood is that the apostolic church was premillennial (or *chiliastic*) in eschatology. If there was a variety of millennial viewpoints in the first centuries, one may conclude that there was no consensus in the earliest church. This paper traces the millennial beliefs of the early centuries of the church.

First Century Jewish and Christian Eschatology

Arthur Cushman McGiffert, translator and commentator of Eusebius' *Church History*, avows that the earliest church was premillennial: "Jewish chiliasm was very common at about the beginning of the Christian era, and is represented in the voluminous apocalyptic literature of that day. Christian chiliasm was an outgrowth of the Jewish, but spiritualized it, and fixed it upon the second, instead of the first, coming of Christ."[1] Arthur Wainwright also affirms,

> The notion of a blessed time that precedes the last judgment is found in Jewish writings of the New Testament period. The Ethiopic Enoch

affirmed that it would last for three weeks, and the Apocalypse of Ezra prophesied a messianic kingdom of 400 years (Enoch 91:12-17; 4 Ezra 7:28-29). It is also possible that the Apostle Paul expected a millennium when he said that Christ's reign would begin with the resurrection of those who "belong to Christ" and continue until "the end" (1 Corinthians 15:20-28). But Paul never indicated the length of that reign. It is the Apocalypse that specifically says that the period will be a thousand years; and it is the Apocalypse that has influenced the Chiliasts in their discussion of the millennium.[2]

In *The Theology of Jewish Christianity* Jean Danielou concurs:

> The conception of a Messianic reign preceding the Last Judgment and the New Creation is to be found as early as Ezekiel, and this made it possible to attach the two types of eschatological prophecy in Scripture, maybe that relating to an earthly triumph of the Messiah, and that speaking of a New Creation to two successive stages in Time. This conception took on a more precise form in the non-canonical apocalypses. It appears in I Enoch and II (4) Esdras 6:20-28, and II Baruch describes the Messianic reign in the imagery of Paradise (XXIX, 4-8). The Revelation of John made use of the same material to describe the times of the Parousia.[3]

In addition, an early Jewish Christian document *The Ascension of Isaiah*, drawing upon and incorporating earlier Jewish material, describes a premillennial scenario.[4]

Millenarianism in the Apostolic Fathers

Of the Apostolic Church Fathers, *The Epistle of Barnabas* is dated by scholars in the late first or early second century, very close to the earliest church. Though it was probably pseudonymous and not written by Barnabas, it nevertheless demonstrates primitive church thinking. Some church fathers such as Origen (though himself not a chiliast) regarded *The Epistle of Barnabas* as sacred Scripture. The author writes in relationship to the week of creation and the "true and false sabbath":

> Attend, my children, to the meaning of this expression, "He finished in six days." This implieth that the Lord will finish all things in six thousand years, for a day is with Him a thousand years.... Therefore, my children, in six days, that is, six thousand years, all things will be

finished. . . . when His Son, coming [again], shall destroy the time of the wicked man, and judge the ungodly; and change the sun, and the moon and the stars; then He shall truly rest on the seventh day [millennium].[5]

This is clearly an early, literal premillennial interpretation. Belief in a seventh glorious millennium following 6,000 years of human history was a common viewpoint among church fathers.

Papias (ca. 60-130), early second century bishop and a disciple of the Apostle John, is credited by church historian Eusebius with a premillennial viewpoint that he claims comes from the apostles and their associates. Eusebius records of Papias:

> Papias, who is now mentioned by us, affirms that he received the sayings of the apostles from those who accompanied them, and he moreover asserts that he heard in person Aristion and the presbyter John. Accordingly he mentions them frequently by name, and in his writings gives their traditions. . . . Amongst these he says that there will be a millennium after the resurrection from the dead, when the personal reign of Christ will be established on this earth.[6]

While these traditions were recorded centuries later and do not have the authority or accuracy of firsthand writings or original manuscripts, nevertheless, they do demonstrate very ancient belief in a premillennial coming of Christ, portrayed as passed on to Papias by the apostles.

Justin Martyr (ca. 100–ca. 165) also expressed a similar millennial concept, claiming that the teaching came from the apostles:

> There was a certain man with us, whose name was John, one of the apostles of Christ, who prophesied, by a revelation that was made to him, that those who believed in our Christ would dwell a thousand years in Jerusalem; and that thereafter the general, and in short, the eternal resurrection and judgment of all men would take place.[7]

Again he writes, "I and others who are right-minded Christians on all points, are assured that there will be a resurrection of the dead and a thousand years in Jerusalem, which will then be built, adorned and enlarged, as the prophets Ezekiel and Isaiah and others declare."[8]

Although some amillennialists claim that Justin Martyr is in their camp because of some ambiguous language which could be interpreted in different ways,[9] it is significant that most scholars, even anti-chiliasts such as postmillennialist founder Whitby recognized and admitted Justin's teaching to be premillennial.[10] Robert Gundry also affirms, "Justin Martyr places the resurrection and gathering of Christians at the beginning of the millennium and equates their hope with Christ's return to earth as prophesied in the OT (Trypho lxxx, lii)."[11]

According to Cambridge professor Brian E. Daley, Theophilus (ca. 115-181/188), bishop of Antioch in Syria, wrote of a new Paradise as a "transformation from a human to a divine mode of life," expressed by Theophilus as a millennial state which is "intermediate between earth and heaven."[12] Melito, a late second-century philosopher and bishop of Sardis, maintained a chiliastic position,[13] as did Hegesippus (130-190).[14]

Irenaeus, as George Eldon Ladd explains, presented the "first detailed outline of prophetic events after the New Testament,"[15] and he "was a thoroughgoing premillenarian, the first, in fact, to give us a premillennial system of interpretation."[16] Irenaeus was a disciple of Polycarp who was a disciple of John. It seems most likely that John's understanding of the millennium was transmitted faithfully to his spiritual grandchild. Further, Robert Gundry notes, "It is inferred that Polycarp was premillenarian because Irenaeus, his pupil, was so, and that Pothinus was premillenarian from the chiliasm of the churches of Vienne and Lyons, over which he presided, and from his association with Irenaeus."[17]

Third Century Church Fathers

Tertullian, whose ministry spanned from the late second century to the early third century, advanced a clear premillennial viewpoint: "But we do confess that a kingdom is promised to us upon the earth, although before heaven, only in another state of existence; inasmuch as it will be after the resurrection for a thousand years in the divinely built city of Jerusalem."[18] Again Tertullian writes:

> When, therefore, the boundary and limit, that millennial interspace, has been passed, when even the outward fashion of the world itself—which has been spread like a veil over the eternal economy, equally a thing of time—passes away, then the whole human race shall be raised again, to have its dues meted out according as it has merited in the period of good or evil, and thereafter to have these paid out through the immeasurable

4

ages of eternity. Therefore after this there is neither death nor repeated resurrections, but we shall be the same that we are now, and still unchanged—the servants of God, ever with God, clothed upon with the proper substance of eternity; but the profane, and all who are not true worshippers of God, in like manner shall be consigned to the punishment of everlasting fire—that fire which, from its very nature indeed, directly ministers to their incorruptibility.[19]

Tertullian writes extensively of the millennial period of time in his defense against the heretic Marcion. It is significant that he uses the premillennial conception as a part of his defense against heresy.

Like *The Epistle of Barnabas*, early church historian Sextus Julius Africanus (ca. 200-ca. 241/245) also held to the characteristic apocalyptic expectation of a glorious millennium following 6,000 years of world history.[20] Commodianus, a North African bishop writing about A.D. 240, presents a millennial scenario following the end of 6,000 years, similar to that of Barnabas, Julius Africanus and Lactantius.[21] Robert Ernest Wallis, a translator of his work, comments, "His Millenarianism reflects the views of a very primitive age, and that without the corrupt Chiliasm of a later period, which brought about a practical repudiation of the whole system."[22] Hippolytus (170-236), a disciple of Irenaeus, likewise places the resurrection and the kingdom of the saints after the return of Christ in literal premillennial fashion following 6,000 years of history.[23]

The excesses of Montanists, who were also chiliasts, brought disfavor to millenarian belief. "The teachings of the Montanists brought such disrepute upon chiliasm that the fathers of the third and following centuries did not show much fondness for those who held or had held these views."[24] Nepos, a third-century Egyptian bishop (230-280) defended chiliasm in the face of rising support for allegorical interpretation. Church historian Eusebius writes that Nepos

> taught that the promise to the holy men in the Divine Scriptures should be understood in a more Jewish manner, and that there would be a certain millennium of bodily luxury upon this earth. As he thought that he could establish his private opinion by the Revelation of John, he wrote a book on this subject, entitled *Refutation of Allegorist*.[25]

Third-century father Methodius (d. 311) "makes the resurrection of Christians coincident with the millennial renewal of nature after the tribulation (*Discourse on the Resurrection* i, 8)."[26] He calls it a "millennium of rest."[27] Methodius wrote further,

> Just as the Jews, after the repose of the Feast of Tabernacles, arrived at the Promised Land, so I too, following Jesus who has passed into the heavens, shall attain to Heaven, no longer living in tabernacles, or rather my own tabernacle no longer remaining as it was, but being transformed after the millennium from a human and corruptible form into angelic greatness and beauty.[28]

Methodius wrote strongly against Origen's allegorical interpretation, defending the traditional millennial viewpoint.[29] Victorinus (d. 304), a Latin-speaking bishop who was martyred during Diocletian's persecution, according to Daley, was "formed in the same millenarian milieu in which Papias, Irenaeus, and most recently Methodius had absorbed the Church's eschatological hope."[30] Although he had moderated and adopted some of Origen's allegorical interpretation of Revelation, he still maintained a premillennial view of the Apocalypse, particularly Revelation 20 and 21.[31]

Lactantius (d. 317) was a pupil of African orator and apologist Arnobius, and a tutor in the court of Diocletian and Constantine. Like many fathers before him, "Lactantius believed that human history was to run a six thousand year course and to be followed by a millennium."[32] Whitby cites additionally Cyprian, Severus and the Council of Nicea as advocates of premillennialism.[33] G.N.H. Peters adds Pothinius (87-177), Tatian (130-190), Cyprian (200-258) and Coracion (230-280).[34] The premillennialism of some may not be as clearly identifiable as others, and space forbids investigation of these claims, but the case for chiliasm is substantial.

The Rise of Allegorical Interpretation and Amillennial Thought

Origen introduced the allegorical method of interpretation in the third century and became one of the early forerunners of amillennialism.[35] His philosophy and hermeneutic swept the church of the third and fourth centuries. Leaders such as Ambrose and church historian Eusebius of Caesarea championed Origen's cause. Augustine, influenced by Greek thought and Origen's allegorical hermeneutics, understood the idea of a millennium symbolically:

> We can measure the response to Origen's methods in the example of Augustine. In his *Confessions*, Augustine tells us that he had been embarrassed in his earlier years by what he thought was a literal reading of the Bible (actually a caricature formed by childhood impressions and Manichean polemics). He was developing an interest in Neo-Platonism as an alternative to Manichean Gnosticism when he heard the Origenistic preaching of Ambrose. It helped him to see Christianity in a completely new light, and soon he became a Christian. The spiritual vision model of eternal life he contemplated through spiritual interpretation was, he believed, confirmed by in his own typically Neo-Platonic mystical visions. After he became a bishop, his writings affirmed the spiritual vision model, and his homilies and commentaries promoted the practice of allegorical interpretation.[36]

When Augustine adopted Origen's viewpoint and developed his own amillennial theology, chiliasm lost favor. Soon chiliasm began to become considered aberrant and schismatic, while allegorical interpretation was becoming dominant and considered orthodox. Arthur Cushman McGiffert, translator and commentator on Eusebius' work, comments,

> Although chiliasm had long lost its hold wherever the philosophical theology of the third century had made itself felt, it still continued to maintain its sway in other parts of the Church, especially in outlying districts in the East, which were largely isolated from the great centers of thought, and in the greater part of the West. By such Christians, it was looked upon, in fact, as the very kernel of Christianity—they lived as most Christians of the second century had, in the constant hope of a speedy return of Christ to reign in power upon the earth.[37]

Dionysius, bishop of Alexandria and a pupil of Origen, wrote a treatise entitled *On the Promises*, in which he defended Origen's allegorism against Nepos (the aforementioned Egyptian bishop who held chiliastic views).[38] His writing had considerable impact. Another chiliastic teacher in the district of Arsinoe in Egypt by the name of Coracion appears to have abandoned his millennial beliefs as the result of a debate by Dionysius. Nevertheless, McGiffert notes, "chiliasm still prevailed in some of the outlying districts of Egypt for a number of generations."[39]

Remnants of chiliastic belief could be found in other locations as well. Jerome mentions Apollinarius (probably the fourth century bishop of Laodicea who died about 390) as a chiliast in connection with Irenaeus.[40] "At the end of the fourth century," Wainwright notes, "the African bishop Quintus Julius Hilarianus accepted Hippolytus's expectation that the millennium would begin about the year 500, which he believed to be 6,000 years after the creation."[41] Eusebius seems to have leaned toward chiliasm in his earlier days, "but after Constantine's acceptance of Christianity, Eusebius revised his attitude."[42]

It is significant that during the third century in some circles in Egypt, authorship of the Book of Revelation was attributed to the Gnostic heretic Cerinthas and denied a place in the canon, "probably because of the millenarian passage in ch. 20."[43] Again in the fourth century, "the Apocalypse still had difficulty in being accepted as scripture, presumably because its opponents believed it to be chiliastic."[44] Yet occasionally hints of chiliasm can be found in some writings evidently clinging to the traditional viewpoint. Firmicus Maternus (ca. 347) was one of those, referring to "the end of centuries"—"a phrase that suggests he accepted the tradition of seeing history as a 'week' of six thousand years, and perhaps that he knew of the millenarian hope as well."[45] Hilary of Portiers maintained the concept of world history as a "week" of 6,000 years, but dropped the belief in a millennium.[46] After this time, chiliasm faded from popularity and amillennialism began to rule as the dominant eschatological position for a millennium.

Conclusions

This brief survey demonstrates that the earliest church overwhelmingly maintained a premillennial viewpoint of the Second Coming of Christ, and later, in the third century, moved toward an allegorical amillennial interpretation due to the influence of Greek philosophy. Some amillennialists even admit that *biblical* writers wrote of a literal millennium:

Undoubtedly the ancient Hebrew prophets announced the advent of a terrible day of Jehovah when the old order of things would pass away. Later prophets foretold a day of restoration for the exiles when all nature would be miraculously changed and an ideal kingdom of David established. The seers of subsequent times portrayed the coming of a truly heavenly rule of God when the faithful would participate in millennial blessings. Early Christians expected soon to behold Christ returning upon the clouds even as they had seen him in their visions literally ascending into heaven. . . . So far as the use of this type of imagery is concerned, millenarianism may quite properly claim to be biblical.[47]

The evidence of the premillennial viewpoint among the early church fathers is so overwhelming that anti-chiliasts are compelled to admit it even while clinging to their own doctrine. William E. Cox, an amillennialist, acknowledges that the earliest post-apostolic church maintained premillennial beliefs: "The historic premillennial belief originated in early post-apostolic times and flourished until the time of Augustine (A.D. 400)."[48] Further, postmillennialist originator Whitby also concedes the point:

The doctrine of the Millennium, or the reign of saints on earth for a thousand years, is now rejected by all Roman Catholics, and by the greatest part of Protestants; and yet it passed among the best Christians, for two hundred and fifty years, for a tradition apostolical; and, as such, is delivered by many Fathers of the second and third century, who speak of it as the tradition of our Lord and His apostles, and of all the ancients who lived before them; who tell us the very words in which it was delivered, the Scriptures which were then so interpreted; and say that it was held by all Christians that were exactly orthodox.[49]

Church historian Philip Schaff agrees: "The most striking point in the eschatology of the ante-Nicene age is the prominent chiliasm, or millenarianism, that is the belief of a visible reign of Christ in glory on the earth with the risen saints for a thousand years, before the general resurrection and judgment."[50]

The issue, then, in the mind of amillennialists and postmillennialists, is not whether or not the Jews and early Christians believed in and expected a literal millennium, but whether they were right in understanding the imagery literally. While Augustine was a great theologian in many respects, his latent Neo-Platonism colored his theology, worldview and, in particular, his eschatology.

It must be acknowledged that not all chiliasts agreed on the details of the millennial scenario. Wainwright explains: "Chiliasts were divided in their opinion about the place of the New Jerusalem (Rev. 21:1-22:5) in the sequence of events. . . . Although they expected a future millennium, Chiliasts had differing views about its proximity."[51] Dispensationists like Walvoord admit that a pretribulation rapture scenario is not apparent in the church fathers: "It must be conceded that the advanced and detailed theology of pretribulationism is not found in the Fathers, but neither is any other detailed and 'established' exposition of premillennialism."[52]

Nevertheless, the overwhelming evidence is that the earliest church was premillennial. Non-chiliasts try to blunt that fact by claiming that "premillennialism finds *slightly* earlier development" (italics mine),[53] thus trying to downplay the plethora of chiliast substantiation. However, with few exceptions, the vast majority of scholars, even from non-chiliast camps, acknowledge that the primitive church and the earliest fathers maintained chiliast views. It is virtually certain that the apostolic church and the apostles understood the coming of Christ to be before the millennial age. If we have unmistakable testimony that the apostles and their disciples and spiritual grandchildren held a chiliastic eschatology, can one's interpretation be better than those who were closest to Jesus and closest to the original apostles? If the earliest church believed that the Second Coming of Christ would take place before a literal millennial age, then we need to return to the historical eschatological roots of the New Testament church.

Endnotes

1. Arthur Cushman McGiffert, *Nicene and Post-Nicene Fathers* (*NPNF*), eds. Philip Schaff and Henry Wace (Grand Rapids: Eerdmans, 1979), 2:1:172, note 19.
2. Arthur W. Wainwright, *Mysterious Apocalypse* (Nashville: Abingdon, 1993), 22.
3. Jean Danielou, *The Theology of Jewish Christianity* (London: Darton, Longman & Todd; Chicago: Henry Regnery, 1964), 377.
4. Ibid., 378.
5. *The Epistle of Barnabas*, Chapter 15, *Ante-Nicene Fathers* (*ANF*), eds. Alexander Roberts and James Donaldson (Grand Rapids: Eerdmans, 1979), 1:146.
6. "Fragments of Papias," 6, *ANF*, 1:154.
7. Irenaeus, "Dialogue with Trypho the Jew," liii, *ANF*, 1:240.

8. Ibid., 1:239.

9. William E. Cox, *Biblical Studies in Final Things* (Nutley, NJ: Presbyterian and Reformed, 1966, 1974), 197-8.

10. Dwight Pentecost, *Things to Come* (Grand Rapids: Zondervan, 1958), 373. Even Cox makes this concession: "The most that could be claimed for Justin Martyr would be to classify him as a very inconsistent premillennialist." Cox, 198.

11. Robert H. Gundry, *The Church and the Tribulation* (Grand Rapids: Zondervan, 1973), 174.

12. Brian E. Daley, *The Hope of the Church: A Handbook of Patristic Eschatology* (Cambridge: Cambridge University Press, 1991), 24; see Theophilus of Antioch, "Theophilus to Autolycus," 2:24; *ANF*, 2:104.

13. McGiffert, *NPNF*, 2:1:203, note 4; Pentecost, 375; see "Remains of the Second and Third Centuries: Melito the Philosopher," Chapter 1, *ANF*, 8:755.

14. Pentecost, 375; see "Remains of the Second and Third Centuries: Hegesippus," *ANF*, 8:763.

15. George E. Ladd, *The Blessed Hope* (Grand Rapids: Eerdmans, 1956), 26.

16. Ibid., 25.

17. Gundry, 178.

18. Tertullian, *Adversus Marcionem*, Book 3, p. 25, cited in Ladd, 27.

19. Tertullian, "Part First: The Apology, " Chapter 48, *ANF*, 3: see also Part 2, Book 3, Chapter 24.

20. Daley, 61; Joel Van Hoogen, "Premillennialism and the Alliance Distinctives," *Alliance Academic Review* (Camp Hill, PA: Christian Publications, 1998), 48 (reprinted in this volume as Chapter 8); see "The Extant Writings of Julius Africanus," 3:18:4; *ANF*, 6:137-8.

21. "Instructions of Commodianus," Chapter 35, *ANF*, 4:209; see also Chapters 43, 44, 80, *ANF*, 4:211, 212, 218.

22. Robert Ernest Wallis, "Introductory Note to the Instructions of Commodianus," *ANF*, 4:201.

23. Ladd, 30-31; Van Hoogen, 48; see Hippolytus, "Treatise on Christ and Antichrist," 2:50, 60, 61, 64, 65; *ANF*, 5:214-9; Hippolytus, "On Daniel," 2:4; *ANF*, 5:179.

24. McGiffert, *NPNF*, 2:1:203, note 4.

25. Eusebius, *The Church History of Eusebius*, 7:24, *NPNF*, 2:1:308.

26. Gundry, 176; see also Methodius, "The Banquet of the Ten Virgins," Discourse 9, Chapter 1, Chapter 5, *ANF*, 6:344, 347.

27. Ibid.

28. Methodius, "The Banquet of the Ten Virgins," Discourse 9, Chapter 5, *ANF*, 6:347 .

29. Daley, 61-64; Methodius, "Discourse on the Resurrection," Part 3, *ANF*, 6:369-377. For more on Methodius' refutation of Origen's interpretation see "Extracts from the Work on Things Created," Chapter 9, *ANF*, 6:379-81.

30. Daley, 65.

31. Ibid., 65-6.

32. Ladd, 28; see also Daley, 66-8; see Lactantius, "The Divine Institutes," 7:25, *ANF*, 7:220 (according to his calculations there were about 200 years left before Christ would return). See also 7:14, *ANF*, 7:211—"at the end of the six thousandth year all wickedness must be abolished from the earth, and righteousness reign for a thousand years; and there must be tranquillity and rest from the labors which the world now has

long endured" (see also "The Epitome of the Divine Institutes," Chapters 71-72, *ANF*, 7:253-5).

33. Pentecost, 373-4.
34. Ibid., 375.
35. Van Hoogen, 49; Craig A. Blaising, "Premillennialism," *Three Views on the Millennium and Beyond*, gen. ed. Darrell L. Bock (Grand Rapids: Zondervan, 1999), 166-7.
36. Blaising, 167-8; see also Pentecost, 20-5; see also Van Hoogen, 49-52, for more on Origen's and Augustine's beliefs.
37. Eusebius' *Church History*, 7:24:1; *NPNF*, 2:1:308, note 1.
38. Eusebius' *Church History*, 7:24:9; *NPNF*, 2:1:309.
39. Eusebius' *Church History*, 7:24:1; *NPNF*, 2:1:308, note 1.
40. *NPNF*, 2:1:206, note 1; see also Wainwright, 34; Pentecost, 373-4.
41. Wainwright, 34.
42. Ibid.
43. Daley, 18.
44. Wainwright, 33.
45. Daley, 93.
46. Ibid., 94-5.
47. Shirley Jackson Case, cited in Pentecost, 18.
48. Cox, 177.
49. Cited in Pentecost, 373.
50. Philip Schaff, *History of the Christian Church*, 2:614; cited in Pentecost, 374.
51. Wainwright, 24.
52. John F. Walvoord, quoted by Kenneth L. Gentry, Jr., "Postmillennialism," *Three Views on the Millennium*, 15.
53. Gentry, 15.

2

Premillennialism

in the Medieval and Reformation Times

• Harold Shelly •

For many, Y2K fatigue is a thing of the past, almost medieval, like something out of the Dark Ages. Yet the idea of a New Age of peace and justice, which existed in those times, lives on, or at least did until 9/11. During tough times people yearn for the parousia of peace and justice. Whenever political and social conditions become unbearable, people look for deliverance, for a messiah who will come and set the captives free. This was certainly true during medieval and reformation times.[1]

Two outlooks toward a millennium dominated medieval and reformation thinking. The first of these, articulated by Augustine of Hippo, is usually called amillennialism. The second is millennialism or chiliasm. The most significant exponent of the latter was Joachim of Fiore in the twelfth century. Immediately one is struck with an incongruity. Augustine wrote on the subject in the early fifth century, much earlier than Joachim. Augustine himself was not ignorant of a chiliastic strain, but he was determined to eradicate it. Still, it lived on. This strain was maintained throughout the early medieval period by many who cherished the Apocalypse of John and embraced the so-called Sibylline Oracles. Whereas Augustine's viewpoint became the prevailing viewpoint of the organized church, the Chiliasts tended to be the outsiders.

Medieval millennialism often became part and parcel of protest movements, whose adherents were usually the downtrodden masses. While the institutional Church preached Apostolic Poverty in theory, in practice it accumulated great wealth. Too often its prelates lived in luxury while they taxed the poor to support their extravagant lifestyle. Thus millennialism had an anti-institutional impulse. Crop failures, famine, death from plagues, conflicts between church and state, and warfare between noble families haunted the populace. Feudal laws made to protect the peasant population were gradually altered to the injury of the poor. It was as if the

Four Horsemen of the Apocalypse—conquest, famine, wars and death—incessantly rode roughshod over medieval Europe. The Crusades against the infidel Turk provided another backdrop for misery and a model for the peasants. Whereas nobility went on their crusades into the Middle East to rescue the Holy Land from the infidel Turk, peasants went on shepherd crusades against faithless churchmen and nobility to create a Holy Land in Europe. False prophets recurrently arose and led people, usually into greater misery. Now back to Augustine.

Aurelius Augustine of Hippo and Millennialism

Augustine of Hippo (354-430), an African, was born in Tagaste and later served the Church in Hippo, located in modern-day Algeria. Indisputably he was the major, definitive theologian of the Latin west. His mother, Monica, a believer, tried to bring him up as a Christian, but his father, Patricius, an unbeliever, won the early days. In his quest for truth he first joined the dualistic Manichaean sect; later he adhered to Neo-Platonic dualism. After a long search for certainty which took him to Rome and Milan, he experienced a decisive conversion in the year 386.

The same year the Goths entered the Empire, Augustine entered the Church; he was then thirty-two years of age. Doubtless a genius, his thinking touches almost all of the doctrines of Western Christianity. In influence he ranks only in back of Paul and Jesus. At the time of the Protestant Reformation, Calvin, Luther and the Catholics all referred to him more than anyone else. Thus, his views on the millennium are of great significance for all of Christendom.

Barbarian intrusion into the Roman Empire increased and non-Christian writers blamed the Christians. In *The City of God*, Augustine's answer to the critics, he sets forth his philosophy (or theology) of history. For him there are two cities recognized by their two loves. Those whose love is holy and good are in the City of God. Those whose love is impure, whose love is for earthly things, are outside the City of God (*The City of God*, IV, 3). It is not, as some pagan writers allege, because of Rome's acceptance of the Christian faith; rather, the Romans got what they deserved. Rome was not the city of God. In this treatise Augustine advanced, among other concepts, the following ideas related to history and the kingdom of God:

1. History has its beginning in the creation, its center in Christ and its consummation in the judgment and transformation of all things.
2. Because God has foreknowledge, He knew that man would be misdirected and evil would come into the world; but He also knew that His grace would bring good from evil.
3. History is divided into two cities formed by alternative loves: the earthly city by the love of self and the heavenly city by the love of God.[2]

Augustine was aware of millennialism, to which many still adhered in spite of repudiation by theologians like Origen.[3] In fact, he admits that he once was a millennialist. Some, he asserts, are enthralled with the idea of a thousand years. In reference to Peter's words (2 Peter 3:8), "one day is with the Lord as a thousand years and a thousand years as one day," they imagine that "there should follow on the completion of six thousand years, as of six days, a kind of seventh-day Sabbath in the succeeding thousand years." He notes, "for I myself, too, once held this opinion." He continues, "they assert that those who then rise again shall enjoy the leisure of immoderate carnal banquets. . . . They who do believe them are called by the spiritual [those who reject the notions of a "carnal" millennium] Chiliasts, which we may literally reproduce by the name Millenarians." To refute this is "a tedious process" he adds. So he proceeds to show how Revelation 20:1-6 should be understood rather than refuting the Millenarians.[4]

So then, how does Augustine explain the thousand-year reference in Revelation? Quite easily, he thinks. John simply "used the thousand years as an equivalent for the whole duration of this world, employing the number of perfection to mark the fulness of time."[5] He continues, "a thousand is the cube of ten. For ten times ten makes a hundred, that is, the square on a plane. But to give this height, and make it a cube, the hundred is again multiplied by ten, which gives a thousand."[6] How clever!

That which John speaks of is the interval between the first and second coming, "which goes by the name of a thousand years." At the end of this indefinite period the devil is loosed for three years and six months and the saints are sheltered, although "the Almighty does not absolutely seclude the saints from his temptation, but shelters only their inner man, where faith resides, that by outward temptation they may grow in grace."[7]

Clearly he does not accept the notion of an earthly 1,000-year reign of Christ on earth following His return to earth after the period of tribulation. But while the Church is expanding, the devil is bound.

At the end of this thousand years, the devil seduces the nations to battle against the "camp of the saints . . . and the beloved city" (Revelation 20:7-10, KJV). This, says Augustine, is when the devil unleashes savage persecution against the church: "the whole city of God is assailed by the whole city of the devil, as each exists on the earth."[8] The camp is "the Church of Christ extending over the whole world," so that wherever the Church is in the whole world, "there it shall be encompassed by savage persecution of all its enemies . . . that is, it shall be straitened, and hard pressed, and shut up in the straits of tribulation, but shall not desert its military duty, which is signified by the word 'camp'."[9]

Thus, Augustine set the stage for medieval doctrine in his denial of a literal 1,000-year reign of Christ on earth after the second coming. Rather, the 1,000 years is a figurative number for the period between the resurrection of Christ and the second coming of Christ. This period he also calls the kingdom of Christ or the kingdom of heaven and the age of the church. The case is settled for Augustine, who "articulated this position, and it became the dominant interpretation in medieval times. His teaching was so fully accepted that at the Council of Ephesus in 431, belief in the millennium was condemned as superstitious."[10] This sounds so final, but millennialism was not so easily dispensed with. If the Fathers at Ephesus thought their anathema would eliminate millennialism, they were sadly mistaken.

The Sibylline Oracles

Circulating throughout the medieval period was a collection of prophetic writings known as the Sibylline Oracles. In ancient Greece people called upon a Sibyl, a female prophet, to reveal the future. Collections of these predictions were highly esteemed in pagan society. Not to be outdone, it seems that Jews and Christians produced their own "oracles," but pretended them to be utterances of Greek sibyls who made prophecies that should lead the nonbeliever to the truth. The collection of Sibylline Oracles consists of fifteen books. Book seven includes eschatological prophecies. Some sections are clearly pagan, some are Jewish and others are of Christian origin or Christian interpolation.[11]

The fourth century Christian apologist, Lactantius, used the Erythraean sibyl, which is favorably quoted by Augustine in his *The City of God*.[12] The prophecy is arranged in such a way that the initial letters—twenty-seven (3x3x3) letters—of each line spell out in Greek, *Jesus Christ of-God Son Savior*. Augustine seems to use this sibyl uncritically. So it was that the Sibylline Oracles could be used by the medieval church with the implicit approval of the great Church Father Augustine.

For many these oracles substantiated the Apocalypse of John. The conquering Christ of the Book of Revelation was the hero. In the sibylline literature the hero was an emperor-type allegedly predicted by Greek prophets.[13] Cohn contends, "Throughout the Middle Ages the Sibylline eschatology persisted alongside the eschatologies derived from the Book of Revelation, influencing them and being influenced by them but generally surpassing them in popularity."[14] These were widely studied and interpreted to reflect contemporary situations. Bad times were foretold; enemies were described as Antichrist and the heros were Christ figures or persons immediately preparing the way for Christ's return in judgment. And the oracles and the Apocalypse allegedly predicted them all. Thus, for many centuries, primitive premillennialism, based on the Apocalypse and the Sibylline Oracles, continued to bolster millennial expectations. A more fully developed millennialism would wait for Joachim of Fiore.

Joachim of Fiore

The major exponent of millennialism in the latter Middle Ages was Joachim of Fiore (ca. 1132-1202).[15] In his system he developed the idea of three ages or dispensations. These are the successive ages of: (1) the Father, (2) the Son and (3) the Holy Spirit, or (1) Law, (2) Grace and (3) "Ecclesia Spiritualis," the age of the Spiritual Church. The latter was to begin about 1260. On the basis of a generation being about thirty years and the generations from Abraham to Jesus being forty-two generations (according to Matthew 1:17), Joachim reasoned that the time from the birth of Christ to the return of Christ must also be forty-two generations. Thus, about 1,260 years after the birth of Jesus Christ, the age of the Son would be completed and the age of the Holy Spirit would begin. The step from this 1,260 years into the 1,000 years of the Apocalypse (Revelation 20:2-7) was easy.[16] Before this Spiritual age, new religious orders would convert the whole world and bring on the new age of the Spirit.

Joachim "identified the resulting new vision with that 'everlasting gospel' which, according to the Book of Revelation, is to be preached to all peoples in the Last Days. . . . Half a century after Joachim's death, *'evangelium aeternum'* had become the slogan of a widespread messianic movement."[17] This *evangelium aeternum* referred to in Revelation 14:6 contains the only use of the word gospel (*euaggelion*) in the Apocalypse. In Revelation 14 John speaks of 144,000 who stand before the throne in constant praise. They are said to be unmarried or virgins (*parthenoi*). Joachim seems to picture them as a vast monastery of celibate monks singing in ecstacy until the judgment day.[18]

This new paradigm of Joachim gained the ascendancy among millennialists in the latter part of the Middle Ages. Franciscan Spirituals saw themselves as the fulfillment of the prophecy. It is even possible that the Franciscan and Dominican Orders were originally approved to keep the fervor of Joachimites under the control of the Church hierarchy. Later Franciscan Spirituals became a thorn in the side of the papacy.[19] Moreover, the new paradigm ran counter to the officially accepted Augustinian view of the millennium.

> Joachim's idea of the third age was of course wholly unreconcilable with the Augustinian view that the Kingdom of God had been realized, so far as it ever could be realized on this earth, at that moment when the Church came into being and that there never would be any Millennium but this. In sponsoring Joachim the Papacy was therefore—quite unwittingly—sanctioning a new form of that chiliasm which for centuries it had been condemning as heretical.[20]

Joachim's new order would supersede the papacy. In the Age of the Spirit, the Church of the Spirit would no longer need the clergy; even written Scriptures would be unnecessary.

Though the papacy, by approving the new mendicant orders and disciplining the Spirituals, may have been able to contain the millennial fever of the thirteenth century, the situation in the late fourteenth and fifteenth centuries proved to be more difficult. England and France were embroiled in the Hundred Years' War; the papacy endured the Babylonian Captivity and the Great Schism, in which England favored one pope and France the other. A peasant girl, Joan of Arc, heard voices and led French armies to victory; an Oxford theologian, John Wyclif, sent out his disciples to proclaim a new gospel throughout England; an academic dean in Prague, John Huss, preached against the evils of the Church.

All of these developments would be declared heretical; Joan of Arc and John Huss would be burned at the stake. In the case of Huss, his followers resisted and the Hussite wars ensued. Again, many saw imminent judgment and the millennium on the horizon.

Taborite Millennialism

Among the followers of Huss were the so-called Utraquists, who desired both bread and wine in Holy Communion. A more moderate group, they returned to the Catholic Church when their demand for "communion in both (*utraque*) kinds" was granted. The more radical of the Hussites continued the struggle against their adversaries, gaining more and more adherents. Members of the movement, which began among the common people and was led by members of the trade guilds, were called Taborites, because they had named their fortified garrison south of Prague Mount Tabor. This designation for their center of operations was not insignificant.[21] Many believed that Mount Tabor between Nazareth and Tiberius was the setting of Jesus' transfiguration. Some also supposed it was the place of the ascension. Several centuries before the Taborites, Crusaders had built a church on Mount Tabor. Now the Taborites were on a new crusade to purify the land and bring in the new age. Purification would precede the Second Coming and the millennium.

The Holy Roman Emperor Sigismund, who after 1420 was also King of Bohemia, gathered a large army to suppress the Taborite movement. The Taborites fought back. "The afflictions now descending on Bohemia, the chiliastic Taborites recognized as the long-expected 'messianic woes'; and the conviction gave them a new militancy."[22] Now they went on the attack against all those they considered evil. Atrocities abounded on both sides. "But what can be said is that it was only amongst the

Taborites that massacre was seen as a way of clearing the way for the Millennium."[23] As soon as they cleansed the land, the Lord would return and they would meet Him in the air. Together they would celebrate the messianic banquet on Mount Tabor and the Millennium, the Third Age of Joachim, would begin.

Alas, fanaticism followed and not the parousia. Although the Taborite movement was wiped out in the battle of Lipany in 1434, Taborite propaganda continued to circulate throughout Europe. Peasants in the German towns bordering on Bohemia continued to harbor chiliastic expectations.

Though many peasant crusades sprang up in various parts of Germany, the most notorious was that led by Thomas Müntzer, sometime visitor to Prague. As Norman Cohn delightfully segues:

> And meanwhile in a different part of Germany—Thuringia, always so fertile in chiliastic myths and movements—Thomas Müntzer was embarking on the stormy career which was to end by making him into a prophet of the egalitarian Millennium, and one whose fame has endured to the present day.[24]

The close of the fifteenth century had seen considerable discontent among the peasants, whose lot in life was degenerating as they fell deeper into serfdom. Germany was seething religiously, economically and socially. Many hoped the emperor would lead them against the repressive princes of the realm; this did not happen. When the peasants heard Martin Luther proclaim that the Christian is a free person in Christ, they concluded they had found a new champion. They were wrong; Luther might understand their plight, but he would not condone rebellion. For him freedom was spiritual, not social or political. When the peasant wars came to Germany in the 1520s, it was Thomas Müntzer, not Martin Luther, who was their champion.

Thomas Müntzer and the Peasant Kingdom

Thomas Müntzer became a follower of Luther shortly after Luther published his *Ninety-five Theses*. In 1519 Luther recommended Müntzer to be pastor of the church in Zwickau. Here Müntzer came in contact with Nicholas Storch, a weaver who had visited nearby Bohemia and absorbed Taborite doctrines. These he passed on to Müntzer. Later

Müntzer himself would travel to Prague to connect with the Hussites. In his "Prague Manifesto" he predicted, "God will do marvelous things with his elect, especially in this country. For here the new Church will arise."[25]

Without employing explicit millennial wording, Müntzer was forecasting the kingdom of the elect that the Taborites had fought to bring to their land. The millennium was near "to be preceded by the ascendency of the Turk as Antichrist."[26] Müntzer also admitted indebtedness to the tradition of Joachim of Fiore.[27]

If Luther preferred the Psalms and the Epistles, Müntzer preferred Daniel and the Apocalypse. In them he found a radical social program; the earthly kingdom of God would come to earth through the elect. Müntzer preached to the princes using Daniel and Revelation. Christ would destroy "the last of the kingdoms of this world, the imperial-papal monarchy" predicted by Daniel. Müntzer urged the princes to join with Christ and His elect, the stone which destroyed the image. When the princes rejected his beckoning, Müntzer joined the peasants on the road to revolution.[28] Chiliasts saw things in the Word which Luther, who urged the princes to have no part in chiliastic schemes and social revolution, could not imagine.[29]

In Allstedt Müntzer clearly threw his lot in with the oppressed peasants. He would lead the saints into the new age of peace, justice and equality. In the terrible Peasants' Wars which ravaged Germany (1524-1525) the princes were at first taken by surprise. But they soon regrouped and unleashed their full fury on the peasants and their supporters. Thomas Müntzer was apprehended in Frankenhausen and put to torture. Although he recanted his teachings, he was beheaded. The princes thus notified the peasants not to rebel against earthly authority.

This should have ended peasant attempts to establish the kingdom of heaven on earth, but it did not; eschatological hopes, ignited by apocalyptic texts and fiery preaching, cannot easily be extinguished. Other Chiliasts kept the promise alive in the volatile days in which they were living. In 1529 the plague again hit central Europe, the price of grain increased and additional taxes were levied on the peasants to support the war against the Turk. The condition of the peasants continued to deteriorate.

Both Luther and Müntzer believed that they were living in the last days and that the kingdom was imminent.

> Just as much as Müntzer, Luther performed all his deeds in the conviction that the Last Days were at hand. But in his view the sole enemy was the Papacy, in which he saw Antichrist, the false prophet. It was by the dissemination of the true Gospel that the papacy would be overcome. When the task had been accomplished, Christ would return to pass sentence of eternal damnation upon the pope and his followers and to found a Kingdom—but a Kingdom which would not be of this world.[30]

Müntzer believed the Elect needed to war against the evil of the Church and of the State; Luther saw their rebellion as utterly evil. For Luther the preaching of the eternal gospel would bring in the kingdom, but not an earthly kingdom.

The Diet of Speier

A frustrated Catholic emperor attempting to enforce conformity on all his subjects called the Imperial Diet to meet at Speier in the spring of 1529. The princes who followed Luther resisted his pressure and issued a protestation. Henceforth these protesters and their followers would be known as "Protestants."[31]

At that same session all the princes, both Catholic and Protestant, agreed together to revive an ancient Justinian law against rebaptism. Henceforth in the Holy Roman Empire those who rebaptized others or refused to baptize infants—commonly branded "Anabaptists"—were forthwith guilty of a capital crime. This became a convenient way of dealing with all those outside the Catholic and Lutheran systems. Those who advocated millennialism—antithetical to the dogma received from Augustine whether they baptized or not—could easily receive the same label. Even the most peaceful Anabaptist became the object of persecution. But the most notorious Anabaptist kingdom would be in the city of Münster.

Melchior Hoffmann and the New Jerusalem

Meanwhile, as peaceful Swiss Anabaptists were fleeing persecution in Ulrich Zwingli's Zurich and spreading out in southern Germany, Austria and Alsace, a new Anabaptist movement appeared in the Netherlands and northwestern Germany. The leader who gave his name to the northern movements was Melchior Hoffmann, a furrier by trade. He had been influenced by Martin Luther and had carried Lutheran teachings along the Baltic to Denmark and into the Netherlands. Not a thoroughgoing Lutheran, he held the same view of the sacrament as Zwingli and, like some of Zwingli's disciples, also came to question infant baptism. Initially Melchior did not advocate rebaptism for adult believers; he urged his followers to "stand still," to wait and not antagonize the civil authorities. Later in Strassburg, along the Rhine, he accepted believer's baptism. The Rhineland had long been a haunt for Chiliasts. Melchior preached "the imminence of the Second Coming and the Millennium" which was "to begin after a period of 'messianic woes' " in the year 1533 "the fifteenth centenary of the death of Christ."[32]

The followers of Melchior Hoffmann multiplied rapidly in the Netherlands where they became known as Melchiorites. His teachings, like those of Thomas Müntzer, had an apocalyptic bent; he predicted the kingdom of God would come to Strassburg about 1533 or 1534.[33] On his fourth visit to the city the authorities put him in prison, where he gladly waited for the coming kingdom. He spent the remainder of his life in a dungeon while the movement went on without him.

The Münster Fiasco

Many followers of Melchior now concluded that the promised kingdom was to be in another location, the episcopal city of Münster beyond the Rhineland, in Westphalia. Münster was founded in 800 by Charlemagne for his newly appointed bishop of the Saxons. In the sixteenth century Münster was the seat of a prince-bishop who seemed to care little for spiritual matters. In 1530 he attempted to sell his bishopric. Lutheran emissaries convinced the citizens to reform their city. Berndt (Bernhard) Rothmann, preaching assistant at St. Mauritz, led the assault on the old church. When the town council came to his support, the prince-bishop fled. The city was divided. Some adhered to the Zwinglian covenantal understanding of the sacraments, but others supported a more Lutheran approach to the sacraments. The division provided an opening for the chiliastic Melchiorites.

Presuming that Münster was now the place where they could establish the kingdom of God, Melchiorites began to arrive from the Netherlands. They persuaded Rothmann to accept their baptism. The bishop, meanwhile, began to organize a siege of the city and non-Anabaptists fled. The Melchiorites invited other Anabaptists to join their new apocalyptic kingdom. On February 23, 1534, they won the town council and Jan Matthijs, a militant Melchiorite, arrived in Münster. Rothmann was reduced to the role of propagandist and matters deteriorated. Their invitation to all Anabaptists in other towns to join them in Münster suggested a "blend of chiliasm and primitivism."[34]

When the prince-bishop and his Protestant allies tightened the siege, John of Leyden proclaimed himself messiah and initiated a Davidic kingdom which would spread over the whole world. As conditions further deteriorated and more men were killed in skirmishes around the city, polygamy was sanctioned in the city. The imagined kingdom of God had become a kingdom of fools. In 1535 the city fell to the prince-bishop and its fanatical rulers were executed.

For generations the tragic fiasco of Münster was used as an example of what these Anabaptists would do if they were not suppressed. Peasants must not take a city; see how they rule![35] Scorned along with the city was any thoughtful consideration of millennialism. All such discourse was unsafe as well as unorthodox. Most Anabaptists returned to the peaceful path toward the kingdom of God, awaiting but not executing God's judgment.

At this point the observation of Robert G. Clouse is worth quoting at length:

> Perhaps the Münster episode led the Protestant Reformers to reaffirm Augustinian amillennialism. Each of the three main Protestant traditions of the sixteenth century—Lutheran, Calvinist, and Anglican— had the support of the state and so continued the same Constantinian approach to theology. Both Luther and Calvin were very suspicious of millennial speculation. Calvin declared that those who engaged in calculations based on the apocalyptic portions of Scripture were "ignorant" and "malicious." The major statements of the various Protestant bodies such as the Augsburg Confession (1, xvii), the Thirty-nine Articles (IV), and the Westminster Confession (chs. 32, 33), although professing faith in the return of Christ, do not support apocalyptic

millenarian speculation. In certain respects, however, the Reformers in-augurated changes which would lead to a revival of interest in Premillennialism. These include a more literal approach to the inter-pretation of Scripture, the identification of the papacy with Antichrist, and an emphasis on Bible prophecy.[36]

This explains the amillennialism of the three main Protestant tradi-tions, but not the eschatology of Menno Simons and the Mennonites, the heirs of the Anabaptist-Melchiorite movement.

Menno Simons and Millennialism

Menno Simons resigned the Catholic priesthood and aligned himself with the so-called Anabaptist movement in 1536. This was the same year the authorities executed the surviving leaders of the Münster Kingdom and the same year John Calvin published the first edition of his *Institutes of the Christian Religion*. The Münster fiasco was still fresh in the minds of many. Peter Simons, possibly Menno's own brother, had joined the move-ment and had died at Oude Klooster (Old Cloister). For Menno the New Jerusalem was a spiritual kingdom which one enters by faith, not by vio-lence. It is the cross of Christ that one must take up, not the power of the sword.

The year after he joined the peaceful wing of the Melchiorites, Menno was ordained an elder and began to exercise leadership. The irenic Menno encouraged the dispirited flock to look for a spiritual kingdom. Others who wished to establish an earthly kingdom of God by force of the sword Menno designated "corrupt sects." Münster had besmirched the whole Anabaptist movement. All who advocated believer's baptism were linked with Münster and said to be the same kind of radical chiliasts who would destroy the whole social fabric if they were given freedom to practice their heresy.

Thus Menno complains in his *Foundation of Christian Doctrine*, "At this point I know right well that we have to hear of Münster, kingdom, polyg-amy, sword, plunder, murder, and the like abominations and scandals which you assert result from baptism." He proceeds to accuse his accusers of using the alleged connection with the "seditious sects and conspiracies" as a justification for their own "blood-shedding."[37]

The idea of an earthly millennium, Menno believed, came from the heretic Cerinthus, who "maintained that the world was created by angels, that Christ was no more than a mere man and had not yet risen, but should rise with us in the future, and thereafter reign one thousand years in the flesh with His saints."[38] Münsterites were in the line of heretics like Cerinthus, not in his camp. Apparently Menno rejected premillennialism as heretical. For Menno, like Augustine, Christ's kingdom was spiritual and eternal, not physical and earthly. Addressing the "corrupt sects" he remonstrates,

> O miserable, erring sheep . . . I have pointed out to the magistrates that the kingdom of Christ is not of this visible, tangible, transitory world, but that it is an eternal, spiritual, and abiding kingdom which is not eating and drinking, but righteousness, peace, and joy in the Holy Ghost.[39]

Moreover, he argued, the "corrupt sects" have a perverted eschatology. In words that sound like an explicit critique of Joachimite eschatology, Menno declares, "You contend that another dispensation is beginning." He saw this as a denial of the Son of God and the Scriptures.[40] Echoing Augustine he insists, "The Scriptures teach that there are two opposing princes and two opposing kingdoms: the one is the Prince of Peace; the other is the prince of strife. Each of these princes had his particular kingdom and as the prince is so is also the kingdom."[41]

The Elect do not bring the kingdom with the sword, but Christ Himself brings punishment on evil when He returns and then the eternal dominion begins. "The Scriptures clearly testify that the Lord Christ must first come again before all His enemies are punished," maintains Menno in *The Blasphemy of John of Leiden*. He continues by quoting a series of New Testament Scriptures to affirm that the coming of Christ is visible. He then goes to Daniel to affirm that Christ is given an everlasting dominion.[42] To counter his critics Menno wrote his *Brief and Clear Confession*. In this concise document he gave a simple creedal statement which includes the following:

> This same man, Christ Jesus, preached, was crucified, died, and was buried. He rose and ascended to heaven and is seated at the right hand of the Almighty father, according to the testimony of all Scripture. From thence He will come to judge the sheep and the goats, the good and the evil, the living and the dead. II Cor. 5:10; II Tim 4:1.

Menno seems not to exceed this in his eschatology. The Mennonite Church, the largest surviving group which traces itself back to Menno and the Anabaptist movement, has historically been amillennial in its eschatology. Its first official confession of faith was adopted in Dortrecht [sic], Holland, in 1632. The Confession affirms a general resurrection where all will be judged before the judgment seat of Christ. The good will be separated from the evil and "as the blessed of their Father, be received by Christ into eternal life . . . and they shall reign and triumph with Christ forever and ever." References cited include Daniel 12:2, First Corinthians 15 and First Thessalonians 4:13. There is no reference to a millennium.[43] Apparently Menno's seventeenth century followers were not Chiliasts either.

Calvin and the Millennium

In 1536, the same year Menno left the priesthood to become a member of a persecuted sect, John Calvin published the first edition of his *Institutes of the Christian Religion*, in which he maintained that French Protestants were neither Anabaptists nor anarchists; they intended neither to destroy the French monarchy nor attempt to establish an earthly kingdom of the saints. What they professed was simply the historic Christian faith. Calvin was a disciple of Augustine, not Joachim.

Calvin was on his way to Strassburg in 1536 to pursue his studies in peace when he stopped off in Geneva. Guillaume Farel, who was leading the Reformed forces, challenged Calvin to remain or risk God's curse on his studies. Fearing God, Calvin stayed and assisted in the reorganization until he and Farel were put out of the city in 1538. Calvin debated Anabaptists in Geneva in 1537 and again during his brief exile in Strassburg (1538-1541). They were probably Melchiorites.[44] Upon his return to Geneva, he further refined his presbyterian system of church government and his Reformed system of theology, usually called Calvinism. In his *Ecclesiastical Ordinances* he promoted the autonomy of the congregation, the independence of Holy Communion and the discipline (the ban) by the church rather than the state. Thus, according to Williams, "Calvinism on the disciplinary side would have appeared closer to Anabaptism than to the magisterial Lutheranism."[45]

In his *Institutes*, Calvin has a quick and easy answer to the question of the millennium. For him there is no such thing as an earthly 1,000-year reign of Christ in any form. Those who hold to such a doctrine are like those who deny the resurrection of the body. The whole notion is passed off as another work of Satan that has "befuddled men's senses." Paul had to defend the resurrection and overthrow those who denied it (1 Corinthians 15:12 ff.). The subsequent dangerous error, in Calvin's mind, was the doctrine of the millennium held by chiliasts:

> But a little later there followed the Chiliasts, who limited the reign of Christ to a thousand years. Now their fiction is too childish either to need or to be worth a refutation. And the Apocalypse, from which they undoubtedly drew a pretext for their error, does not support them. For the number "one thousand" [Revelation 20:4] does not apply to the eternal blessedness of the church but only to various disturbances that awaited the church, while still toiling on earth.[46]

Note the expressions *fiction, childish, pretext* and *error*. Apparently Calvin was not impressed with those who understood John to be expounding a literal 1,000-year reign of Christ on earth after His parousia. Moreover, Calvin repudiated all the teachings of those commonly branded Anabaptist, finding them not "to be worth a refutation."

Worse than this, he contended, they bring dishonor to Christ: "Those who assign the children of God to a thousand years in which to enjoy the inheritance of the life to come do not realize how much *reproach* they are casting upon Christ and his Kingdom."[47] In fact, he claimed they are guilty of making Christ's kingdom a temporary realm and denying the power and grace of God:

> In short, either such persons are *utterly ignorant* of everything divine or they are trying by a *devious malice* to *bring to nought* all the grace of God and power of Christ, the fulfillment of which is realized only when sin is blotted out, death swallowed up, and everlasting life fully restored.[48]

Thus this "dishonorable" teaching is comparable to a repudiation of the resurrection, an essential teaching of Scripture. Undeniably Calvin set the standard for Reformed theology; his stinging phrases, such as *devious malice, utterly ignorant, cast reproach*, help one understand why not a few of his followers easily dismiss premillennialism.

It would be in the seventeenth century that premillennialism entered the magisterial denominations. In 1527 two books were published, *The Beloved City* by the Reformed theologian Johann Heinrich Alsted, and *Clavis Apocalyptica* by the Anglican Joseph Mede.[49] Both advocated premillennialism; nevertheless, premillennialism remained a minority view until the nineteenth century. Augustine had prevailed.

Endnotes

1. Principal works drawn upon include the following: John Baille, ed., *Library of Christian Classics*, 26 vols. (London: SCM, 1953-69). Norman Cohn, *The Pursuit of the Millennium: Revolutionary Messianism in Medieval and Reformation Europe and its Bearing on Modern Totalitarian Movements*, 2nd ed. (New York: Harper, 1961). F.L. Cross and E.A. Livingstone, eds., *Oxford Dictionary of the Christian Church* (New York: Oxford, 1957 & 1974). Walter A. Elwell, ed., *Evangelical Dictionary of Theology* (Grand Rapids: Baker, 1984). Robert G. Clouse, ed., *The Meaning of the Millennium: Four Views* (Downers Grove: InterVarsity, 1977), hereafter cited as *Meaning*. George H. Williams, *The Radical Reformation* (Philadelphia: Westminster, 1952).
2. Frank N. Magill, *Masterpieces of World Philosophy in Summary Form* (New York: Harper & Row, 1961), 258-63.
3. Robert G. Clouse, "Views of the Millennium," *Evangelical Dictionary of Theology*, Walter A. Elwell, ed. (Grand Rapids: Baker, 1984), 716, hereafter cited as "Views."
4. Augustine, *The City of God*, 20, 7, 518.
5. Ibid.
6. Ibid., 519.
7. Ibid., 20, 8, 521.
8. Ibid., 20, 11, 527.
9. Ibid., 528.
10. Clouse, *Meaning*, 9.
11. "The Sibylline Oracles," *Oxford Dictionary of the Christian Church*, 1252-3.
12. *The City of God*, 18, 23, 426-8. "The sibyl of Erythrae certainly wrote some things concerning Christ which are quite manifest. . . ." He notes that the Latin translation is bad, but in the Greek the first letter of each line forms the words, literally, "Jesus Christ of-God Son Savior." This is the phrase which was made into the acrostic *ichthus*, the Greek word for "fish," commonly used as a symbol for Jesus by the early church.
13. Constantine, by favoring the Church in the fourth century, had set a precedent for messianic emperor figures to come.
14. Cohn, 18.
15. His major works are *Liber Concordiae Novi ac Veteris Testamenti*, *Expositio in Apocalysium* and *Psaltarium Decem Cordarum*. See "Joachim of Fiore," *The Oxford Dictionary of the Christian Church*, 727.
16. Note also the use of "1260" in the Apocalypse (11:3, 12:6, 14:20). The only other use of the phrase "one thousand" (*chilioi*) is in Second Peter 3:8, where Peter reminds us that one day and a thousands years are alike to God. Forty-two months are also spoken of

in the Apocalypse (11:2, 13:5). If the forty-two months equal 1,260 days and if the days are transitioned into years, the system works. Commenting on the reign of the first beast of Revelation 13, A.B. Simpson uses the 1,260 as the years of his political power, which he surmises begins in 610 with "the decree of [the Eastern Roman Emperor] Phocas establishing the supremacy of the Pope." This brings him to 1870, the year "when the death blow was finally struck at the temporal power of the papacy" (A.B. Simpson, *Heaven Opened: or Exposition of the Book of Revelation* [Nyack, NY: Christian Alliance Publishing, 1899], 131-2). Apparently Simpson reckoned that much of Revelation was actually history by his times, possibly the indirect influence of Joachimite eschatology.

17. Cohn, 99-100.

18. Simpson disagrees. "The word 'virgins' is used in the masculine here to denote a life severed and separated from all illicit and unholy things. . . . The Bible nowhere casts a slur on lawful marriage as a less holy state than celibacy" (Simpson, 144). Simpson considers Revelation 14 to be concerned with holiness and missions. "It is very significant that the Holy Spirit has here grouped together two movements which are the peculiar spiritual features of our days. One is the movement for Scriptural holiness and the other the great missionary movement to give the Gospel as a witness immediately to the nations" (Ibid., 146). The words of John are contemporary. The message of judgment is also important. "Is this not a marked feature of the missionary movement of this Age?" asks Simpson (Ibid., 148).

19. Franciscan Spirituals may have influenced some sixteenth century Anabaptists.

20. Cohn, 100-1.

21. Mount Tabor had a long history in Israel. On the occasion of the enslavement of Israel by the Canaanites, God called Deborah, the prophetess and judge, to emancipate the Israelites (Judges 4-5). She commissioned Barak to ascend Mount Tabor and gather an army for the deliverance of God's people. Coming down into the valley of Jezreel at the base of Mount Megiddo, he defeated the Canaanites "by the waters of Megiddo" (Judges 5:19). The sole reference to Megiddo in the New Testament is in the Apocalypse. John foresees the gathering of the kings for "the battle of the great day of God Almighty. . . . And he gathered them together into a place called in the Hebrew tongue Armageddon" (Revelation 16:14, 16). The fifteenth-century Taborites could not miss the connection between old Mt. Tabor and the eschatological Battle of Armageddon. Additionally Cohn proposes that the Taborites named the local river Jordan and their city Tabor for the Mount of Olives. "While the former became the Jordan, the latter became the Mount of Olives where Christ had foretold his parousia (Mark XIII), where he had ascended to heaven and where, traditionally, he was expected to reappear in majesty" (Cohn, 230).

22. Ibid., 225.

23. Ibid., 226.

24. Ibid., 252.

25. In Hans J. Hillerbrand, *The Reformation: A Narrative History Related by Contemporary Observers and Participants* (New York: Harper and Row, 1964), 224.

26. Williams, 46. "Characteristic of the *Prague Manifesto* is the open espousal of the Storchite-Taborite chiliasm which justifies the violence of the elect" (Ibid., 49).

27. Müntzer does this in his *Von dem gedicheten Glauben* (Ibid., 51).

28. Williams, 54.

29. "The elect friends of God will learn to prophesy.... God will do marvelous things with his elect," wrote Müntzer in his *Prague Manifesto* (Hillerbrand, 223-4). Williams observes, "Luther with his argumentation from the written Word and Müntzer with his argumentation out of the compulsion of the Spirit could never have debated from the same platform" (Williams, 57).

30. Cohn, 261.

31. See "Resolution of the Minority," B.J. Kidd, *Documents Illustrative of the Continental Reformation* (Oxford: Clarendon Press, 1911), 243-4.

32. Cohn, 279.

33. In his *Exposition of the XII Chapter of Daniel* he predicted the end of the world in 1533 (Williams, 261).

34. Ibid., 288.

35. It seems even some Protestants preferred a Catholic prince-bishop over an Anabaptist peasant kingdom. Luther's prince might turn his territory into a Protestant state; Zwingli might convince the Town Council to change the religion of the canton; Calvin might agree to overthrow the authority of the bishop and establish a Reformed clerocracy; but peasants must endure affliction from both Catholic and Protestant rulers.

36. Clouse, "Views," 716-7.

37. *The Complete Writings of Menno Simons, c. 1496-1561*, tr. and ed. Leonard Verduin (Scottdale, PA: Herald Press, 1956), 197.

38. Ibid., 199.

39. Ibid., 217. The "corrupt sects" included the mob at Münster, the Batenburgers and the Davidians, other Dutch fanatics, usually labeled Anabaptists.

40. Ibid., 219.

41. Ibid., 554.

42. Ibid., 47-8.

43. *Confession of Faith and Minister's Manual*, comp. J.F. Funk (Scottdale, PA: Mennonite Publishing, 1942), 31.

44. In Geneva he debated John Bomeromenus of Strassburg and John Stordeur of Liege. In Strassburg he convinced the latter to turn to the Reformed faith. After Stordeur died, Calvin married his widow, Idolette de Bure (Van Buren), who gave Calvin his only child (Williams, 587, 591).

45. Ibid., 596. This may be a factor which later induced many former Dutch Melchiorites to espouse the Reformed faith.

46. John Calvin, *Institutes of the Christian Religion*, ed. John T. McNeill, tr. Ford L. Battles (Philadelphia: Westminster, 1960), 3.25.5, II, 995. Calvin made numerous editions of his *Institutes*. All quotations come from the 1559 Latin edition, not the first in 1536, thus reflecting his mature estimation of Anabaptism. Williams (598), however, argues that Calvin called a diverse group of his critics "Anabaptists" and "did not clearly distinguish between his opponents."

47. Calvin, II, 995.

48. Ibid., II, 996 (italics mine).

49. Clouse, *Meaning*, 10-1, 213 (fn. 4).

3

Premillennialism

and the Holiness Movement in the Late Nineteenth and Early Twentieth Centuries

• Steven L. Ware •

In their 1891 song "When He Comes," A.P. Cobb and J.H. Fillmore expressed their excitement which flowed from an expectation of Jesus' imminent return to earth:

> Are you ready for your Lord should He come;
> Are you ready for your summons home?
> Does your anxious spirit burn, His appearing to discern;
> Are you ready if your Lord should come?
>
>
> Oh, be ready for Him when He comes, when He comes,
> Oh, be ready for Him when He comes;
> Be it midnight, be it morning, when He gives the solemn warning,
> Oh, be ready, be ready when He comes.[1]

In a similar vein, in his 1896 work entitled *The Holy Spirit*, A.B. Simpson exulted in what he perceived as the increasing clarity of understanding of God's eschatological plan for all creation when he stated,

> The most remarkable sign that we are in the last days and that the mystery of the ages is about to be finished, is the wondrous light which the Holy Ghost has shed on the interpretation of prophecy in our time. . . . The brightest and soundest scholarship of the age is on the side of premillennial truth. The wonderful events of our time are the beginning of those overturnings which are to bring in the kingdom of Christ and His millennial reign.[2]

Nearly a decade earlier, in the first chapter of his first significant work dealing with eschatology—*The Gospel of the Kingdom* (1887)—Simpson compared and contrasted postmillennialism and premillennialism. And in the second and third chapters he made it clear that he viewed premillennialism as more solidly based in Scripture.[3]

We should be aware of the fact, however, that Simpson was certainly not alone in his preference for premillennial eschatology. In the larger holiness movement in which he participated,[4] premillennialism enjoyed increasing popularity in the late nineteenth and early twentieth centuries—the decades of the movement's primary theological and ecclesiastical formation. This chapter will explore that popularity, the reasons for its rise in this time period and its place in their understanding of church history.

The Shift Toward Premillennialism

In his *Lectures on Prophecy*, Methodist revivalist Henry Clay Morrison derided postmillennialists for promising the kingdom of God on earth while the apparent conditions of the world were only getting worse, and backed up his contention with Scripture and the history of Judaism.

> The postmillennial teaching of the Lord's coming no more harmonizes with the teachings of the New Testament than the Jewish notion of the Messiah appearing as King of kings and Lord of lords at His first coming into the world harmonizes with the Old Testament teaching. . . . What are we to think of men who, in the light of these words of Jesus will persist in telling us that our Lord delays His coming for ten, fifty, one hundred thousand, or perhaps one million years; and that the ecclesiastical forces of this world will bring all men into a state of perfect peace and righteousness before the Lord comes? Meanwhile, an apostate church is tearing up the Bible, denying the deity of Christ, defending and excusing sin, and ridiculing the idea of Christian holiness.[5]

Morrison was joined in his judgment and in his leanings toward premillennial eschatology by numerous other holiness leaders of the era. In fact, Kenneth Brown contends that with the deaths of Phineas Bresee in 1915 and Charles Fowler in 1919, the holiness movement had no leaders capable of mediation between premillennial and postmillennial views. So with the rise of C.W. Butler to the presidency of the National Holiness Association in 1928, the transformation to premillennialism was complete.[6]

Morrison and Simpson were just two of numerous well-known preachers and writers of the late nineteenth and early twentieth centuries associated with what became known as the holiness movement. Most of these leaders and their followers had spiritual roots in one of the predominant Protestant church bodies, most often Methodism. The holiness movement began after the Civil War with the largely postmillennialist vision it had received from its Methodist forebears—the conviction that a pure church can convert the entire world and therefore initiate the millennium—a 1,000-year period of peace and prosperity which would end with the return of Christ. By the beginning of the twentieth century, however, a premillennialist vision had begun to become predominant among holiness leaders—a vision which retained hope for changing the world through the conversion of individuals to the lifestyle of Christian holiness, but which largely avoided political involvement and shifted ultimate responsibility for changing the world to Christ Himself at His return.[7]

The most popular strain of premillennialism which arose in this period became known as *dispensational* premillennialism. Largely attributed to the teachings of John Nelson Darby and the Plymouth Brethren in England, dispensationalism was popularized through the Bible and prophecy conferences which were attended by many Methodist ministers in the late nineteenth century, as well as by numerous Baptist, Presbyterian and Congregational ministers. Dispensationalism was popularized perhaps even more by the publication of Cyrus I. Scofield's *Reference Bible*,[8] which included copious study notes interpreting scriptural texts with dispensational ideology. Although certainly not all premillennialists of this period, especially among the holiness movement, were dispensationalists, the teaching of premillennialism which made it stand out from postmillennialism was the claim that Christ would return to earth in judgment before the beginning of the promised millennium. This meant that all efforts toward the creation of a perfect society, even those sponsored by Christian organizations, would be ultimately futile and declared as incomplete by Christ at His return.[9]

Reasons for the Shift

Why the change in eschatological orientation? Several factors are readily identifiable. Because of the rise of new and threatening issues such as Darwinian evolution (and its applications to society which became known as "Social Darwinism"), biblical criticism and the comparative study of religions, and social developments such as the change from agrarian and rural to industrial and urban society, American churches seem to have encountered a general crisis of faith, whether consciously or unconsciously. The *millennium* many had anticipated as the result of evangelical revivals in the early and mid-nineteenth century, the abolition of slavery and the Northern victory in the American Civil War failed to materialize. Consequently, religious matters in the late nineteenth century have been described by historians in terms of conflict and creativity, realignment and reorganization, and as the "spiritual crisis of the Gilded Age."[10]

The most stubborn resistance to the rise of premillennialism in the holiness movement seems to have come from those who attempted to maintain their connections to Methodism and other established church bodies, and who were therefore more reluctant to leave and form their own organizational structures. As Charles Jones demonstrates, members of the first generation of leaders of the National Holiness Association such as John Inskip strove to maintain that relationship, and were therefore more resistant to new doctrines such as premillennialism.[11] And Dayton notes that even as late as 1931 A.M. Hills, a postmillennialist, faced a dilemma when writing the first systematic theology for the Church of the Nazarene. Hills, formerly a Congregationalist and a student of Charles Finney at Oberlin, "solved the problem by producing a systematic theology with two eschatologies, a postmillennial one penned by himself and a premillennial one penned by a leader of that perspective."[12]

Brown has demonstrated that many Methodists, some of whom became leaders in the holiness movement, were heavily involved in the Bible Conference movement—more traditionally associated with Reformed evangelicals. While the evidence is inconclusive, this could be a major source for premillennialism in the holiness movement. So while Phineas Bresee retained his commitment to a postmillennial vision, even while allowing the contributions of premillennial writers to *Nazarene Messenger*—which he edited—he was in an increasingly shrinking camp of holiness leaders by the early twentieth century.[13]

On the other hand, it could be argued that the internal theological dynamics of the holiness movement naturally lent themselves to the development and growth of premillennialism.[14] Using the long life and experiences of his grandfather (John Lakin Brasher, 1868-1971) as an example, Lawrence Brasher records that at the end of the nineteenth century southern Methodism "looked with increasing dismay upon the recent, dynamic wedding of the second blessing and premillennialism, a combination that not only gave doctrinal offense to the church but that also seemed to give the holiness movement extraordinary new power."[15] By being linked to premillennialism, sanctification ". . . quickly acquired new meaning as the required initiation preparing believers to meet the coming Lord. In the cleansing, sometimes ecstatic, moment of the second blessing, the sanctified proleptically experienced the glory of the awaited second coming."[16]

Sanctified believers therefore viewed themselves as participating in a great worldwide revival which was to produce a purified church immediately preceding Christ's return to earth. Furthermore, sanctified believers were hastening Christ's return by proclaiming the gospel message to all people, which was a necessary prerequisite to His return.

The connection between premillennialism and evangelism, however, is seen nowhere more clearly than in the writings and activities of Albert Benjamin Simpson, founding personality of The Christian and Missionary Alliance. Like many of his colleagues in the holiness movement, Simpson adopted premillennialism early on, as evidenced in the aforementioned comments in *The Gospel of the Kingdom* (1887). In addition, in the same work he stated that the simultaneous revival of the doctrines of holiness and the second coming of Christ were not a mistake, but part of God's plan to prepare His people for the end. In agreement with many other premillennialists, he argued that true Christians would be "raptured," or removed from earth before the beginning of the seven-year-long Great Tribulation,[17] and would therefore not be present during the period of God's judgment upon sinful humanity. That judgment was then to be followed by a literal 1,000-year reign of Christ on earth.[18]

The connection between premillennialism and world missions is seen as well in the hymnody of the Alliance, with some hymns written by Simpson himself. Of particular note are hymns of missionary concern for individual geographical areas, such as Simpson's *The Dark Soudan*:

> They are dying in the dark Soudan,
>   that lies by the Niger's shore.
> Let us save them while alone we can,

'ere for them the harvest time is o'er.
Every day a thousand lost ones die,
   ninety missions in darkness lie;
Let us listen to their pleading cry,
   as it echoes from that heathen shore.[19]

Like many leaders in the Bible Conference movement in the late nineteenth century, Simpson was intensely interested in the place of the Jews in biblical prophecy. The growing popularity of Zionism had given him the expectation that the millennium was near, since he viewed the return of Christ as intimately connected with the re-establishment of the political state of Israel. The weakened condition of the Ottoman Empire—which exercised political control over Palestine at that time—and the advent of "the Great War" (World War I) led him to expect that the establishment of a Jewish state and the return of Christ could not be far away.[20]

Simpson's eschatological awareness was not based solely on political events, however. He bemoaned the rise and influence of Darwinism, biblical criticism, naturalistic philosophy, worldliness in the church and widespread skepticism in the established churches regarding Christ's return. Yet even these negative signs he viewed as unmistakable signs of Christ's imminent return, because alongside these negative developments were the widespread evangelistic successes occurring around the world. Like many of his contemporaries, he viewed these successes as the beginning of the "latter rain," a special outpouring of the Holy Spirit upon all humanity just before the "harvest" to take place at Christ's return.[21]

Restoring the New Testament Church

Part and parcel with the eschatological significance of the experience of entire sanctification was the perception by holiness adherents that they were participating in the restoration of the Christian church to the power, polity and piety with which it had begun in the apostolic era. Nearly universal among Protestants through the nineteenth century was an understanding of Church history which interpreted the late ancient and medieval eras as periods of decline and apostasy from the true Christian faith taught by Jesus and the apostles, followed by a gradual restoration of New Testament Christianity since the beginning of the Protestant Reformation.[22]

This interpretive scheme of Church history is clearly seen in Simpson's introduction to *The Gospel of the Kingdom*, where he describes the premillennial return of Jesus to earth as

> . . . the supreme hope of the primitive Church for nearly three centuries. Only when a proud empire and a formal Church began to look for their inheritance in this world, and talk of the Pope as the Lord, and the emperor's dining-room as the "New Jerusalem," did they abandon the reality of this "blessed hope" for the vague spiritualizing interpretation which has since taken possession of so many minds.

But then he began to detail the good news of the restoration of true Christianity:

> When Luther awoke the sixteenth century from the unhallowed dreams of the night of ages, to prepare for the day of the Son of Man, he did not at once restore the whole Gospel from the fetters of darkness and error. It was a good deal that he should give us back the doctrine of justification and Christ's free and saving grace. It has been reserved for others in the succeeding generations to unfold the fullness of the Gospel of the grace of God, the healing life and power of Christ, and the Gospel of the kingdom.[23]

With minor variations, one finds in the writings of numerous holiness and pentecostal leaders of the late nineteenth and early twentieth centuries a kind of litany of the restoration of true Christianity which began with the Protestant Reformation in the sixteenth century. It was stated perhaps most succinctly by pentecostal writer H.S. Maltby in 1913:

> During the Reformation God used Martin Luther and others to restore to the world the doctrine of justification by faith. Rom. 5:1. Later on the Lord used the Wesleys and others in the great holiness movement to restore the gospel of sanctification by faith. Acts 26:18. Later still he used various ones to restore the gospel of divine healing by faith (Jas. 5:14, 15), and the gospel of Jesus's second coming. Acts 1:11. Now the Lord is using many witnesses in the great Pentecostal movement to restore the gospel of the baptism with the Holy Ghost and fire (Luke 3:16; Acts 1:5) with signs following. Mark 16:17, 18; Acts 2:4, 10:44-46, 19:6, 1:1-28:31. Thank God, we now have preachers of the whole gospel.[24]

While one can certainly detect pentecostal biases or scriptural interpretations in Maltby's statement, he was reflecting an understanding of Church history which pentecostals had adopted from their roots in the holiness movement, with minor variations concerning the role of speaking in tongues as evidence of baptism in the Holy Spirit. The common perception among participants in both holiness and pentecostal revivals was that they were witnessing the church's full restoration to apostolic norms in their generation. Eschatological awareness, perhaps especially among premillennialists, was therefore supported by the perception that they were witnessing God's final acts in preparation for Christ's return.

Following a long-standing Protestant tradition with such examples as Luther, Calvin, Baxter and Wesley, holiness leaders viewed Roman Catholicism as an illegitimate institution which had, in the name of Christ, in fact driven people away from Christ.[25] Moreover, they interpreted numerous eschatological portions of Scripture as prophetic of a period of spiritual decline and corruption, which they viewed as having begun in the second century with the development of formal liturgies, the use of Greek philosophical concepts in Christian theology and the patronage of the wealthy after the legalization of Christianity under Constantine. Spiritual decline and corruption continued through the Middle Ages, personified in the politically powerful papacy.

God did not allow the church to languish forever in corruption, however, and began the process of restoring the church to New Testament standards with the Protestant Reformation, as noted above. Again standing in a long Protestant tradition, both images and numbers in Scripture were interpreted in *historicist* fashion by holiness leaders in understanding their place in God's eschatological plan. For instance, Simpson interpreted the seven parables of Jesus in Matthew 13 as descriptive of successive ages of church history.[26] Likewise, the letters to the seven churches in Revelation chapters 2 and 3 were interpreted as descriptive of the Church's progress through history. Furthermore, the numbers in Revelation were interpreted in the "day-year" method. For instance, the 1,260 days of the woman's protection in the wilderness (Revelation 12:6) were interpreted by Simpson as a period of 1,260 years beginning with the declaration of Byzantine Emperor Phocas in A.D. 610 concerning the right of the bishop of Rome to rule Western Europe, which is also seen as the beginning of the reign of the Beast (Antichrist). Twelve hundred and sixty years past 610 brings us to 1870—the date when the Papal States ceased to exist.[27]

Back to Eschatology

Given the privilege of seeing such earth-shaking events—the dissolution of the Papal States, the destruction of World War I, increased Jewish immigration to Palestine under British occupation, the increasing sinfulness of modern society and the widespread successes of evangelical revivals—many leaders in both holiness and pentecostal circles concluded that the return of Christ was nothing less than imminent. The revivals in which they participated were seen as the "latter rain," which would bring on the spiritual harvest just before Jesus' return. Their critical mission was to proclaim the gospel message to all peoples. Beyond the accomplishment of that goal and the unfolding of worldly events prophesied in Scripture, they could simply look forward to the blessed hope of Jesus' return and the consequent beginning of the millennium of peace and righteousness. With that consciousness, they were certainly ready for His coming.

Endnotes

1. A.P. Cobb and J.H. Fillmore, "When He Comes," R. Kelso Carter and A.B. Simpson, eds., *Hymns of the Christian Life: New and Standard Songs for the Sanctuary, Sunday Schools, Prayer Meetings, Mission Work and Revival Services* (New York: Christian Alliance Publishing Company, 1891), No. 378.

2. A.B. Simpson, *The Holy Spirit, or Power from on High: An Unfolding of the Doctrine of the Holy Spirit in the Old and New Testaments* (Harrisburg, PA: Christian Publications, 1975 [1896]), 279, 283.

3. A.B. Simpson, *The Gospel of the Kingdom: A Series of Discourses on the Lord's Coming* (New York: Christian Alliance, 1887), 13ff, 24. The introduction to this work contains one of Simpson's earliest mentions of the "Fourfold Gospel" of Christ as Savior, Sanctifier, Healer and Coming King (9), which became the doctrinal backbone of The Christian and Missionary Alliance. The full explanation of his fourfold scheme is found in another book published a few years later—*The Fourfold Gospel* (New York: Christian Alliance, 1890). Pentecostal evangelist Aimee Semple McPherson, born in the same year in which *The Fourfold Gospel* was published, seems to have largely borrowed from it, whether consciously or unconsciously, to outline the theological distinctives of her International Church of the Foursquare Gospel in 1922.

4. Oddly enough, pentecostal author Edith L. Blumhofer separates Simpson from the holiness movement by consistently associating him with other non-holiness evangel-

ical leaders of the same period who disagreed with holiness soteriological categories (*Restoring the Faith: The Assemblies, Pentecostalism, and American Culture* [Urbana, IL: University of Illinois Press, 1993], 25, 29-30), but makes no mention of him with regard to the holiness movement. Likewise, in her doctoral dissertation Blumhofer identifies Simpson with non-holiness evangelicals such as Dwight L. Moody, Adoniram Judson Gordon and Reuben Archer Torrey, contrasting "these evangelicals," with their emphasis on the ministry of the Holy Spirit, over against holiness leaders who stressed only inward purity (Edith L. Waldvogel, "The Overcoming Life: A Study in the Reformed Evangelical Origins of Pentecostalism" [Ph.D. Dissertation, Harvard University, 1977], 24-5), thus ignoring the groundswell of pentecostal language which had been building in holiness circles since before the Civil War. See Donald W. Dayton, "From 'Christian Perfection' to the 'Baptism of the Holy Ghost'," Vinson Synan, ed., *Aspects of Pentecostal-Charismatic Origins* (Plainfield, NJ: Logos, 1975), 39ff; D. William Faupel, *The Everlasting Gospel: The Significance of Eschatology in the Development of Pentecostal Thought* (Sheffield, England: Sheffield Academic Press, 1996). An association of Simpson with non-holiness evangelicals is somewhat understandable, given his Presbyterian heritage and affinities for Keswickian teachings on the Holy Spirit. It ignores, however, his writings which make his affinities for holiness soteriological categories unmistakably clear, such as *The Fourfold Gospel*.

5. Henry Clay Morrison, *Lectures on Prophecy* (Louisville: Pentecostal Publishing House, 1915), 80, 83.
6. Kenneth O. Brown, "Leadership in the National Holiness Association, with Specific Reference to Eschatology, 1867-1919" (Ph.D. Dissertation, Drew University, 1988), 282-3.
7. Brown, 288, 297. For a discussion of Protestant social reform before the American Civil War see Timothy L. Smith, *Revivalism and Social Reform: American Protestantism on the Eve of the Civil War* (Baltimore: Johns Hopkins University Press, 1957).
8. *The Scofield Reference Bible: Holy Bible, Authorized King James Version* (New York: Oxford, 1909).
9. The theology and historical rise of premillennialism are discussed thoroughly in Clarence Bass, *Backgrounds to Dispensationalism* (Grand Rapids: Eerdmans, 1960); Ernest R. Sandeen, *The Roots of Fundamentalism: British and American Millenarianism, 1800-1930* (Chicago: University of Chicago Press, 1970); and Timothy P. Weber *Living in the Shadow of the Second Coming: American Premillennialism, 1875-1982* (Chicago: University of Chicago Press, 1983). Donald Dayton sounds a note of caution in associating dispensational premillennialism with pentecostalism, noting that pentecostals have usually adopted periodizations of human history and applied to the church certain biblical texts which non-pentecostal dispensationalists have relegated to the millennial kingdom. He also notes that dispensational thought is less prevalent in the holiness-oriented branches of pentecostalism. See Dayton, *Theological Roots of Pentecostalism* (Peabody, MA: Hendrickson, 1987), 145-6.
10. See Weber, chapter 1; Paul A. Carter, *The Spiritual Crisis of the Gilded Age* (DeKalb, IL: Northern Illinois University Press, 1971). Weber includes a convenient diagram of the varieties of Christian millennialism on page 10.

11. Charles Edwin Jones, *Perfectionist Persuasion: The Holiness Movement and American Methodism, 1867-1936* (Metuchen, NJ: Scarecrow, 1974), chapter 6, "The Come- Outers."

12. Dayton, 164. See A.M. Hills, *Fundamental Christian Theology* (Pasadena, CA: C.J. Kinne, 1931), II, 339ff.

13. Brown, 110ff, 279.

14. See Dayton, 164-7.

15. John Lawrence Brasher, *The Sanctified South: John Lakin Brasher and the Holiness Movement* (Urbana, IL: University of Illinois Press, 1994), 37-8. Brasher explains that his grandfather held postmillennial views until the event of his sanctification, at which time he turned radically toward premillennialism, feeling that it provided a much greater impetus for his evangelistic ministry (62-3). This was in line with the perception of many southern holiness premillennialist church members that the special power with which their preachers delivered their sermons was a sign of the close of the age. See Brasher, 221 *n9*.

16. Brasher, 62.

17. The concept of a pretribulation rapture seems to have been the limit of Simpson's agreement with dispensational theology. As Franklin Arthur Pyles asserts, Simpson otherwise disagreed with the futurist orientation of dispensationalism and instead was an historicist in his eschatological interpretation of the biblical book of Revelation. See Pyles, "The Missionary Eschatology of A.B. Simpson," David F. Hartzfeld and Charles Nienkirchen, eds., *The Birth of a Vision: Essays on the Ministry and Thought of Albert B. Simpson* (Camp Hill, PA: Christian Publications, 1986), 30-5.

18. A. B. Simpson, *The Gospel of the Kingdom*, 13ff, 24, 292f, 300. George D. Watson went a step further in a rather controversial direction when he claimed that only sanctified Christians would be "raptured" from the earth before the Great Tribulation, and that unsanctified believers would be left to suffer its horrors: "The bride of Christ does not comprise all of those who are saved, but a select company out from that body who has been conformed to Christ in His life and sufferings and ministry in a special degree" (*The Bridehood Saints* [Cincinnati: God's Revivalist Office, 1913], 4). In an earlier work he stated that "only those who are really saints, and who have made a covenant by the complete sacrifice of themselves to God, shall be gathered up" (*Steps to the Throne* [Dallas: Holiness Echoes 1898], 109).

19. A.B. Simpson, "The Dark Soudan," *Hymns of the Christian Life* (South Nyack, NY: Christian Alliance, 1897), No. 200. See also No. 201, "I'm Going to the Congo," and No. 204, "Beautiful Japan."

20. Simpson, *The Gospel of the Kingdom*, 165ff, 221ff; Simpson, "Israel in the Light of Prophecy and Providence," *Living Truths* 4 (August 1904):439. This view was shared by Henry Clay Morrison, who stated that the deliverance of Palestine from Turkish control was a fulfillment of biblical prophecy. See Percival A. Wesche, *Henry Clay Morrison: Crusader Saint* (Wilmore, KY: Asbury Theological Seminary, 1963), 177. For a broader discussion of Zionist sympathies and eschatological expectations among conservative evangelicals in this period, see Weber, chapter 6. Weber limits his discussion, however, to those of conservative Reformed traditions, mentioning Methodists only once (169). He also mentions the holiness movement only once, and that in connection with the combined emphases of premillennialism and world evangelism found in The Christian and Missionary Alliance (78-9).

21. Simpson, *The Gospel of the Kingdom*, 187ff, 214; Simpson, *The Coming One* (New York: Christian Alliance, 1912), 190-1. A thorough explanation of the early rain/latter rain interpretation of church history was written by an early pentecostal author, David Wesley Myland, in *The Latter Rain Covenant and Pentecostal Power* (Chicago: Evangel Press, 1910).

22. A most succinct explanation of this understanding of church history is a 1917 sermon by pentecostal evangelist Aimee Semple McPherson, "Lost and Restored." See *Lost and Restored, and Other Sermons* (Los Angeles: Foursquare Publications, 1989), 7ff.

23. Simpson, *The Gospel of the Kingdom*, 10-11.

24. H.S. Maltby, *The Reasonableness of Hell* (Santa Cruz, CA: privately printed, 1913), 82-3. Cited from Dayton, *Theological Roots of Pentecostalism*, 19-20. Restorationism was more pronounced in the early history and theology of some pentecostal church bodies, such as the Church of God (Cleveland, Tennessee). See Charles W. Conn, *Like a Mighty Army, Moves the Church of God* (Cleveland, TN: Church of God Publishing House, 1955), 7-16.

25. See Martin Luther, "Against the Roman Papacy, an Institution of the Devil" (1545), Eric W. Gritsch, ed., *Luther's Works* (American Edition, Philadelphia: Fortress Press, 1966), Vol. 41, 263-4, 376; John Calvin, *The Necessity of the Reformation* (New York: S.W. Benedict, 1844 [1544]), 11; Richard Baxter, "The Protestant Religion Truly Stated and Justified," William Orme, ed., *The Practical Works of the Reverend Richard Baxter* (London: James Duncan, 1830), I, 658; John Wesley, "A Short Method of Converting all the Roman Catholics in the Kingdom of Ireland," *The Works of John Wesley* (London: Wesleyan Conference Office, 1872), X, 130-1.

26. Simpson, *The Gospel of the Kingdom*, 91-4.

27. Simpson, *The Coming One* (1912), 83-84. For a fuller explanation, see Steven L. Ware, "Restoring the New Testament Church: Some Varieties of Restorationism in the Holiness Movement in the Late Nineteenth and Early Twentieth Centuries" (Ph.D. Dissertation, Drew University, 1998), 93-105.

Bibliography

Primary Sources

Baxter, Richard. *The Practical Works of the Reverend Richard Baxter*. Orme, William, ed. London: James Duncan, 1830.

Calvin, John. *The Necessity of the Reformation, to Which Is Appended the Articles of Agreement on the Sacramentarian Question Between the Churches of Zurich and Geneva*. New York: S.W. Benedict, 1844 [1544].

Hills, A.M. *Fundamental Christian Theology*. 2 vols. Pasadena, CA: C.J. Kinne, 1931.

Hymns of the Christian Life: New and Standard Songs for the Sanctuary, Sunday Schools, Prayer Meetings, Mission Work and Revival Services. Carter, R. Kelso, and Simpson, A.B., eds. New York: Christian Alliance Publishing Company, 1891.

Luther, Martin. *Luther's Works*. American Edition. Pelikan, Jaroslav, and Lehmann, Helmut T., eds. Philadelphia: Fortress Press, 1966.

McPherson, Aimee Semple. *Lost and Restored, and Other Sermons*. Los Angeles: Four-square Publications, 1989.

Morrison, Henry Clay. *Lectures on Prophecy*. Louisville, KY: Pentecostal Publishing Company, 1915.

The Scofield Reference Bible: Holy Bible, Authorized King James Version. New York: Oxford, 1909.

Simpson, Albert Benjamin. *The Coming One*. New York: Christian Alliance, 1912.

———. *The Fourfold Gospel*. New York: Christian Alliance, 1890.

———. *The Gospel of the Kingdom: A Series of Discourses on the Lord's Coming*. New York: Christian Alliance, 1887.

———. *The Holy Spirit, or Power from on High: An Unfolding of the Doctrine of the Holy Spirit in the Old and New Testaments*. Harrisburg, PA: Christian Publications, 1975 [1896].

———. "Israel in the Light of Prophecy and Providence." *Living Truths* 4 (August 1904): 439.

Watson, George Douglas. *The Bridehood Saints*. Cincinnati: God's Revivalist Office, 1913.

———. *Steps to the Throne*. Dallas: Holiness Echoes, 1898.

Wesley, John. *The Works of John Wesley*. London: Wesleyan Conference Office, 1872.

Secondary Sources

Aspects of Pentecostal-Charismatic Origins. Synan, Harold Vinson, ed. Plainfield, NJ: Logos, 1975.

The Birth of a Vision: Essays on the Ministry and Thought of Albert B. Simpson. Hartzfeld, David F., and Nienkirchen, Charles W., eds. Camp Hill, PA: Christian Publications, 1986.

Blumhofer, Edith L. *Restoring the Faith: The Assemblies of God, Pentecostalism, and American Culture*. Urbana, IL: University of Illinois Press, 1993.

Brasher, John Lawrence. *The Sanctified South: John Lakin Brasher and the Holiness Movement*. Urbana, IL: University of Illinois Press, 1994.

Brown, Kenneth O. "Leadership in the National Holiness Association, with Special Reference to Eschatology, 1867-1919." Ph.D. Dissertation, Drew University, 1988.

Conn, Charles W. *Like a Mighty Army, Moves the Church of God*. Cleveland, TN: Church of God Publishing House, 1955.

Dayton, Donald W. *Theological Roots of Pentecostalism*. Peabody, MA: Hendrickson, 1987.

Faupel, David William. *The Everlasting Gospel: The Significance of Eschatology in the Development of Pentecostal Thought*. Sheffield, England: Sheffield Academic Press, 1996.

Jones, Charles Edwin. *Perfectionist Persuasion: The Holiness Movement and American Methodism, 1867-1936*. Metuchen, NJ: Scarecrow, 1974.

Niklaus, Robert L., Sawin, John S., and Stoesz, Samuel J. *All for Jesus: God at Work in The Christian and Missionary Alliance for Over One Hundred Years*. Camp Hill, PA: Christian Publications, 1986.

Waldvogel, Edith L. "The Overcoming Life: A Study of the Reformed Evangelical Origins of Pentecostalism." Ph.D. Dissertation, Harvard University, 1977.

Ware, Steven L. "Restoring the New Testament Church: Some Varieties of Restorationism in the Holiness Movement in the Late Nineteenth and Early Twentieth Centuries." Ph.D. Dissertation, Drew University, 1998.

Weber, Timothy P. *Living in the Shadow of the Second Coming: American Premillennialism, 1875-1982.* Chicago: University of Chicago Press, 1983.

Wesche, Percival A. *Henry Clay Morrison: Crusader Saint.* Wilmore, KY: Asbury Theological Seminary, 1963.

4

Premillennialism

A.B. Simpson, Sanctification and the C&MA

• Samuel J. Stoesz •

"And this gospel of the kingdom will be preached in the whole world as a testimony to all nations, and then the end will come" (Matthew 24:14) are the words of Jesus that have challenged the Alliance movement from its initial beginning. The Great Commission given to the church in Matthew 28:18-20 is recognized as a premillennial kingdom goal—". . . go and make disciples of all nations . . . to the . . . end of the age."

I. A Coming Kingdom—A Call to a Crucial Message

During the forty days between His resurrection and ascension, Jesus instructed His disciples regarding the kingdom of God. Its globalization would come through the expansive witnessing power of the Holy Spirit in the church at Jerusalem, extending to Judea, Samaria and to the ends of the earth (Acts 1:3-8).

Dr. A.B. Simpson, founder of The Christian and Missionary Alliance, believed that this globalization task was essential to the Church's very nature and function; that obedience to the Great Commission would speed Christ's return to establish God's kingdom (2 Peter 3:11-13). Jesus clearly said, "All authority in heaven and on earth has been given to me. Therefore go. . . . And surely I am with you always, to the very end of the age" (Matthew 28:18-20). The command with promise motivated Simpson to publish an evangelical missionary magazine—*The Gospel in All Lands*—the first of its kind.[1] He held a missionary convention in his pastorate, the New York Gospel Tabernacle in 1884, and described it in his magazine. This resulted in numerous invitations from various denominational churches for similar events, each lasting eight to ten days with emphasis on the deeper life and missions. Five were sponsored in large urban centers in 1885 and in 1900 Simpson noted that the calls for conventions far exceeded the possibility to engage them.[2] Auxiliaries called "branches"

47

originated to sustain the message and challenge between annual conventions wherever they were regularly established.

Contrary to the initial intentions of the founder, the branches eventually became churches. In 1974 a public announcement was made at annual council that the Alliance was no longer an interdenominational missionary society, as formerly identified, but had become a denomination of churches.[3] The Alliance movement has now spread not only throughout North America but is also currently in sixty-two countries of the world.[4]

To Simpson, the premillennial coming again of Jesus to set up His kingdom was the preparatory message Jesus preached: "Repent, for the kingdom of heaven is near" (Matthew 3:2). It was the warp and woof of all scriptural revelation. The vision and faith of the Alliance movement is best understood by examining premillennialism as it was accepted by the founder and to inquire as to its continuing relevance for today.

II. A Coming Kingdom— A Call to a Realism of Faith

Simpson viewed the millennial kingdom as a triumphant fulfillment of the Great Commission. He understood uniquely how strongly creation is tied to divine redemption in Scripture. Biblically, creation and redemption are interdependent in Jesus' gospel of the kingdom. Man, the vice-regent of creation, is commissioned to conquer and to exercise dominion over all creation (Genesis 1:28). This mandate was not rescinded (see Psalms 8:1-8; 115:16), though the human race fell through disobedience and allegiance to Satan. The redeemed and glorified church is to rule over creation in the kingdom to come (2 Timothy 2:12; Revelation 5:10; 20:4, 6). The Great Commission, therefore, is to fulfill man's original mandate. Globalization of the gospel, Simpson believed, will speed Christ's return and restore dominion to redeemed man.

The premillennial consummation is in anticipation of Christ's personal and physical appearing in triumphal glory to reign with His Church. Meanwhile, the Church is promised Christ's presence and power to overcome Satan's domain which He has usurped through man's allegiance to Him. Christ's kingdom, now present in mystery form, will become manifest triumphantly when Jesus returns to earth. The kingdom cannot be etherealized by spiritualzation. The earth will be regenerated (*paliggenesia*, Matthew 19:28, KJV) after Christ's coming and believers, as priests of God and of Christ, will reign with Him on earth for 1,000 years (Revelation 20:6).

The many promises in the Old Testament of an earthly restored order when the Messiah comes will be fulfilled. The Old and the New Testaments are simply components of one revelation that promises a redemption of earth as well as of believers. The Old describes man in paradise lost, the New concludes with a vision of man in a new heaven and a new earth. The book of Revelation provides greater detail of a transitional period of 1,000 years. Satan will be bound for that period, after which he will be loosed for a short time and then cast into a lake of fire (Revelation 20:10). Mortal inhabitants of earth and glorified saints of heaven will worship God and every knee will bow and every tongue confess that Jesus Christ is Lord (Isaiah 45:23-24; Philippians 2:10; Romans 14:11).

The added detail of a millennial period is no doubt given to establish the realism of completing the universal redemptive process predicted in both Testaments. Simpson objected strenuously to amillennial and postmillennial positions, saying that the rejection of a restored earthly kingdom "takes out of God's Book all reality and makes everything merely a dream as vague as the fooleries of Christian Science."[5] The millennium begins with the restored kingdom and ends when the transition is complete, followed by a new heaven and earth. The realism of a physical and personal return of Christ and a physical resurrection of the saints in which heaven and earth are spiritually and physically reconciled (Colossians 1:19-20) is in essence the burden of Simpson in *The Gospel of the Kingdom*.[6]

To Simpson the power of the gospel includes a transforming power in the present world. The challenge of saints to overcome the world (Revelation 3:21) is not only to save souls but also to exercise Christ's power and authority by fulfilling God's purpose in creation-history. The Church is God's divine agency, now being trained and educated to rule with Christ in His coming kingdom. The Scriptures boldly assert that the kingdom of the world under Satan will become the kingdom of our Lord and of His Christ and that He will reign forever and ever (11:15).

True Christian spirituality has a commonality with creation that concretizes faith. The natural and the divine are blended in Jesus Christ, who is fully man as well as fully God. Christ Himself is the hope of the world of creation as well as man's salvation.

There are many phenomenal questions for which human answers are impossible. How will every eye see Jesus Christ when He comes (1:7)? Who and by what manner do the mortal inhabitants of earth come into existence during the millennium? How can the glorified saints who accompany Jesus on thrones judge mortals on earth (20:4)? What kind of roles will various saints have to rule and judge, or be in charge of many things (Matthew 25:21)? The Apostle Paul called such unsolved questions a wisdom for the mature but conversely a conundrum to the unregenerate mind. He associated Isaiah 64:4 with the believer's hope and said, "No eye has seen, no ear has heard, no mind has conceived what God has prepared for those who love him" (1 Corinthians 2:9). Again the Scriptures say, "The secret things belong to the LORD our God, but the things revealed belong to us and to our children forever" (Deuteronomy 29:29).

Jesus took a resurrected physical body to glory and He will come again to earth in a like manner as He was seen going into heaven (Acts 1:10-11). Pentecost came about when Jesus was glorified (John 7:39). It was Jesus who with the Father sent the Holy Spirit to impart His own nature to His children and to share with them the purpose of creation. Scripture asserts that all of creation waits in eager expectation for the glory to be revealed in believers and to receive with them a liberation from decay. Creation will be brought into the glorious freedom experienced by the children of God when they are glorified (Romans 8:18-22).

Surely it is true that man's redemption is paramount as expressed in John 3:16-17. The redeemed Church is to reach every human creature in the world with the gospel, but this is not exclusive of its relationship to the world of creation. Jesus was specific when He said that repentance and forgiveness of sins will be preached to *all* nations (Luke 24:47) and that believers will be witnesses in Jerusalem, and in all Judea and Samaria and to the ends of the earth (Acts 1:8). God is interested in the whole world of creation and has certain delight in it as when He created it (Genesis 1:10, 13, 18, 21).

The kingdom of God in mystery form, represented in the Church, will reclaim, by Jesus' blood and by the testimony of the saints, Satan's kingdom of usurped authority. Christ's power, authority and presence are promised to the Church not only to globalize the gospel but also to mitigate evil even though the world will not be Christianized. A conflict of the ages will climax this age with tribulation as the final harvest of earth's redemption and Satan's defeat comes to an ultimate end.

While engaged in research for the centennial history *All for Jesus*, I was amazed how Simpson projected the need of the gospel in various countries in his early publication of the missionary magazine. In detail he described countries not only geographically and demographically, but also their language, climate, history, culture and pagan worship. He described the devastation sin made on their economy, family relationships, the bondage of women, the tyranny of rulers, the plight of physical maladies, the cruelty caused by superstition and the oppression of pagan idolatry.[7] The hope of these countries Simpson recognized as the gospel.

An incident is frequently told of a close associate of Simpson's who awakened in the night to hear groaning intercession. He dared to investigate by peering through a crack in Simpson's study door and saw him kneeling with his arms embracing a large world globe with tears moistening its surface.

The royal priesthood of believers (1 Peter 2:9) is presently given a global stance of authority by being led in triumphal procession despite fierce opposition (2 Corinthians 2:14). Faith need not shrink though pressed by every foe. Satan is not only a personal foe but also one who with his minions seeks to hold territories under his sway (see Daniel 10:12-13). Royal priests, however, believe that the gospel can defeat him and will challenge him on his own ground of devastating influence. The church planted in Satan's territorial domain is a stake of claim over which the gates of hell will not prevail (Matthew 16:18).

III. A Coming Kingdom— A Call to Sanctified Living

Simpson viewed sanctification of believers as essential to the premillennial global mission of the church. Holiness of life to Simpson was not sinlessness, perfectionism or the filling of the Spirit with an evidence sign, but an identification and union with Christ Himself that imparts by the Holy

Spirit Christ's own nature and life (Colossians 1:27). The Christ who in His earthly ministry said that the works He did were not of Himself but of the Father who dwelt within Him, also promised, "If a man remains in me and I in him, he will bear much fruit; apart from me you can do nothing" (John 15:5). Pentecost demonstrated that the power and authority of Christ's gospel was for all people and languages because Christ Himself was glorified (Acts 2:5-39).

Perhaps the greatest weakness of the Church is in its search for a personal possession of power and worthiness. Instead, all that is accomplished for eternity is what Jesus Christ Himself does for us, in us and through us as His saints. Abiding in union with Him to fulfill His purpose and will makes servanthood fruitful—not our worthiness, sinlessness or personal power. If by faith believers abide in union with Him, He will abide in them and they are sheltered by His blood and promised to bear much fruit. Sin is an obstruction to faith and obedience, but to walk in the light volitionally is to be blameless and free with continuous cleansing (1 John 1:7).

Satan exercises all his expertise to defeat the Church by accusing saints day and night (Revelation 12:10). He accuses them of weakness, unworthiness and sins of omission and commission. He only needs to distract them from Christ's sufficiency for power and authority to do God's will. The human self-nature desires to earn its own right for authority and power, whereas a transformed Christlike nature relinquishes all such rights and looks only to Him.

Simpson believed that as members of the Church volitionally set themselves apart for Christ and His kingdom, they were holy for the indwelling power of His Spirit. Obedience to Christ's commission was an obedience of life in every vocational calling. This would gift the Church as a whole for its global task. The Church is called, Simpson believed, to position itself in message and vision on the fullness and sufficiency of Christ Himself to fulfill its high calling.

IV. A Coming Kingdom— A Call to the Church as God's Agency

Simpson viewed The Christian and Missionary Alliance as a cooperative servant of the Church for the fulfillment of its premillennial high calling.

The impact of initial beginnings on the present is too much overlooked. The Fourfold Gospel was an identity slogan of a core faith. Though initially the Alliance was an interdenominational missionary society and not a church per se, it is still its organic dynamism—Christ as Savior, Sanctifier, Healer and Coming King. Premillennially, Christ is Coming King, leading His church on a global mission and in triumphal procession (2 Corinthians 2:14) for a glorious manifestation of the kingdom. In this, Simpson idealized, all evangelical churches could join with no conflict in major doctrine. The Alliance, Simpson wrote, "is not an ecclesiastical body in any sense, but simply a fraternal union of consecrated believers in connection with the various evangelical churches. It does not organize distinct churches, or require its members to leave their present church connection, but helps them to work together in a broader fellowship of sympathy, testimony and service."[8]

Today, we smile at this but it was not a deception. The policy remained as long as Simpson lived and beyond. He explained frequently that the New York Gospel Tabernacle, his pastorate, was a church affiliated with the Alliance. The policy statement, however, reveals the all-embracing vision that motivated Simpson and the significance and scope with which he held the Fourfold Gospel, not as a piecemeal expression of faith, but as a core organism.

Too often we fail to consider the historical context in which bold venture becomes necessary, especially when on an uncharted and untried course. The Church at large was failing in its obedience to the Great Commission—that was too obvious. The risk of sending missionaries without adequate support of intercessory involvement, proper training, an organic faith dynamic that would unite the church at home with the missionary on the front lines—these were essential issues. Financial support was to Simpson a side issue. The physical risks missionaries would encounter was a reality that could not be avoided. A missionary church at home should be as responsible and committed as the missionary it sends.

Dr. Simpson's close friend and confidante, Dr. A.J. Gordon of Boston, began missionary training institutes. The dean of the Boston Institute, Dr. F.L. Chapell, served an Alliance branch in Bridgeport, Connecticut, for years and lectured on occasion at Nyack. Both Simpson and Gordon were deeply committed to the doctrine of divine healing. Simpson's strongest critics were in regard to this doctrine, even though he never sponsored a public and protracted healing campaign.

No doubt Simpson and Gordon were aware of Paul's sufferings depicted in Second Corinthians 11, and of his healing ministry. They knew of the intense suffering of William Carey, the father of modern missions, and of Adoniram Judson and David Brainerd. Did not the promised presence and authority of Jesus include healing of physical suffering? Did not Jesus and His apostles have such ministry?

The Fourfold Gospel represented a scope, a configuration and an integrated focus involving the whole twentieth-century evangelical church.

The Alliance branches operated with increasing ambivalence after Simpson's death. While branches sought to assure churches that no proselytism was intended, many members of branches considered it their church. But while missionaries were being trained under high academic standards of the time at the Missionary Training Institute, lay superintendents for the branches received a six-week course of training "off campus."

Perhaps the biggest influence toward a church-like operation of the branches came in the early 1920s when the fundamentalist movement against liberalism caused many trained ministers in the denominations to resign their churches and accept leadership in Alliance branches. But the need to be the church and to model the missionary mandate was a slow and painful process.

Today, church planting at home and in missionary service has become a major priority of The Christian and Missionary Alliance. Training national pastors for churches planted by missionaries is recognized as highly important. If indigenous churches are to become missionary in the context of their culture, they must be adequately trained to meet the challenge. Not only Bible training institutes but graduate theological schools are also increasing. The turnabout is more revolutionary than has yet been estimated.

V. A Coming Kingdom—A Call to the Holistic Nature of the Church

The globalized call of the Church as given in Matthew 28:18-20 demands an holistic perspective regarding the nature and function of the

Church. The rendering of this passage in the King James Version may suggest that "Go ye into all the world" is an imperative. A more literal rendering may be, "All power is given unto me in heaven and on earth; as you go into all the world. . . ." Globalization is a lifestyle for every believer and for the corporate Church. The Church's nature and function includes world missions—not as an extra piece of baggage, but as its very being. The local church, as a home base for missionary outreach, models its nature by evangelism and baptizes converts to teach them to observe all that Jesus has commanded, which is discipleship formation.

This extends to the formation of the corporate nature and function of the Church. Evangelism and missions, with a grounded faith in the power and authority of Jesus, will extend evangelism at home to missions worldwide. New converts will be identified as "in Christ" and "in the Church" by baptism, and be taught to *observe* all that Jesus commanded.

The holistic nature of the Church is to experience Christ's own power and presence by the Holy Spirit to proclaim the kingdom of God as Jesus did. The kingdom of God was not only important to Jesus' ministry on earth, but also became the theme of His teaching to the disciples after His resurrection. The doctrine of premillennialism is more than prophetic curiosity; it involves a realism that should motivate the Church with a global vision.

To bring into alignment what the Alliance believes and how it functions efficiently and effectively in the full scope of its operation and profession of faith is a very necessary consideration. The fast change of our times and the enormous mixture of communication—academically and technologically—deepens the urgency. The harvest is most plenteous and the laborers so few, we must by God's grace pray and seek divine wisdom to integrate holistically the full scope of our divine mandate. This is not to claim that the Alliance is superior to other churches or denominations; it is our particular calling and responsibility that ought to be fully embraced.

Endnotes

1. Robert Niklaus, John Sawin and Samuel Stoesz, *All for Jesus* (Camp Hill, PA: Christian Publications, Inc., 1986), 37. By the time Simpson's first missionary convention

was held, *The Gospel in All Lands* had ceased publication and was replaced by *The Word, the Work and the World*, a predecessor of the current magazine, *Alliance Life*.

2. *The Story of the C&MA* (New York: Alliance Press, 1900), 6.

3. "The C&M Alliance Converts to Denominational Status," *Eternity*, August 1974, 8.

4. Due to the active missions program of the Alliance and the volatility of sociopolitical conditions across the globe, the actual number of countries in which the Alliance is involved is subject to frequent change.

5. A.B. Simpson, *The Coming One* (New York: Christian Alliance Publishing, 1912), 16.

6. A.B. Simpson, *The Gospel of the Kingdom* (New York: Alliance Press, 1890), 19-20.

7. See early editions of Simpson's missionary magazine, *The Gospel in All Lands*.

8. *The Story of the C&MA*, 3.

Current Considerations

Premillennialism

the Scriptures and Convergent Issues

• K. Neill Foster •

A well-known seminary president has said that within ten years few evangelical organizations will retain their premillennial stance. That trend among evangelicals creates a powerful concern that in the abandonment of premillennialism much more may be surrendered than is immediately apparent. This essay reflects that concern.

To speak of premillennialism is to immediately identify oneself with traditional evangelicalism and with a fervent belief in the return of Jesus Christ. It also implies a certain view of Scripture, particularly of the book of Revelation, in that the six biblical references to 1,000 years are all contained in Revelation chapter 20. (There are other biblical passages which support the concept of a 1,000-year reign of Jesus Christ, but the twentieth chapter of Revelation is the key.)

Related issues to be addressed in this paper include definitions, history, hermeneutics and biblical authority as it interfaces with a number of biblical concerns. Some attention will also be paid to the positions of the Reformers and the era in which premillennialism emerged anew in the evangelical context. Strategic biblical arguments for the premillennial belief will be brought forward. Finally, the potential impact of amillennialism on the missionary mandate will be examined, and the propensity of amillennialism toward liberalism and evolution will be explored.

I. Definitions

A. *Millennialism* can be described as the belief that there will be a righteous rule of 1,000 years on this earth: "Israel will be the center of that kingdom and Jerusalem will be the capital of it. All nations will come to worship at Mount Zion."[1] Implicit in the concept of millennialism is the idea that Christ the Ruler will return before the millennium as Revelation 20 clearly indicates.

B. *Premillennialism* can therefore be described as the express belief that Jesus Christ will indeed return before the millennium described in Revelation 20 and that He will rule and reign for 1,000 years.

C. *Postmillennialism* may be described as follows: "Those who believe Christ will not return until after the millennium are called post-millenarians."[2] The practical anticipation is that the Church through its activity and influence will so permeate society that the kingdom of God will be fashioned before the King appears. The prophecies of both Testaments are not literal but are spiritualized.

D. *Amillennialism* is the disbelief in the literal meaning of the millennial passages in Revelation 20; this view ultimately can be traced to Origen. Whitby, as cited in Haldeman, following the hermeneutics of Origen, taught for example that "all the promises of the kingdom should be taken in a spiritual and allegorical sense."[3] The abandonment of the grammatical/historical "plain sense" hermeneutic is essential to the embrace of amillennialism.

II. History and Premillennialism

Historical patterns on any given subject have profound significance. Nowhere is this more true than in Church history. And in the case of premillennialism, the facts of history are of special impact.

The earliest church fathers were premillennial, as Paul L. King well illustrates elsewhere in this book of essays. Thiessen flatly says that "the early church was premillennial"[4] and Fisher (in a comment of interest to me since I have come to this conclusion on my own) blames the Montanistic heresy of the second century with its prophetic eccentricities for the overthrow of chiliasm in the early Church.[5] Unfortunately, in the early Church, millennialism (i.e., chiliasm) was thought by some to be both sensual and "grossly materialistic."[6] After Origen, it is nearly impossible to overestimate Augustine's formidable contribution in the intervening centuries. Through his influence and writings (including *The City of God*), amillennialism became the *de facto* theology of the Church. With the Reformation and the historic return of the Church to the Bible, belief in the soon coming of Christ reemerged. Luther, Melancthon, Calvin and Knox may all be cited as fervent believers in the return of Jesus Christ.[7] Belief in the *imminent* return of Jesus Christ unfortunately did not extend to premillennialism among the Reformers. Their view of Scripture, however, made the re-emergence of premillennialism likely, if not inevitable.

Indeed, there was a tremendous surge in premillennial belief in the nineteenth and twentieth centuries. And, predictably, the surge was built upon the sturdy view of Scripture embraced earlier by the Reformers. Evangelical leaders crowded the premillennial platform. A.B. Simpson was among them.[8] Thiessen says, ". . . there has been a return to the position of the early Church. Charles Wesley, Isaac Watts, Bengel, Lange, Godet, Ellicott, Trench, Alford, the Bonar brothers and most of the outstanding evangelists of the past and present generations have espoused the premillennial position."[9] From Thiessen's perspective in the mid-twentieth century, he remained optimistic: "During the last sixty years there has been a renewed emphasis upon this blessed hope."[10]

However, as indicated earlier, premillennialism is currently under assault and is being repudiated on many sides.[11] One possible factor in the decline of premillennialism is weariness in regard to the ongoing controversies over pre- and post-tribulational views of the second coming of Jesus Christ. These controversies among dispensational premillennialists, along with present eccentricities in the charismatic/prophecy movements, may have combined to erode belief in premillennialism.

Premillennialism is under attack by academics and theologians, but the common people seem to hear it gladly, as evidenced by the incredible sales of the Left Behind series, which is both premillennial and pretribulational.

Finally, a new interest in Reformed theology sometimes also carries with it a casual disdain for the tenets of premillennialism. In seeking to be Calvin-like and Luther-like, the new "reformers" have not extended their passion for the full authority of Scripture to eschatology. And the long shadow of Augustine's amillennialism has lingered too. These caveats notwithstanding, the biblical arguments for premillennialism are several and strong.

III. Scripture and Premillennialism

Many sections of the Bible can be summoned to advance premillennialism. I include six of these passages here:

1. Revelation 20:1-6 affirms the concept of 1,000 years six times, and it also affirms the rule and reign of a king, specifically Christ's rule. To overthrow or abandon premillennialism, Revelation 20 must be attacked.

2. First Corinthians 15:23-28 references the coming of Jesus Christ and associates it with His rule and reign. This is a strong premillennial passage in that Jesus Christ is portrayed as the conquering monarch, clearly ruling and reigning. Amillennialism and postmillennialism do not fit this passage.

3. Daniel 7:13-14 describes the coming of the Son of Man in the clouds and His subsequent rule. All people, nations and languages will serve Him. It sounds very much like Revelation 20:1-7. Premillennialism fits like a glove.

4. Isaiah 11:2-10 describes the wolf and the lamb dwelling together and a ruler's ensign which "the Gentiles [shall] seek." The ruler here is from "the root of Jesse" and again this scene from the prophet synchronizes with the New Testament passages on the millennium, Revelation 20 and First Corinthians 15.

5. Psalm 2:6-9 gives the description of a king on the holy hill of Zion. The uttermost parts are included, along with the heathen. He rules with a rod of iron. Again, a king ruling in a millennium-like ambiance is in view.

6. Other Scriptures which could be summoned to the premillennialist cause but upon which I will not comment include Isaiah 65:20, 25; Psalm 45:4; Ezekiel 37:27-28; Ezekiel chapters 40-48 (especially 43:19-27, 45:20-21); and Zechariah 14:16-21.

These and yet other Scriptures describe the rule and reign of the Lord Jesus Christ in terms that best fit the premillennial view.

IV. Systematic Theology and Premillennialism

The biblical text is carefully ordered, and God's workmen are to go about correctly dissecting and dividing the sacred Word. Moreover, it can be done rightly (2 Timothy 2:15).

Biblical truth is linear in nature. History is directional. It is going somewhere. It is finally eschatological and apocalyptic: "In the beginning, God . . ." (Genesis 1:1). And a grand climax is coming: "Amen. Come, Lord Jesus" (Revelation 22:20). The ordering of biblical doctrines is essential to biblical understanding. Paul's admonition to Timothy was to divide the Word of God rightly (2 Timothy 2:15).

Premillennialism is part of a serious systematic theology which Professor John Frame has described as follows: ". . . any study that answers the question, 'What does the whole Bible teach us today?' about any given topic."[12] If one takes both the Old Testament anticipation of the kingdom, the inauguration of the kingdom in the life of Jesus Christ, along with the New Testament's description of the millennial kingdom rule of Jesus Christ, one tends to become both millennial, i.e., believing in the millennium, and premillennial, i.e., believing that Jesus Christ will set up His kingdom before the millennium and will rule for 1,000 years. Systematic theology frames the path to premillennialism. The doctrine of last things is inevitably a part of systematic theology.[13]

V. Biblical Interpretation and Premillennialism

The interpretation of Scripture is a significant issue when dealing with the Bible. The application of hermeneutics is an honorable occupation for all who wish to understand what the Bible says. It has been called "the science which teaches the principles of interpretation. Biblical hermeneutics in particular is the science which determines the principles of the interpretation of the Holy Scriptures."[14] An emphasis on the clarity or perspicuity of Scripture reemerged at the time of the Reformation, and we have the Reformers to thank for the contemporary encouragement to read and seek to understand Scripture and to be ruled by it. Plain people should be able to read plain Scripture and plainly understand.

However, hermeneutics has been abused. Chiliasm, or as we prefer, premillennialism, took a jolt early in Church history when Origen, a universalist of sorts, came up with a new hypothesis, suggesting that the biblical "promises of the kingdom should be taken in a spiritual and allegorical sense."[15] That was a hermeneutical shift from the way the early Church believed. Indeed, Thiessen calls Origen "the father of modern postmillennialism."[16]

The spiritualization of the millennial passages continued under Augustine, though he himself hints that at one time he had been a millennialist.[17] As history moved toward the modern era, the Church became increasingly less attached to government, less ready to believe that secular power along with the Christian message would usher in the millennial kingdom. Augustine, though tempted with the millennial view, persisted also in allegorical hermeneutics. The Reformers basically rescued the Church from Augustine's hermeneutical prison, restored the authority and clarity of Scripture and endorsed the priesthood of all believers. In such an atmosphere, millennialism in its "pre-" form could once again emerge. Not surprisingly, two centuries after Luther, premillennialism was back. Believing Revelation 20 literally was back in style.

Agenda Hermeneutics

Today's hermeneutical adventurers have not exactly returned to the allegorical method, which tossed out premillennialism, but have established new ways, modern ways, to circumvent the plain statements of Scripture. A sometimes appropriate cultural hermeneutic, for example, can be a Corban-like way to get around Scriptures one may not like (Mark 7:11). Casuistry, it is called. Evangelicals are tempted in the twenty-first century by agenda hermeneutics from the twentieth century.

- Homosexuals who wish to be Christian ministers must first invent a permissive hermeneutic for the Bible before they can convince themselves or others of their legitimacy.

- Egalitarian/feminist views of the Bible require Scripture-twisting which even Clark Pinnock, no biblicist himself these days, called "hermeneutical ventriloquism."[18]

- Those who wish to advance universalism (or its little sister, inclusivism) must have an agenda hermeneutic to negate John 14:6 in which Jesus claims that He is the way, the truth and life and that no one comes to the Father except through Him.

- Dampening down hell's eternal fire also requires a certain agenda hermeneutic. If one begins with the *a priori* argument that hell simply could not be eternal, one must then get around texts like Matthew 25:46, where eternal life and eternal fire are locked together with the same Greek words in the same verse.

Modern examples of agenda hermeneutics could be enlarged beyond this section, but time and space do not allow. My estimation is that evangelicals are presently being tempted with about 100 kinds of interpretation, nearly all of them suspect and agenda-driven.

What kind of hermeneutic, then, overturns premillennialism? The "problem" passage—if one is interested in abandoning premillennialism—is Revelation 20. John, by the Holy Spirit, had the audacity to mention 1,000 years six times. Further, Revelation 21 describes heaven, which no one wants to abandon or explain away. What is needed for the abandonment of premillennialism is a judicious application of the "spiritualize-all-prophecy" hermeneutic to Revelation 20, taking care not to disturb Revelation 21 (and the reality of heaven) with the interpretation. The evidence is clear: In current evangelicalism this hermeneutical dance is underway, the elimination of premillennialism pending in some parts.

It would be possible to reserve the arguments just made for millennialism alone. However, Revelation 20 has Jesus Christ the King on the scene. Believers are to rule and reign with a present, ruling, reigning Christ. That is a premillennial implication.

VI. *Inerrancy and Premillennialism*

The very words of Scripture are important. "Inerrancy" and "plenary" are words which describe a view of Scripture which focuses on the actual words of the ancient text. Jesus talked about "jots" and "tittles" never passing away (Matthew 5:18). Paul made profound arguments on the singular and plural forms of a single word in the Old Testament (Galatians 3:16). Is the Bible to be trusted when it says, "they will be priests of God and of Christ and will reign with him for a thousand years" (Revelation 20:6)? Some of the newer translations shy away from John's declaration that believers will be "kings and priests" (1:6). The Greek word is plainly "kings." Reigning with Christ in a literal way during the millennium requires a perspective of Christ as the ruling King of kings. Plain statements of Scripture have to be overturned or set aside in order to avoid belief in Christ as King in the millennium.

"It could not be said that all amillennialists deny the verbal, plenary inspiration of the Scriptures . . . [yet] it seems to be the first step in that direction. The system of spiritualizing Scripture is a tacit erosion of the doctrine of the verbal, plenary inspiration of the Scriptures. . . ."[19]

Some amillennialists do tend toward eroded views of Scripture. This is an exceptionally worrisome tendency, but it is not a rule; some amillennialists are anything but weak on Scripture.

Our Error

From the amillennial view, the fundamental error of premillennialism is the view of Scripture that tends to be embraced by us as chiliasts.[20] If that "fundamental error" is the verbal and plenary view of inspiration, we plead joyfully guilty! In formal terms, premillennialism is a natural outgrowth of the grammatical/historical pattern of interpretation.

Loraine Boettner makes a remarkable admission, speaking to a premillennialist as an amillennialist, when he flatly says, "It is generally agreed that if prophecies are taken literally, they do foretell a restoration of the nation Israel in the land of Palestine with the Jews having a prominent place in that kingdom and ruling over the other nations."[21]

VII. Christology and Premillennialism

Christ is the King in the premillennial view of eschatology. Indeed, He is the King of kings and Lord of lords (Revelation 19:16). His kingdom has been anticipated (Psalm 2:6-12; Matthew 3:2), has arrived (Zechariah 9:9-10; Luke 4:18) and is still coming (Matthew 24:14). And we are to pray for it as the Lord's prayer makes clear (6:10). All of those statements amplify the broadly based biblical and Christological teaching about the King and the kingdom of God. Gerhard Kittel says, "In the general linguistic usage, it is to be noted that the word *basileia*, which we usually translate realm, designated first of all the existence, the character, the position of the king. Since it concerns a king, we would best speak of his majesty, his authority."[22]

To abandon the concept of a literal millennium presents the necessity of belief in a King without a literal kingdom. If there is no millennium, one has to wonder about the plain statements of Scripture and the hundreds of biblical references about the kingdom of God which are disenfranchised. Millennialism is implicit if there is a soon-coming King.

Christological Reality

Ultimately the kingship of Jesus Christ is an unalterable, nonnegotiable Christological reality. Ladd sums it up: "... the millennial reign of Christ will be the [Christological] manifestation in history of the lordship and sovereignty which is his already."[23]

Alliance evangelist Joel Van Hoogen refers to premillennialism in a Christological context as well. "The Alliance teaching on the centrality of Christ in the history of the world is evidenced by its unwillingness to be sidetracked into focusing upon God's dealing with the nation Israel as the primary key for understanding eschatology. Rather, the focus remained on Christ. ..."[24]

VIII. *Biblical Holiness and Premillennialism*

Two Scriptures are very emphatic here: "And every man that hath this hope in him purifieth himself, even as he is pure" (1 John 3:3, KJV); "And the very God of peace sanctify you wholly; and I pray your whole spirit and soul and body be preserved blameless unto the coming of our Lord Jesus Christ" (1 Thessalonians 5:23, KJV). If the millennium is not real, then is the Lord really coming, and is there anything to get ready for and be pure about? Or if the millennial dawn arrives after the whole world abandons sin and gradually converts to Christianity, how does present-tense holiness connect to an event that may be a thousand years hence? (An important caveat here: It is a stretch to blame amillennial thought for the pervasive carnality of weak believers.)

A.B. Simpson saw premillennialism as a great and powerful instrument in the life of a believer. "This is an intensely practical truth—a great lever that will uplift the world into a fitness to receive Him. It is intimately associated with holiness. 'He that hath this hope purifieth himself even as He is pure' (1 John 3:3)."[25]

The Apostle Paul yearned for his coming crown, but also believed there would be a crown for those that "love his appearing" (2 Timothy 4:8, KJV). The author of Hebrews wrote, "Follow peace with all men, and holiness, without which no man shall see the Lord" (Hebrews 12:14, KJV).

This is not the place to present a thorough exposition of the doctrine of holiness in the New Testament, but simply to say that this soundly biblical doctrine is there, and it is unavoidable. It is part of the authentic Christian message and is biblically linked to the return of Jesus Christ. Premillennialism is a theological option which stimulates a vibrant personal faith and encourages, even demands, an ardent pursuit of holiness. (I admit, however, that some Reformed amillennialists do take injunctions to holiness very seriously.)

IX. *Imminence and Premillennialism*

"Watch therefore: for ye know not what hour your Lord doth come" (Matthew 24:42, KJV). There is a thread of imminence about Christ's return winding all the way through the New Testament. "Strange it is," says A.J. Gordon, "that we have reached an age where it is counted an eccentricity to love His appearance and a theological error to cry with the best-loved apostle, 'Even so come, Lord Jesus!' "[26] For A.B. Simpson, a strong factor in his turn to premillennialism was the element of watchfulness admonished in Scripture. "Another reason firmly impressed on my mind was the use of the word *watch*. If a thing is not imminent, why watch for it? If the millennium was to come first, that and not His coming, would be the event to watch for. If that word [*watch*] means anything, it means that He might come anytime."[27]

X. *The Missiological Mandate and Premillennialism*

The "end" was connected to the Great Commission by the Lord Jesus Christ. "And this gospel of the kingdom shall be preached in all the world for a witness unto all nations; and then shall the end come" (24:14, KJV). A.B. Simpson was focused resolutely on this biblical mandate. Simpson preached "that our Lord's return was imminent; it awaited no future event, and was dependent only on the completion of world evangelism."[28]

For a more current view of the connection between the missionary mandate and premillennialism, Keith Bailey once summarized the views of The Christian and Missionary Alliance as follows:

> The return of Jesus Christ is premillennial. The literal manifestation of Christ's rule over the nations of the world and His reign over Israel will not come about until His Second Coming. For now, the Church here on earth persists in the task of world evangelism while

she waits for the coming of her Lord (Matt. 24:14). From the perspective of the Bible, the soon coming of Jesus Christ is a strong motivation for world missions.[29]

Dispensational premillennialism, which is traced back to Darbyism[30] in the current era, suggests that Israel will finish the missionary mandate during the tribulation days.[31] That dispensational view, while generally missionary in perspective, can tend to erode missionary passion by suggesting that someone else will finish the task. You will find, however, that the overwhelming majority of premillennialists, including dispensational premillennialists, believe that the King is coming and that the missionary mandate must be relentlessly pursued.

Now back to Simpson. In an essay entitled, "The Missionary Eschatology of A.B. Simpson," Franklin Pyles says of Simpson, "Every single point of his end-time thinking had a definite impact on his plan to preach the gospel across the world. And, at the same time, his missionary theology guided his eschatology, for if a point of prophecy had no impact on missionary strategy, he had little concern for it."[32] At the end of his essay, Pyles observes, "The current divorce between our missionary practice and our eschatology can be overcome by again asserting the strengths of premillennialism: A real kingdom will soon be inaugurated on this earth by the personal presence of Jesus Christ."[33]

XI. Conclusion

The authority of the Scriptures is integrally related to premillennialism. An eroded view of Scripture may facilitate both amillennialism and postmillennialism while not necessarily being unique to them. The debate should never rest on the varieties of eschatological interpretations. *It should rest rather and always on the full authority of Scripture and the hermeneutic to be applied to prophecy.* Donald Wiggins cautions, "I believe the fundamental problem [with the amillennial view] is a blindness to a literal approach to prophecy carried over in the historical Reformed tradition."[34]

A.B. Simpson seems to have "muddled through" with many of his changing views on prophecy, but there never was any doubt about his resolute view of Scripture. For many years, until 1992, his "Christ in the Bible Series" commentary on the book of Revelation was not kept in print by

Christian Publications, the publishing house he founded. In that same year, the series was renamed *The Christ in the Bible Commentary* and reissued with these comments placed at the beginning of Revelation:

> As you read this final volume of the series you may understand why it was not kept current. It was not simply that Simpson's view of a partial rapture ran counter to the prevailing evangelical opinion in the first half of the century. . . . Simpson was unashamedly in love with Jesus Christ, and he longed for His return. Simpson was concerned for a lost world of people, and he worked night and day for their evangelization. He was persuaded [biblically] that world evangelization must precede the end-time events portrayed in *Revelation*.[35]

A church historian might further observe that the first three centuries of the Church, along with the last two centuries, have been the most predominantly missionary centuries in the entire history of the Church. Is it coincidental that premillennialism is connected with the grand expansion of the Christian Church? I think not. Do theological dalliances with amillennialism and postmillennialism have a frightful missiological cost? Do they tend to impede obedience to the missionary mandate? If so, they must be resisted—for the sake of the still-lost world. Groups like The Christian and Missionary Alliance play with amillennialism or postmillennialism at their profound peril.

For the Alliance, at stake ultimately is the "Missionary" in the name.

Warnings from the Elders

Wendell Grout, long-time pastor of the First Alliance Church in Calgary, Alberta, put it this way: "Have you ever seen a premillennial liberal?"[36] The answer is self-evident. And one more warning from yet another elder: Harold O.J. Brown, of academic fame among evangelicals, recently cited a friend[37] as saying that noting a person's stand on an issue is only one part of the equation. One needs as well to see which way the person is leaning.

To abandon premillennialism as some have done, "leans."

Does it "lean" finally toward the denial of inerrancy and authority of Scripture? Possibly. It would be better in my view never to have been premillennial than to have been premillennial and then to have abandoned it.

Endnotes

1. Henry C. Thiessen, *Lectures in Systematic Theology* (Grand Rapids: Eerdmans, 1952), 282-3.
2. Jesse Forrest Silver, *The Lord's Return* (New York: Revell, 1914), 37.
3. M.I. Haldeman, *History of the Doctrine of Our Lord's Return* (Philadelphia: Philadelphia School of the Bible, 1914), 26.
4. Thiessen, 470.
5. George P. Fisher, *History of the Christian Church* (New York: Charles Scribner's Sons, 1902), 84ff.
6. Charles L. Feinburg, *Millennialism* (Chicago, IL: Moody, 1982), 42.
7. Haldeman, 23ff.
8. A.B. Simpson, "How I Was Led to Believe in Premillennialism," *Communicate*, June 2000.
9. Thiessen, 471.
10. Ibid.
11. K. Neill Foster, "Calgary Assembly 2000," *Alliance Life*, October 2000, 31-2.
12. Wayne Grudem, *Systematic Theology* (Grand Rapids: Zondervan, 1994), 21.
13. Millard J. Erickson, *Christian Theology* (Grand Rapids: Baker, 1983), 23. Cf. also George Eldon Ladd, *The Gospel of the Kingdom* (Grand Rapids: Eerdmans, 1959).
14. Charles C. Ryrie, *The Premillennial Faith* (New York: Loizeau Brothers, 1953), 34.
15. Haldeman, 26.
16. Thiessen, 471.
17. Harold P. Shelley, "Premillennialism in the Medieval and Reformation Times," *Essays on Premillennialism* (Camp Hill, PA: Christian Publications, 2002), 14-6.
18. Clark H. Pinnock, "Biblical Authority and the Issues in Question" in *Women, Authority and the Bible* (Downers Grove, IL: InterVarsity, 1986), 57-8.
19. Ryrie, 34-5.
20. Ibid., 36.
21. Robert G. Clouse, *The Meaning of the Millennium* (Downers Grove, IL: InterVarsity, 1977), 95.
22. Gerhard Kittel and Gerhard Freidrich, eds., *Theological Dictionary of the New Testament* (Grand Rapids: Eerdmans, 1949), 579.
23. Clouse, 32.
24. Joel Van Hoogen (2000, www.christianpublications.com/periodicals/communicate/no1page2.htm).
25. A.B. Simpson, "How I Was Led to Believe in Premillennialism," *The Christian and Missionary Alliance Weekly*, November 13, 1891.
26. William Bell Riley, "The Historical Ministry of Premillenarianism," *The Biblical Evangelist*, November-December 2000.
27. Simpson, 298-9.
28. Lindsay Reynolds, *Rebirth, the Redevelopment of The Christian and Missionary Alliance in Canada* (Toronto, ON: The Christian and Missionary Alliance in Canada, 1992), 10.
29. Keith M. Bailey, *Bringing Back the King* (Colorado Springs, CO: The Christian and Missionary Alliance, 1992), 84.
30. Millard J. Erickson, *Contemporary Options in Eschatology* (Grand Rapids: Baker, 1977), 132.

31. William R. Goetz, *Apocalypse Next* (Camp Hill, PA: Christian Publications, 1996), 362.
32. Franklin Pyles, "The Missionary Eschatology of A.B. Simpson," *Birth of a Vision* (Camp Hill, PA: Christian Publications, 1994), 32.
33. Pyles, 44.
34. Donald Wiggins, written comments on an early manuscript of this paper, March 2002.
35. K. Neill Foster, editorial comments in *The Christ in the Bible Commentary* (Camp Hill, PA: Christian Publications, 1992), vol. 6, 407.
36. Telephone conversation with Wendell Grout, March 2001.
37. Conversation with Harold O.J. Brown, Fall 2001.

Bibliography

Bailey, Keith M. *Bringing Back the King.* Colorado Springs: The Christian and Missionary Alliance, 1992.

Boettner, Loraine. "Postmillennialism," *The Meaning of the Millennium: Four Views.* Downers Grove, IL: InterVarsity, 1977.

Brown, H.O.J. Conversation with the author, Fall 2001.

Clouse, Robert G., ed. *The Meaning of the Millennium.* Downers Grove, IL: InterVarsity, 1977.

Draper, Kenneth L. "Simpson and Alliance Eschatology" (1998). Available online at http://online.cbccts.ca/alliancestudies/draper/l12_esch.html

Erickson, Millard J. *Christian Theology.* Grand Rapids: Baker, 1983.

————. *Contemporary Options in Eschatology.* Grand Rapids: Baker, 1977.

Feinburg, Charles L. *Millennialism.* Chicago, IL: Moody, 1982.

Fisher, George P. *History of the Christian Church.* New York: Charles Scribner's Sons, 1888.

Foster, K. Neill. "Discernment, the Powers and Spirit-speaking." Pasadena, CA: Fuller Seminary unpublished dissertation, 1988.

————. "Publisher's Foreword." *Christ in the Bible Commentary,* vol. 6. Camp Hill, PA: Christian Publications, 1992.

————. "Calgary Assembly 2000." *Alliance Life.* October, 2000.

Goetz, William R. *Apocalypse Next.* Camp Hill, PA: Christian Publications, 1996.

Grenz, Stanley J. *The Millennial Maze.* Downers Grove, IL: InterVarsity, 1992.

Grout, Wendell. Conversation with the author, March 2001.

Grudem, Wayne. *Systematic Theology.* Grand Rapids: Zondervan, 1994.

Haldeman, M.I. *History of the Doctrine of Our Lord's Return.* Philadelphia: Philadelphia School of the Bible, 1914.

Hartzfeld, David F. and Charles Nienkirchen, eds. *Birth of a Vision.* Camp Hill, PA: Christian Publications, 1994.

Kaiser, Walter C., Jr. and Moises Silva. *An Introduction to Biblical Hermeneutics.* Grand Rapids: Zondervan, 1994.

Pinnock, Clark H. "Biblical Authority and the Issues in Question," *Women, Authority and the Bible*. Downers Grove, IL: InterVarsity, 1986.

Pyles, Franklin. "The Missionary Eschatology of A.B. Simpson." *Birth of a Vision*. Camp Hill, PA: Christian Publications, 1994.

Reynolds, Lindsay. *Rebirth, The Redevelopment of The Christian and Missionary Alliance in Canada*. Toronto: The Christian and Missionary Alliance in Canada, 1992.

Riley, William Bell. "The Historical Ministry of Premillenarianism." *The Biblical Evangelist*. November-December 2000.

Ryrie, Charles C. *The Premillennial Faith*. New York: Loizeau Brothers, 1953.

Silver, Jesse Forrest. *The Lord's Return*. New York: Revell, 1914.

Simpson, A.B. "How I Was Led to Believe in Premillennialism." *The Christian and Missionary Alliance Weekly*, November 13, 1891.

———. "How I Was Led to Believe in Premillennialism." *Communicate*. June 2000.

Thiessen, Henry C. *Lectures in Systematic Theology*. Grand Rapids: Eerdmans, 1952.

Walvoord, John F. *The Millennial Kingdom*. Grand Rapids: Zondervan, 1959.

6

Premillennialism

Jesus Christ and the Church

• Keith M. Bailey •

A sequence of events lies at the very heart of premillennialism. Jesus Christ must return before the millennial kingdom can be openly manifested to the world. Christ stands at the center of this awesome eschatological event. The genius of Christianity is the incarnation of the eternal Christ followed by His sinless life, His death on the cross, His resurrection from the dead, His ascension into heaven and His position at the right hand of the Father. These great redemptive events form the backbone of New Testament Christology but they do not exhaust the subject. A full understanding of Christology takes in the offices, reign, glory and judgment entailed in His literal 1,000-year reign over all the earth and its peoples. The full display of Christ's glory awaits His return to set up the kingdom.

The Ruler of the Kings of the Earth

One of the great Christological passages in the New Testament is found in the book of Revelation:

John, to the seven churches which are in Asia:

Grace to you and peace from Him who is and who was and who is to come, and from the seven Spirits who are before His throne, and from Jesus Christ, the faithful witness, the firstborn from the dead, and the ruler over the kings of the earth. To Him who loved us and washed us from our sins in His own blood, and has made us kings and priests to His God and Father, to Him be glory and dominion forever and ever. Amen.

Behold, He is coming with clouds, and every eye will see Him, even they who pierced Him. And all the tribes of the earth will mourn because of Him. Even so, Amen.

"I Am the Alpha and the Omega, the Beginning and the End," says the Lord, "who is and who was and who is to come, the Almighty." (1:4-8, NKJV)

The Apostle John brings together in this doxology a magnificent display of the powers, perfections, glory, offices and attributes of the Lord Jesus Christ. Here is strong evidence that the teaching of premillennialism has its own contribution to the New Testament doctrine of Christ. John ranges in his treatment of the eternal Christ from His preexistence, His days in the flesh, to His coming kingdom. The work of Christ cannot be complete without His literal reign over the nations of the earth. The Greek expositor H.C.H. Lenski calls this passage the signature of Christ's deity.[1] It is plain that the glory of His second coming is part of the signature of Christ's deity. The return of Christ has deeper implications than the proper close of history. It will be the long-awaited vindication of His glory and His right to reign, won at Calvary.

What are the precise aspects of Christology related to eschatology and premillennialism in particular? There are five that we will consider in this study. The first of these is found in Revelation 1:5, where Christ is called "the ruler over the kings of the earth" (NKJV). At no time while Christ was upon earth did He rule over the nations and at no time since His ascension to heaven has He literally exercised rule over the nations on earth. Christ's use of His kingly right over the earth is part of the *eschaton*.

While prophets portray the kingdom of God as everlasting, they maintain that a critical aspect of that kingdom is a literal reign of Christ over the nations of the world. This phase of the kingdom of God is commonly called the Millennium, because Revelation 20 says that this reign will last 1,000 years. This concept echoes all through the Bible. Across the ages the prophets have been calling for Messiah's glorious reign over Jews and Gentiles. The Psalmist says, "Yes, all kings shall fall down before Him; All nations shall serve Him" (Psalm 72:11, NKJV). The whole of Psalm 72 deals with the universal reign of Messiah.

The second Psalm brings this doctrine into clearer focus. It is evident from the use of this passage in the New Testament that it refers to Christ. The Psalmist describes a rebellion of the nations against God and His Son Jesus Christ. The Father has predetermined that the nations will be subjugated to Christ. God affirms the placement of Christ as King. God says to His Son,

> "Ask of Me, and I will give You
>   the nations for Your inheritance,

And the ends of the earth for
   Your possession.
You shall break them with a
   rod of iron;
You shall dash them to pieces
   like a potter's vessel." (2:8-9, NKJV)

Some want to interpret this verse as a promise for world evangelism but that is not its meaning. Christ does not propagate the gospel with an iron scepter. This divine word has application to the coming day when Christ returns as King of kings. Biblical prophecy shows Christ returning to the earth in great power and glory to take immediate and full control of the chaotic international situation described in Revelation 19:17-21. After subjugating the nations, Christ will judge them from His throne of glory (Matthew 25:31-45). Revelation 19:15 says, "Now out of His mouth goes a sharp sword, that with it He should strike the nations. And He Himself will rule them with a rod of iron. He Himself treads the winepress of the fierceness and wrath of Almighty God" (NKJV).

Add to the above Scripture the prediction of Zechariah, which details the events of Christ's second coming in relation to His governmental rule over the world. Zechariah presents the return of Christ to the earth at a time of international war. With great victory Christ puts down every enemy and in the words of the prophet He becomes "King over all the earth" (Zechariah 14:9, NKJV). The multiple testimony of the Scriptures leaves no doubt as to the literal and earthly reign of our Lord over the nations immediately following His second advent. Any effort to spiritualize these passages falls short of sound hermeneutics. A whole Christology calls for Christ to rule as King of kings, and no such reign has yet occurred. The church is still waiting for the Coming King. The prophetic expectations can only be satisfied by the literal, visible, personal and bodily return of Jesus Christ, followed by the public establishment of His kingdom over all terrestrial affairs.

The King of the Jews

Deeply instilled in the Old Testament prophets lies the hope that when Messiah comes, He will take up His throne as a descendant of David and be king over Israel. When Pilate ordered a placard over the cross of Jesus which read "The King of the Jews," he had no idea of the far-reaching implication of that title. The New Testament fills in the details of what it means that Jesus Christ is King of the Jews. The angel Gabriel's announcement of the virgin birth of Christ to Mary prophesied this royal baby's future work. Luke's record says, "He will be great, and will be called the Son of the Highest; and the Lord God will give Him the throne of His father David. And He will reign over the house of Jacob forever; and of His kingdom there will be no end" (Luke 1:32-33, NKJV).

When the kingship of Christ is considered christologically it must be pointed out that Christ will be King over Israel in a very special way—a sovereign rule that must be distinguished from His universal rule over Gentile governments. The roots of the concept of Messiah's rule over Israel go back to near the end of David's reign. God made a covenant with David that his seed would reign forever over Israel. The incarnate Christ comes from the line of David and will fulfill the covenant God made with David so long ago.

Near the close of David's reign over Israel he shared with Nathan the prophet his strong desire to build a temple for the Lord. God spoke to David through Nathan that he was not to build the temple but that his son would build it. At that time God revealed to David a covenant that would make his throne everlasting. The Lord said, "Your house and your kingdom shall be established forever before you. Your throne shall be established forever" (2 Samuel 7:16, NKJV). The prophet Hosea said of Israel,

> For the children of Israel shall abide many days without king or prince, without sacrifice or sacred pillar, without ephod or teraphim. Afterward the children of Israel shall return and seek the LORD their God and David their king. They shall fear the LORD and His goodness in the latter days. (Hosea 3:4-5, NKJV)

In a few words the prophet bridges the history of Israel from the suspension of the kingdom until the last days when Christ returns to rule as their King.

It was always God's intention that His covenant people should be under a theocratic kingdom. It was for this reason God was offended with Israel's request for a human king. God is the rightful King over Israel and that divine plan will be renewed at the Second Coming of Christ. Israel's spiritual renewal is associated with that eschatological event. Jeremiah says,

> "Behold, the days are coming,"
>> says the LORD,
> "That I will raise to David a
>> Branch of righteousness;
> A King shall reign and prosper,
> And execute judgment and righteousness in the earth.
> In His days Judah will be saved,
> And Israel will dwell safely;
> Now this is His name by
>> which He will be called:
>> THE LORD OUR RIGHTEOUSNESS."
>> (Jeremiah 23:5-6, NKJV)

Jeremiah shows the theocratic kingdom over Israel to have international domain. The whole world will be ruled by Israel's King, the Lord Jesus Christ. The fulfillment of these prophecies awaits the premillennial reign of Christ. Israel, for centuries the tail of the nations, will become the head. From Jerusalem Christ will rule the world in righteousness, peace and justice. He who must reign as King of kings must also reign as king over Israel as the prophets have promised.

Lifting the Curse from Creation

The premillennial coming of Jesus Christ will benefit the natural creation. After the fall of man God told Adam He would curse the earth and man would continue to deal with the adverse effects of the curse (Genesis 3:17). The curse on the natural earth has some astounding theological implications. The Apostle Paul relates the release of creation from the curse to the events of final redemption:

> For the earnest expectation of the creation eagerly waits for the revealing of the sons of God. For the creation was subjected to futility, not willingly, but because of Him who subjected it in hope; because the creation itself also will be delivered from the bondage of corruption into the glorious liberty of the children of God. For we know that the whole creation groans and labors with birth pangs together until now. (Romans 8:19-22, NKJV)

Nothing in the earthly ministry of Jesus, nor the long centuries of the church's history, even comes close to this expectation. It waits for the blessed hope of Christ's second advent followed by the manifestation of the kingdom of God on earth.

Darrell Bock, professor of New Testament studies at Dallas Theological Seminary, says of the gospel of Christ, "Its power will extend into the complete unending redemption for us and the creation."[2]

The Romans passage associates the liberation of creation with the glorification of God's people. Paul specifies the creation's deliverance to be from corruption. Christ as the Redeemer will be the immediate agent of this great work. He subjected the natural world to the curse and He alone can lift it. The outworking of this truth will take place when Christ returns and begins His reign over the earth. The creation earnestly awaits this redemptive work of Messiah.

This doctrine has its roots in the Old Testament. The prophets spoke of radical changes in the natural order at the time of Messiah's rule. Isaiah said,

> The wolf also shall dwell with the lamb,
>   The leopard shall lie down with the young goat,
> The calf and the young lion and the fatling together;
>   And a little child shall lead them.
> The cow and the bear shall graze;
>   Their young ones shall lie down together;
> And the lion shall eat straw like the ox.
>   The nursing child shall play by the cobra's hole,
> And the weaned child shall put his hand in the viper's den.
>   They shall not hurt nor destroy in all My holy mountain,
> For the earth shall be full of the knowledge of the LORD
>   As the waters cover the sea. (Isaiah 11:6-9, NKJV)

Irrespective of the efforts to spiritualize this passage and others like it, the plain sense of the Word of God is unavoidable: The kingdom of Christ on earth will bring about a change in the natural order consistent with the deliverance of that order from the curse.

It is the Romans 8 passage which relates the restitution of the natural world to the glorification of God's people. H.P. Liddon, renowned Anglican scholar of the Greek New Testament, brings this truth into focus:

... on account of God and in order to satisfy His will, without the will of nature itself, but with the appended condition of a hope that not merely the children of God, but irrational nature as well, would be delivered from the bondage which consists in corruption, into the freedom which consists in the glory of the children of God.[3]

What incredible glory will characterize the Second Advent of the Lord Jesus Christ! The release of His redemptive power will exceed all that has ever transpired in ages past. Christ's appearing and His kingdom will introduce planet Earth to the glad day for which it has been longing.

Isaiah and Amos both prophesy of great productivity from the land during millennial days:

> The wilderness and the wasteland shall be glad for them,
>   And the desert shall rejoice and blossom as the rose;
> It shall blossom abundantly and rejoice,
>   Even with joy and singing.
> The glory of Lebanon shall be given to it,
>   The excellence of Carmel and Sharon.
> They shall see the glory of the LORD,
>   The excellency of our God.
>
> Strengthen the weak hands,
>   And make firm the feeble knees.
> Say to those who are fearful-hearted,
>   "Be strong, do not fear!
> Behold, your God will come with vengeance,
>   With the recompense of God;
>   He will come and save you."
>
> Then the eyes of the blind shall be opened,
>   And the ears of the deaf shall be unstopped.
> Then the lame shall leap like a deer,
>   And the tongue of the dumb sing.
> For waters shall burst forth in the wilderness,
>   And streams in the desert.
> The parched ground shall become a pool,
>   And the thirsty land springs of water;
> In the habitation of jackals, where each lay,
>   There shall be grass with reeds and rushes.

A highway shall be there, and a road,
 And it shall be called the Highway of Holiness.
The unclean shall not pass over it,
 But it shall be for others.
Whoever walks the road, although a fool,
 Shall not go astray.
No lion shall be there,
 Nor shall any ravenous beast go up on it;
 It shall not be found there.
But the redeemed shall walk there,
 And the ransomed of the LORD shall return,
 And come to Zion with singing,
 With everlasting joy on their heads.
They shall obtain joy and gladness,
 And sorrow and sighing shall flee away. (35:1-10, NKJV)

"Behold, the days are coming," says the LORD,
 "When the plowman shall overtake the reaper,
 And the treader of grapes him who sows seed;
 The mountains shall drip with sweet wine,
 And all the hills shall flow with it.
I will bring back the captives of My people Israel;
 They shall build the waste cities and inhabit them;
 They shall plant vineyards and drink wine from them;
 They shall also make gardens and eat fruit from them.
I will plant them in their land,
 And no longer shall they be pulled up
 From the land I have given them,"
 Says the LORD your God. (Amos 9:13-15, NKJV)

The prospect of renewed fertility takes on a new significance for modern Christians. They are well aware of the pollution of the air, land and water by man. Even the secular world sees the seriousness of this problem. At His kingdom, the Lord Jesus Christ will not only lift the curse from the earth, but will also restore it to its optimum productivity. This implies the cleansing and restoration of all of the systems of nature. The weather, rainfall, plant life, insects and other forces and creatures of nature will work in harmony to bring abundant fruitfulness to the earth. It will be normal for the first time since the Garden of Eden. What a testimony of the unlimited power of Jesus Christ!

The Judge

Not much is said in theological literature or in modern preaching about our Lord's holy office of judge. Perhaps it is because the reality of His judgment role awaits His premillennial coming. In the Old Testament at the placing of the ark of the covenant into the tabernacle David composed a wonderful Psalm.

> Let the heavens rejoice, and let the earth be glad;
>> And let them say among the nations, "The LORD reigns."
> Let the sea roar, and all its fullness;
>> Let the field rejoice, and all that is in it.
> Then the trees of the woods shall rejoice before the LORD,
>> For He is coming to judge the earth. (1 Chronicles 16:31-33, NKJV)

David, with the inspiration of the Holy Spirit, looked to the time of Messiah's reign when the theocratic kingdom would enjoy its ultimate triumph in human history. The crowned Christ comes not only to rule but also to judge. J.A. Seiss, a Lutheran theologian well known for his works on premillennialism, saw a strong correlation between the kingdom and judgment. He said, "In a general sense, then, and as presenting a key to this whole subject, we might say that the judgment of God is the administration of the government of God."[4]

Premillennialism sees the judgment as a progression in events rather than a general judgment as advocated by Reformed theology and other amillennialists. It would be difficult to reconcile the judgments of the nations, the judgment seat of Christ and the great white throne judgment with the concept of a general judgment. These judgments occur in vastly different contexts. His judgment of the Church will take place after the rapture of the Church. As a function of His kingly office, the Lord Jesus Christ, at His second advent, will judge the nations over which He is taking authority. The judgment of the wicked (the great white throne judgment) will come after the 1,000-year reign, described as follows:

> Then I saw a great white throne and Him who sat on it, from whose
> face the earth and the heaven fled away. And there was found no place

for them. And I saw the dead, small and great, standing before God, and books were opened. And another book was opened, which is the Book of Life. And the dead were judged according to their works, by the things which were written in the books. The sea gave up the dead who were in it, and Death and Hades delivered up the dead who were in them. And they were judged, each one according to his works. Then Death and Hades were cast into the lake of fire. This is the second death. And anyone not found written in the Book of Life was cast into the lake of fire. (Revelation 20:11-15, NKJV)

The Conqueror

The literal reign of Christ for a thousand years is essential to the final subjugation of Satan and the forces of darkness. When Christ died on the cross, He spoiled principalities and powers and made a show of them openly, triumphing over them on the cross. Alongside that great victory lies the fact that Satan continues his diabolical activities to the present hour and dares to make war on the saints.

The seeming paradox is answered by the truth that God permits the continued activity of the evil one to test the Church and to strengthen the loyalty of believers. But this arrangement is not eternal. There must come a time in history when the devil and his demons no longer have access to mankind and the world.

Satan is called the god of this world. His claim to Christ at the temptation was not an empty boast. This fallen world has been under his rulership for all the centuries. During this time, the victory of Christ may be claimed by faith as final, and may defeat the devil in individual situations. At the coming of Christ's millennial kingdom all of this will be changed. Christ the King will take up His rightful authority over the world. One of the first acts of Christ's second advent will be the total subjugation of the powers of hell and their confinement in the pit.

The kingdom of Christ will be like heaven on earth, for Satan cannot touch it. Mankind will be free of the deception and the seduction of the mastermind of evil. Satan can throw no shadow on the pure light of the kingdom of God on earth. In the scheme of eschatology, premillennialism alone offers prospect of the total defeat of the evil one within the boundaries of time and space history.

The conquest of Calvary will be fully displayed as the crowned Christ rules the earth in righteousness and peace during the Millennium.

Revelation 20:1 describes the manner of Satan's defeat. Christ is so in control, He dispatches an ordinary angel to bind and dispose of our ancient foe. At the close of this millennium, Satan will be released briefly. In true character, he masses an army of rebellious souls to attack the city of God. But the mighty power of the Conqueror, Christ Jesus, puts him down immediately and vanquishes him forever in the lake of fire. Not only did Christ win a victory over Satan spiritually, but He will also terminate his activity for eternity. Christ's literal rule of righteousness on earth will bring out in full every dimension of His Calvary victory.

The Church

As premillennialism shows Christ in all His glory, so it displays the bridal Church in its ultimate destiny. The last mention of the Church in the New Testament refers to her as the Bride (Revelation 21:9). Before Christ comes out of heaven with the saints, an event called the marriage supper of the Lamb will take place in heaven (19:9). The raptured believers, clothed in the fine linen of saints, will eat at that glorious supper in the immediate presence of the Bridegroom, the Lord Jesus Christ. It is toward this event that every Lord's Supper has pointed since the first supper in the Upper Room.

The New Testament passage that most completely details the rapture of the Church is First Thessalonians 4:13-18. That Scripture says the Church is to be caught away to be with her Christ and "shall always be with the Lord" (NKJV). Where the Bridegroom is, there will be the Bride. When the Bridegroom comes in glory to this earth, His Bride will be with Him. The fine linen representing righteousness will be the clothing of the bridal Church coming out of the heavens with Christ (19:14).

What are the implications of this scene? Where will the Church be when Christ rules this world? Does the Church have a role in the coming kingdom? Does this truth have a bearing on the present earthly life of a believer? The Bible does give us some clear answers to these questions. Unfortunately, this is an aspect of Christian doctrine largely unknown to modern evangelical Christians. A solid study of biblical premillennialism can make this truth real to Christians today. When rightly understood, it is a strong incentive to selfless service and practical holiness.

The starting place to understand the role of the Church in the millennial kingdom is the Garden of Eden. God told Adam he was to have dominion over every living thing on earth. Man's fall in sin brought an end to his kingship that can only be restored in the redemptive work of Christ. It has always been the divine intention that man in right relationship to his Creator would be a king. The blood-bought, Spirit-born Church is destined to enjoy in the kingdom, the dominion lost by Adam in the fall. Jesus said to His disciples, "Do not fear, little flock, for it is your Father's good pleasure to give you the kingdom" (Luke 12:32, NKJV).

The Scriptures in more than one way open up to us the nature of the Church's role in the manifest kingdom of Christ. In the parable of the mina, Jesus speaks of the faithful "ruling over ten cities," and some over "five cities." The truth of the parable is obedience and faithfulness now in light of the prospects for us in the kingdom.

The Apocalypse beginning in the first chapter describes the Church as kings and priests unto God:

> . . . and from Jesus Christ, the faithful witness, the firstborn from the dead, and the ruler over the kings of the earth. To Him who loved us and washed us from our sins in His own blood, and has made us kings and priests to His God and Father, to Him be glory and dominion forever and ever. Amen. (Revelation 1:5-6, NKJV)

To the church at Thyatira, Christ promised, "And he who overcomes, and keeps My works unto the end, to him I will give power over the nations" (2:26, NKJV). To the lukewarm Laodicean church, Jesus said, "To him who overcomes I will grant to sit with Me on My throne, as I also overcame and sat down with my Father on His throne" (3:21, NKJV). The head of the Church intends for the true saints to share His rule in this kingdom age.

The Apostle John records a song he heard when elevated to heaven during his Patmos vision. It is the rejoicing of the redeemed in heaven as they look on the Lamb of God,

> You are worthy to take the scroll,
> And to open its seals;

For you were slain,
> And have redeemed us to God by Your blood
> Out of every tribe and tongue and people and nation,
> And have made us kings and priests to our God;
> And we shall reign on the earth. (5:9-10, NKJV)

Some translations that follow this Wescott-Hort-style manuscript of the Greek text translate "us" and "our" as "they" and "their." While this difference is construed by some scholars to mean that the twenty-four elders were not in the redeemed company (the Church), it has no bearing on the fact that the blood-bought Church shall reign on earth. Regardless of the position one takes on the Greek text, this passage is consistent with the previous references to the Church's rule with Christ.

The Church without question is a heavenly people and to be distinguished from Israel, God's earthly people.

The next mention of the reigning Church comes in Revelation 20:4-6:

> And I saw thrones, and they sat on them, and judgment was committed to them. Then I saw the souls of those who had been beheaded for their witness to Jesus and for the word of God, who had not worshiped the beast or his image, and had not received his mark on their foreheads or their hands. And they lived and reigned with Christ for a thousand years. But the rest of the dead did not live again until the thousand years were finished. This is the first resurrection. Blessed and holy is he who has part in the first resurrection. Over such the second death has no power, but they shall be priests of God and of Christ, and shall reign with Him a thousand years. (NKJV)

The reign of the Church, about which the elders sang in Chapter 5, is here explained as a reign with Christ for a thousand years. Verse 4 makes it clear that more than martyrs are to reign with Christ. The revelator saw thrones occupied by those with judicial power prior to any mention of the martyrs. It is the whole Church that is to reign with Christ on earth for 1,000 years.

The saints are depicted as seated on thrones. Thrones were promised to the overcomers. The twenty-four elders sat upon thrones. The word "throne" is used widely in Revelation and always speaks of power, authority and dominion. The bridal Church will reign with Christ.

87

When the reign of the Church is discussed, the question of how it relates to Israel during these days of the millennium should be considered. Israel will be fully restored and enjoying her status as the head of all the nations in this world. The Jews who make up Israel in that day will not be martyrs or those who died or were raptured by the return of Christ. They will be a flesh-and-blood, earthly people. They will be the Jewish remnant spared through the Great Tribulation. As has been already established, Christ will be their King. The problem is, how will the Church reign over the earth at that same time?

Those who make up the bridal Church will be priests and kings unto God. We cannot safely go beyond Scripture in determining what the reign of the Church will be like. It is not yet fully revealed, but we do know that the rule of the Church will include judgment (1 Corinthians 6; Revelation 20:4) and a priestly function. The heavenly Church will rule with Christ on earth.

Israel fully restored, politically and spiritually, will rest in the full possession of the promises with Jerusalem as its capital. Ezekiel speaks of the prince in his revelation of the millennial temple. Christ as King over Israel will delegate a prince to represent Him in the holy city (Ezekiel 44:1-4; 46:1-18).

The moral, spiritual and governmental affairs of all the nations of the earth will be the jurisdiction of Jesus Christ, the King of kings. He has indicated clearly that His Bride, the Church, will share this reign with Him. Jesus said to the church at Thyatira that those who overcome will have power over the nations. Such an amazing prospect is meant to be more than a curiosity. It is an incentive to so walk with Christ now in order to be fitted for whatever assignment He may be pleased to give us in that day.

The Christian worships, serves, witnesses and trains for the future responsibility of being a priest and king unto God in the age to come. We are deciding now whether our rule will be over five cities or over ten cities (Luke 19:12-27). Taking all the New Testament says on this subject, it can be said that obedience, fruitfulness and victory over the world, the flesh and the devil will determine our level of rule in the coming kingdom. The Apostle Paul, in one brief theological statement, confirms this truth: "If we endure, we shall also reign with Him" (2 Timothy 2:12, NKJV). It comes as a shock to many (perhaps most) Christians that they are destined to be kings.

In the British royal family tradition, the Prince of Wales knows from the beginning that he is to be king some day. From early childhood, the prince is taught and shaped for his regal responsibility in the future. The Scripture advises us that we are to be kings and it is just as necessary for us as for the Prince of Wales to be fitted for our roles as royal priests in the kingdom of God.

Premillennialism is not meaningless speculation about the future. It is revelation from God Himself as to the close of history. Man sees history as going out with a whimper. God sees history going out in 1,000 years of glory with Christ and His Bride in the center of things on planet Earth. The 1,000-year reign will be the ultimate expression of Christ the Redeemer in human history.

Without the millennial reign of Christ on earth, the prophets do not make sense. The doctrine of premillennialism gives Christianity a forward look and a perspective of hope. Premillennialism, more than any other theological system of eschatology, provides the stage for the full realization and public display of the kingdom of our Lord Jesus Christ in accordance with the Scripture. It is the glorious unveiling of all Christ's redemptive offices. The millennium is not a carnal utopia, but ultimate spirituality made possible by the presence of the King of eternity. To the enlightened Christian there is a personal aspect to this doctrine. Being a true child of God through Christ is going to eventuate in each believer being a participant in this holy reign.

Conclusion

Among the great doxologies is the one found in Paul's first letter to Timothy, which reaches a high watermark in the exaltation of Christ:

> I urge you in the sight of God who gives life to all things, and before Christ Jesus who witnessed the good confession before Pontius Pilate, that you keep this commandment without spot, blameless until our Lord Jesus Christ's appearing, which He will manifest in His own time, He who is the blessed and only Potentate, the King of kings and Lord of lords, who alone has immortality, dwelling in unapproachable

light, whom no man has seen or can see, to whom be honor and ever-lasting power. Amen. (1 Timothy 6:13-16, NKJV)

The apostle has in mind as he takes up this subject the second advent of Christ: "He will manifest in His own time, He who is the blessed and only Potentate." This is the only place in the New Testament where this title of Christ is found. It is superior to all other titles, greater than King of kings and Lord of lords. It is evident that Paul believed the manifestation of this office by Christ awaits His second coming. It has a season and it will be shown at that time. The season for the blessed and only Potentate will be the millennial kingdom established by Christ at His return.

Christ will rule for eternity over all things. But this divine plan calls for a final age in time-and-space history prior to the eternal age when Christ will exercise all of His offices, authority and dignity before men on earth. Not one of His perfections will be overlooked in that day. The lowly, bat-tered, crucified Nazarene will stand triumphant on Mount Zion. All the world shall bask in the glory, splendor and dignity of the crowned Christ.

Endnotes

1. H.C.H. Lenski, *Interpretation of Revelation* (Minneapolis: Augsburg, 1961), 53.
2. Darrell Bock, *Christianity Today*, February 7, 2000, a7.
3. H.P. Liddon, *Explanatory Analysis of St. Paul's Epistle to the Romans* (Minneapolis: James and Klock, 1977 reprint), 135.
4. J.A. Seiss, *The Last Times* (Louisville, KY: Pentecostal Publishing House, 1878), 141.

7

Premillennialism
and the Kingdom of God

• Eldon Woodcock •

The kingdom of God, a central theme of biblical theology, is especially important for biblical eschatology. As Alva J. McClain has stated: "No adequate system of biblical eschatology can possibly be constructed apart from the history and meaning of the concept of the kingdom of God."[1]

I. The Key Concepts

The Greek word, *basileia*, means kingship, royal power, royal rule, kingdom.[2] In the Septuagint it was often used to translate the Hebrew word, *malkut*.[3]

The kingdom of God involves His rule over all that He created by the exercise of His sovereign power and authority.

Biblical references to the kingdom of God exhibit a tension between at least three pairs of polarities. These texts picture God's kingdom as both (1) eternal and temporal; (2) universal and local; (3) immediate (ruled directly by God) and mediate (ruled by God through an appointed representative).[4] The most plausible way to make sense of these tensions is to recognize some texts as referring to God's universal kingdom and others as indicating limited portions of that kingdom.

II. The Universal Kingdom of God

God's universal eternal kingdom extends continuously throughout the entire realm of His creation from eternity past to eternity future. David referred to this kingdom when he described Yahweh as "enthroned as King forever" (Psalm 29:10) and designated Yahweh's kingdom as "an everlasting kingdom" (145:13).[5] David also stated, "The LORD has established his throne in heaven, and his kingdom rules over all" (103:19). Since God has authority over both nature and people, His purposes will inevitably be accomplished.[6] Those who reject or rebel against Him have no effect upon the reality and effectiveness of His rule.

III. *The Mediatorial Kingdom of God*

Within God's universal eternal kingdom are limited realms in which God has delegated (or will delegate) His authority to selected human individuals or groups to rule over certain areas during certain intervals of time. This has been designated God's mediatorial kingdom which is temporal, local and mediate.[7] Since it occurs within human history, God's mediatorial kingdom, in its various forms, is the portion of His universal kingdom that has received the most attention in Scripture. Biblical data concerning God's mediatorial kingdom are especially significant with regard to a premillennial eschatology.

God's mediatorial kingdom has three elements.[8] (1) God ruled through His chosen instruments, who represented Him to the people and the people to Him. This involved the functions of king, prophet and priest. Usually the ruler exercised only one of these functions, but occasionally would exercise two (e.g., Ezekiel) or even all three (e.g., the Messiah). (2) God's mediatorial rule involved the earth or some part of it. (3) His representative was human.

A. God's Mediatorial Kingdom as Revealed in the OT Historical Books

1. *The Prepatriarchal Period*

References to the mediatorial kingdom of God during this period are minimal. God did give man the capability of ruling and the authority to rule over all other earthly life forms (Genesis 1:26-28). Nevertheless, after the fall, the bulk of mankind was dominated by increasing wickedness.[9] In the absence of godly mediatorial rulers, God periodically exercised His sovereign authority to judge and to punish (3:14-19; 4:10-12; 6:5-7; 11:5-9).

2. *The Patriarchal Period (Genesis 12-50)*

Although retaining His sovereign authority over the entire world, God rejuvenated His mediatorial kingdom by focusing upon a people that He would bring into existence, i.e., Israel.

God revealed Himself and made promises to Abraham concerning his physical descendants through Isaac, Jacob and Jacob's sons (12:1-3; 13:14-17; 15:18-21; 26:2-6; 28:13-15). Although not functioning as kings, each of these Hebrew patriarchs was evidently a leader of his clan. From his twelve sons, Jacob designated Judah as the one whose descendants would produce a line of kings to rule Israel (49:10; cf. 17:6; 35:11).

3. The Abrahamic Covenant

From the patriarchal period on, there was a close relationship between the mediatorial kingdom of God and the covenants that God made concerning Israel.

God formalized His promises to Abraham in the foundational covenant known as the Abrahamic Covenant. These promises stipulated that (1) Abraham's descendants were to be numerous and become a great nation (12:2; 13:16) and (2) Abraham's specified descendants were officially granted the land from the Euphrates River to the River of Egypt (15:18-21).[10] On the basis of this land grant, Abraham's descendants were to possess this land God had promised to them (hence the name "the Promised Land").[11] God specified that this covenant would apply only to Abraham's descendants through Isaac (17:19; 26:2-5) and Jacob (28:10-15; 35:9-13).

The ritual by which the Abrahamic Covenant was established made it clear that it was unconditional (15:7-21).[12] Later God confirmed His covenant promises to Abraham when He swore by Himself that He would fulfill them (22:15-18). By doing this, God used the ultimate supreme authority as the basis for His oath (Hebrews 6:13-20). As a result, God guaranteed His unconditional covenant with Abraham concerning selected physical descendants as unchangeable and irrevocable.[13]

4. The Mosaic Period (Exodus-Deuteronomy)

During the Mosaic period God moved the focus of His mediatorial kingdom from the clans descended from Abraham through Isaac to the Hebrew nation emerging from those clans. God's deliverance of the Hebrews from Egypt (the Exodus) was a significant event in this development (Exodus 14-15).

Although never designated a king, Moses nevertheless exercised his God-given authority as a ruler (Acts 7:35). He was prophet and priest, both representing God and His will to the Hebrews and representing them before God, especially in intercessory prayer (Deuteronomy 18:15; 9:25-29). He anticipated the kings that would later reign over Israel (17:14-20). He functioned as a judge, handling cases and resolving disputes that were brought to him (Exodus 18:13-16). Moses was thus the first ruler over the specific nation that comprised the mediatorial kingdom of God at this time.

5. *The Mosaic Covenant (Exodus-Deuteronomy)*

A function of the Mosaic Covenant was to operate as Israel's constitution, defining the structure of her government during this stage of God's mediatorial kingdom and indicating the spiritual and moral elements in the lifestyle that the Hebrews were to follow.[14]

The political structure of the mediatorial kingdom of God during and after the Mosaic period was to involve a leader (centuries later, a king) whose primary responsibility was to learn and to enforce the Mosaic Covenant (Deuteronomy 17:18-20).[15] That leader was not to intrude upon the responsibilities of religious leaders who conformed to Mosaic laws.

The Mosaic form of the mediated kingdom of God supported the religious practices stipulated by the Mosaic Covenant.[16] It required a close correlation between religious practice and moral behavior. Neither was sufficient without the other.

This covenant was clearly conditional, as indicated by the "if" clause (Exodus 19:5). It stated clearly that obedience would bring blessing and success while disobedience would produce punishment and disaster (Deuteronomy 28). God would make an obedient Hebrew nation "a kingdom of priests and a holy nation" (Exodus 19:6). This is the first biblical association of the term "kingdom" with God's rule.

6. *The Charismatic Period*[17] *(Joshua, Judges, 1 Samuel 1-7)*

Charismatic leaders were those whom God had raised up, gifted and empowered to perform the tasks that He had prepared them to do. During this period these people were mostly military leaders. Victory in battle demonstrated the presence of their charismatic endowment. As a result, they were often given judicial and political authority.

During this period these charismatic leaders functioned as God's intermittent representative rulers in His mediatorial kingdom.[18] On occasion, they acknowledged Yahweh as Israel's King (Judges 8:23; 1 Samuel 12:12).

7. *The Hebrew Monarchy (1 Samuel 8-30; 2 Samuel; 1-2 Kings; 1-2 Chronicles)*

Reacting against the inadequacies of charismatic leadership and no longer aware of God's beneficial providence, the Hebrews sought to solve their problems by means of a monarchy. This foolish and futile approach involved their replacing God with government.[19] As a result of this change, the Hebrews experienced intolerable oppression, including compulsory governmental service (military, agricultural, industrial), burdensome taxation, property confiscation and political corruption (1 Samuel 8:7-20).[20]

God intended for His kingdom program to move through a line of kings descended from Judah and beginning with David (1 Chronicles 28:4-5). After the rupture of Israel into two Hebrew kingdoms, God caused His mediatorial kingdom to continue with the Davidic line of kings over the southern Hebrew kingdom of Judah.[21]

The failure of Judah to be a distinctive kingdom under God, indicated by her disobeying the requirements of the Mosaic Covenant, led to her temporary exile in Babylon. About that time, the departure of the *shekinah* glory from the temple indicated God's termination of His mediatorial kingdom in Judah.[22] God transferred that authority to Babylon and other Gentile empires (Daniel 2:37ff).[23] He would still fulfill His Messianic promises to His covenant people. Nevertheless, they would not experience His mediatorial rule until Jesus Christ's second coming.[24]

8. *The Davidic Covenant*

The key eschatological promise made in the Davidic Covenant is summarized in this statement by God through Nathan to David: "Your house and your kingdom will endure forever before me; your throne will be established forever" (2 Samuel 7:16, cf Psalm 89:34-37). David's house (or dynasty) referred to the royal line of Hebrew kings who would be physically descended from David.[25] David's throne indicated his right to rule that God had given to him and his royal descendants.[26] David's kingdom meant the political entity over which David and his royal descendants would reign.[27]

The Davidic Covenant was unconditional. God's promise to establish David's kingdom forever precludes any conditions which, if not met, would lead to its termination. God reaffirmed His promises made in this covenant even after many failures by the Hebrew nation to follow Him (e.g., Jeremiah 23:5-6).[28] This could hardly have been the case had the covenant depended upon Hebrew obedience. The Davidic Covenant was as secure as the sun and the moon (Psalm 89:37). Since it was unconditional and has not yet been fulfilled, the Davidic Covenant must be fulfilled in a yet future time.[29]

The Davidic Covenant did not require a continuous occupation of the Davidic throne by a Davidic king.[30] In fact, as Allen stated:

> But even with the defeat of Judah and the destruction of Jerusalem, the line of David was not extinguished, nor was the throne of David (the right to rule) abrogated. The line was devoid of power and the throne was empty, but the "house" continued. That line continued all the way to . . . the birth of Jesus of Nazareth in the ancestral home of the family of David.[31]

For after Jehoiachin, no royal Davidic descendant occupied the Davidic throne to rule until the Lord Jesus Christ in whom the Davidic line ended. When Jesus died, He had no son. Yet His resurrection enabled Him to succeed Himself. As Allen stated: "He who is the eternal Son of God . . . is the adopted royal Son of God [in fulfillment of the Davidic Covenant]."[32]

The future fulfillment of the Davidic Covenant suggests at least three eschatological developments:[33] Israel will be (1) preserved as a nation; (2) restored to the land promised her by God; and (3) ruled by David's prime descendant, the Lord Jesus Christ. This covenant laid the foundation for later prophetic pronouncements.

B. God's Mediatorial Kingdom as Revealed in the OT Prophetic Books

The mediatorial kingdom of God is a major theme in the OT prophets, especially in its future Messianic manifestation. Thorough coverage would require a large book; thus, only a concise survey will be attempted.

1. Its Coming

Although often predicting future events, the OT prophets did not always indicate the chronological relationships of these events to each other. They specified no precise date for establishing the predicted Messianic kingdom.

The coming of the future Messianic kingdom will be sudden and catastrophic.[34] The Lord of the kingdom will come suddenly to judge and punish the wicked (Malachi 3:1-5), who will be rapidly destroyed like burning stubble (4:1). He will pour out His wrath upon the Gentile nations (Isaiah 13:9-11; 26:21).

2. Its Government

a. Its Form

The future kingdom envisioned by the OT prophets will be a monarchy, ruled by the Davidic Messianic King. On this occasion, the promises made in the OT covenants, especially the Davidic Covenant, will be fulfilled (Jeremiah 33:20-22).

b. Its King

The Lord will raise up a Davidic King who will bring His people to follow God's laws (Ezekiel 34:23-24; 37:24-25). The Hebrews will seek the Lord their God and their Davidic Messianic King under whom they will live in the last days (Hosea 3:5).

The future Messianic King will be designated "the Holy One of Israel among you" (Isaiah 12:6). With righteousness, wisdom and power perfectly balanced in His government, He will judge justly and equitably (11:1-5; Jeremiah 23:5-6).

The future Davidic Messianic King will shoulder the full responsibilities of His government (Isaiah 9:6-7). He will administer all functions of government—judicial, legislative and executive (33:22). This is much too formidable a project for a mere man. In order to achieve this objective, the future Ruler will need to be both divine and human. Thus He is called both "Prince of Peace" and "Mighty God" (9:6). For He is the only One who can handle these responsibilities efficiently and justly.

In His administration the Messianic King will exercise His threefold function as Prophet, Priest and King. He will thus possess both supreme religious authority and supreme political authority.

c. Its External Organization[35]

The levels of authority in the future governmental structure will be, in descending order: (1) the Messianic King who is the Lord (Zechariah 14:9); (2) the resurrected saints of the Most High (Daniel 7:18, 27); (3) the living people from the nation of Israel (Isaiah 60); (4) the Gentile nations (Micah 4:2).

d. Its Extent and Duration

It will be worldwide, including all nations on the entire earth (Isaiah 2:2-4; Zechariah 14:9). These texts focus on the *earthly* setting of the kingdom. It will be everlasting (Isaiah 9:6-7; Daniel 7:13-14). This fits the idea of the postmillennial merging of the mediatorial kingdom with the universal kingdom of God.[36]

3. *Its Blessings*

a. Spiritual Benefits

The future Messianic mediatorial kingdom will be characterized by widespread salvation. People will drink from the waters of salvation and be clothed with the garments of salvation (Isaiah 12:3; 61:10). God will remove believers' sins (Micah 7:19). He will convey many redemptive blessings upon believing Israelites including cleansing from sin, regeneration, providing new hearts and placing His Spirit within them (Ezekiel 36:24-38).[37] He will bring healing to His people's incurable wounds (Jeremiah 30:12, 17). The redeemed will respond with everlasting joy (Isaiah 51:11).

b. Ethical Benefits

During the future mediatorial Messianic kingdom people will live by high moral standards, for many will come to Jerusalem in order to learn and to follow God's ways, i.e., the ways of His Law (2:3). Hebrew teachers will instruct their people in God's ways that will define their lifestyle (30:20-21). With their children receiving God's teaching, they will be established in righteousness (54:13-14).

c. Social Benefits

The complete abolition of war will be very beneficial. Nations will neither fight nor train their people for war (Micah 4:3). This will eliminate the massive destruction of life and property that war brings, for

God's abolishing of war and weapons will enable people to live securely, safely and without fear (Isaiah 2:4; Micah 4:4; Hosea 2:18).

In the future mediatorial Messianic kingdom there will be complete social justice. People will benefit from their labor, whether construction or agriculture (Isaiah 65:21-23). They will experience the delights of marriage (Jeremiah 33:10-11). These conditions will only be possible during the reign of the divine Messianic King.

d. Political Benefits

The most desirable social reforms are unlikely to be implemented without effective governmental administration.[38] The OT prophets anticipated some aspects of future political structures.

The future mediatorial Messianic kingdom will have international authority. A new world order consisting of one world government by sinful men would be very dangerous to desirable lifestyles and to genuine governmental justice. The OT prophets saw the solution to this problem in the Messianic King whose reign will be characterized by righteousness in all of His judgments and policies (Isaiah 2:4; 9:6-7). With Messianic judgments resolving disputes, military actions will become unnecessary, irrelevant and no longer used.

The future Messianic kingdom will be on the earth with Jerusalem as its capital (24:23). Jerusalem will be the center from which God's Law will go out (2:3). It will be refortified, beautified and enriched (60:10, 13, 17).

God will regather the dispersed Hebrews from all over the world and restore them to the land He had promised them (Jeremiah 31:10-11; 32:37; Ezekiel 37:21-22). From here, Israel will rule over other nations (Isaiah 14:2). At that time many foreigners will recognize God's being with His people and will want to go with them, yielding to their God (Zechariah 8:23; Micah 4:1-3).

e. Physical Benefits

In the future mediatorial Messianic kingdom there will be substantial and beneficial changes in earth climates. Abundant rainfall will eliminate famines and produce bountiful crops (Isaiah 30:23-25; Ezekiel 34:29).

There will be substantial geological changes, especially from violent earthquakes that will cause splits in the earth's crust (Isaiah 24:19), overturn mountains (Ezekiel 38:19-20) and split the Mount of Olives, causing water to flow out of Jerusalem (Zechariah 14:4, 8). These changes will cause waters and rivers to flow from the mountains and in the desert, enriching the soil (Isaiah 30:25; 35:6-7; 41:18-20). Even the Dead Sea will be changed into a freshwater lake that will support fish and other life (Ezekiel 47:8-12).

Aided by God's miraculous provisions of water, the barren wastelands, useless for agriculture and incapable of supporting life, will be transformed into rich, productive soil (Joel 2:21-24; Ezekiel 34:26-27). The desert will become fruitful and yield bountiful crops (Isaiah 32:13-15; 35:1-2). The fields will be so productive that the processes of plowing, reaping and treading grapes will overlap each other (Amos 9:13). God will accomplish these things by pouring out His Holy Spirit (Isaiah 32:15).

In that day God will make drastic changes in the nature of wild animals. No longer predators, they will live peacefully with each other and will not even threaten or harm small children (11:6-8). This will involve substantially changed eating patterns for both people and animals.

In that day there will be neither physical diseases nor deformities. For God will heal the blind, deaf, lame and mute (35:5-6). No one living in Zion will even claim to be sick (33:24). With no diseases to threaten them, people will experience long life, considering a normal life span to greatly exceed a century (65:20).

In that day there will be no ordinary disasters that will injure people, hamper their capabilities or prematurely terminate their lives. People will be free from attacks by wild animals, violent storms, famine and armies (Ezekiel 34:23-31). God will protect His people from misfortune and futile toil (Isaiah 65:23).

f. Religious Benefits

Under their King-Priest (Zechariah 6:12-13), the nation Israel will fulfill her destiny to be "a kingdom of priests" (Exodus 19:6; Isaiah 61:6). Others will recognize Israel as a people blessed by God (Isaiah 61:9). The Levitical priests in their function of administering the various offerings will be prominent in Israel's religious leadership (Jeremiah 33:17-22).[39]

As in the political realm, Jerusalem will be known as the religious center of the future mediatorial Messianic kingdom. Jerusalem will be acclaimed as a center of righteousness (Isaiah 1:26), the Lord's presence

(60:14), the word of God (2:3), and worship by the nations (Zechariah 14:16-19). In that day there will be no freedom of religion. People will worship the only true God according to only the principles that He has revealed.

g. The Role of the Messianic King

The characteristics of the future Messianic kingdom will result from the policies of the Messianic King, for He will reign in righteousness (Isaiah 32:1), thereby producing the benefits described in the preceding section.

Thorough examination of the OT prophetic data makes it clear that the future mediatorial Messianic kingdom will be a literal, earthly, political kingdom with many physical features. Its Ruler will be the divine Messianic King-Priest. His government will be a monarchy extending over the entire earth. These observations make it evident that this Messianic Ruler will arrive before His setting up His kingdom, i.e., that the Messiah's second coming must precede His governing His millennial kingdom.

C. The Mediatorial Kingdom of God as Revealed in the Gospels

1. Announcement of the Mediatorial Kingdom of God

The Gospels identify Jesus as the King of this kingdom. Before Jesus' birth an angel informed Mary that God would give her Son the throne of David from which He will reign forever (Luke 1:32-33). John the Baptist, Jesus and Jesus' disciples all announced the kingdom of God as near (Matthew 3:1; 4:17; 10:7).[40]

Jesus supported His announcement of His kingdom by doing numerous impressive miracles, especially healings and exorcisms (4:23-24; 9:35). His miracles were so clearly authentic that even His enemies could not deny or ignore them (John 11:47-48).

Jesus' miracles made it clear that "the kingdom of God has come upon you" (Luke 11:20, NKJV). He taught that that kingdom was among them—in the Person of the King (17:2-21).[41]

2. The Identity of the Mediatorial Kingdom of God

Although much debated, the most plausible conclusion is that the kingdom announced by the Lord Jesus Christ was identical to that presented

101

by the OT prophets.[42] The Gospels often refer to some aspect of the kingdom that fulfills an OT prophecy concerning it. For example, Jesus Christ's triumphant entry into Jerusalem fulfilled an OT prophecy as to how the Messianic King would do that (Matthew 21:4-5; Zechariah 9:9).

The kingdom proclaimed by Jesus Christ had characteristics similar to that anticipated by the OT prophets. Jesus presented its most basic moral standards as rooted in the Law and Prophets. These included His teachings on personal ethics (Matthew 19:17-19), social relationships (Matthew 5:21-48), condemning social injustice (23:23-24) and Temple corruption (Mark 11:15-17). He indicated the physical nature of His kingdom by His miracles, which were largely physical in their effects (Matthew 11:2-5).

3. The Rejection of the King and His Kingdom

In the Gospels the mediatorial kingdom of God and its King are inextricably connected.[43] That kingdom cannot be established on earth without the King's being physically present. Conversely, rejection of the King involves rejection of His kingdom. This was a Jewish issue, since announcements of His kingdom were made exclusively to the Jews (10:5-6).

Jewish rejections of Jesus as the Messiah occurred often and became increasingly vehement throughout His ministry on earth. These rejections included His being driven out of His home synagogue at Nazareth (Luke 4:16-30), the attributing of Jesus' miracles performed by the power of the Holy Spirit to demonic power[44] (Matthew 12:22-32; Mark 3:20-30) and the hostile confrontation at the Feast of Tabernacles (John 7-8). Jesus' rejection finally culminated in His crucifixion. As a whole, the Jews rejected Jesus as the Messiah, along with His kingdom over which He will yet reign.[45]

4. Christ's Preparation of His Disciples for the Interregnum

Rejected by the Jews who had had Him crucified, Jesus departed by means of His resurrection and ascension. Thus both the Messianic King and the Messianic kingdom departed together. Anticipating these developments, Jesus instructed His disciples concerning His mediatorial kingdom that would exist from His death to His second coming, when He establishes His prophesied Messianic kingdom. This period is what McClain designated the interregnum.[46]

Jesus began His instruction with a series of parables depicting His mediatorial kingdom (Matthew 13). The parable of the sower pictures a sowing of seed with varied responses represented by different types of soil (13:1-9, 18-23). The parable of the wheat and weeds portrays a sowing of weeds by an enemy (13:24-30). It pictures the infiltration of the kingdom by followers of the evil one (13:36-43). The parables of the mustard seed and the yeast depict a gigantic expansion of the kingdom which includes both good and evil elements (13:31-33).[47] The parable of the catch of good and bad fish in the fishing net also pictures the inclusion of both righteous and wicked within the kingdom (13:47-50). At the end of the age, God will gather the righteous and remove the wicked from His kingdom by means of His judgment (13:40-43, 49-50).

Later the Lord Jesus Christ announced that He would create a new entity: His Church (16:15-18). From His perspective at that time, this was to be a future development. He used the Greek word, *ekklesia*, to designate this entity. An *ekklesia* is an assembly or congregation, usually with some sort of ruling function.[48] Jesus gave to Peter and to His other disciples authority in His kingdom (16:19; 18:18).[49] This implies that all who proclaim Jesus as the Messianic King have this authority.

Although consistently rejected, Jesus went to Jerusalem where He performed His final series of Messianic acts. These included His requisitioning of a donkey which He rode into Jerusalem, fulfilling Messianic prophecy and His cleansing of the temple of its corrupt and lucrative financial activities (21:1-13; Zechariah 9:9). During His approach to the city His disciples proclaimed Him as the King (Luke 19:38). Nevertheless, the Jews as a whole continued to reject Him as their Messianic King. In response, Jesus told some kingdom parables against them (Matthew 21:28-45).

In His eschatological discourse given on the Mount of Olives that overlooks Jerusalem, Jesus prophesied concerning His second coming and related events (Matthew 24-25). He pictured His second coming as sudden, unexpected, obvious, accompanied by astonishing events and great power and glory (24:27-30). Since no one knows when it will occur, He warned His disciples to be constantly alert, watching for it (24:36-44). On the occasion of His second coming in all of His glory, He will sit on His throne (25:31). He will exercise His royal authority by judging the nations, separating those who will participate in His kingdom from those who will be expelled into the eternal fire (25:31-46, especially verses 34, 41). These actions picture the Messianic King as exercising His royal authority *at the beginning* of His establishing the Messianic kingdom anticipated by the OT prophets.

D. The Mediatorial Kingdom of God as Revealed in Acts

For forty days the risen Christ instructed His disciples concerning the kingdom of God (Acts 1:3). When they asked Him if He planned to restore the kingdom of God to Israel at that time, He replied that it was not for them to know when that event will occur, that it will happen at a future time set by God's authority (1:6-7). Later Peter stated that God will restore everything (presumably including that kingdom) when He sends the Christ (3:19-21). This is another indicator that the Lord Jesus Christ will return before He establishes His Messianic kingdom.

On the day of Pentecost, Peter reminded his Jewish audience of Jesus' authenticating ministry (2:22). Even though He had been crucified, Jesus Christ's resurrection and ascension had qualified Him to sit on the throne of David (2:24-32). Nevertheless, most Jews rejected the Messianic King and His servants who proclaimed Him.[50]

In Acts, the term "kingdom of God" includes both the mediatorial kingdom and the Church.[51] For both Philip and Paul, proclaiming the kingdom of God evidently referred to both present and future aspects of the Mediatorial kingdom (8:12; 19:8; 20:25; 28:23, 31).[52]

The statement that one needs to "go through many hardships to enter the kingdom of God" (14:22) evidently refers primarily to the future mediatorial Messianic kingdom.[53] The people involved were Christians who had already entered the present mediatorial kingdom by means of the new birth (John 3:5). The future kingdom will be preceded by a time of terrible troubles and afflictions.

E. The Mediatorial Kingdom of God as Revealed in the Epistles

Most epistolary kingdom texts point to the future mediatorial Messianic kingdom of God as central in the future of Christians.[54] Christians will be called to it (1 Thessalonians 2:12), brought to it (2 Timothy 4:18), inherit it (James 2:5), be worthy of it (2 Thessalonians 1:5) and receive it—a kingdom that cannot be shaken (Hebrews 12:28).[55]

Paul connected the future kingdom with Christ's appearing, i.e., His second coming (2 Timothy 4:1). He described the future resurrection of believers as occurring at the second coming of Christ after which will come the end when He will turn His kingdom over to God the Father (1 Corinthians 15:23-24). That future Messianic kingdom will begin at Christ's second coming and will continue until He gives it to His Father.[56] These two texts provide yet another indication that Christ's second coming will be premillennial. When Christ will give His kingdom to His Father, that kingdom will merge into God's eternal, universal kingdom.

F. The Present Mediatorial Kingdom and the Church

It is important to recognize the kingdom of God and the Church as distinct entities.[57] In the NT *ekklesia* is never used to refer to the kingdom of God. An *ekklesia* (church) is a congregation or assembly ruled by the people.[58] A kingdom consists of people governed by an authoritative ruler who establishes policy. The synoptic Gospels often mention the kingdom of God as being preached. Yet only Matthew mentions the church (three times), and that as a future entity. In Acts the focus moves from kingdom to Church. The Epistles mention the kingdom, but emphasize the Church.

Yet the Church is integrally related to the mediatorial kingdom of God in its present aspect.[59] God is preparing in the Church those who will reign with Christ in the future Messianic kingdom. The Church receives some blessings of the kingdom.

The functioning of Church people in relation to the kingdom has been well stated:

> As to their persons, they are citizens of the kingdom: as to their existence they are the fruit of the message of the kingdom: as to their nature they are the organism of the kingdom: as to their task they are the ambassadors of the kingdom.[60]

The present mediatorial kingdom of God that followed Christ's first coming neither replaced nor fulfilled the prophesied Messianic Davidic kingdom.[61] In the former kingdom Christ's rule involves a limited portion of His Father's authority and power that He will exercise in the latter kingdom. It will be in that future kingdom that the Lord Jesus Christ will fulfill the Messianic prophecies about His rule as King.

G. The Mediatorial Kingdom as Revealed in the Apocalypse

1. Introduction

The Book of Revelation begins with an introductory vision and several exhortations to the seven churches of Asia (Revelation 1-3).[62] Then it mostly pictures a series of future judgments and punishments in which God will pour out His wrath upon a world system characterized by anti-Christ perspectives (4-18).

A new song stated, "You have made them to be a kingdom and priests to serve our God, and they will reign on the earth" (5:10).[63] This text pictures the redeemed as sharing God's rule in the future Messianic kingdom which is explicitly stated to be an earthly kingdom. God's program is steadily moving toward this kingdom as its goal.[64]

The seventh angel announced, "The kingdom of the world has become the kingdom of our Lord and of his Christ, and he will reign for ever and ever" (11:15). Thomas' perceptive comments on this text are significant:

> Jesus will return and assume the throne of His father David in this future crisis, at which time He will replace the satanically energized sovereignty of the world rulers that has prevailed for so long. The whole theme of Revelation is the purging of evil from the world so that it can become the domain of the King of kings (cf. 19:16). Only a physical kingdom on earth will satisfy this.[65]

2. The Millennial Kingdom (19:11-20:6)

This section of the Apocalypse pictures the final stage of the mediatorial kingdom of God—the Messianic millennial kingdom. It begins with a vivid portrayal of the second coming of the Lord Jesus Christ to establish His prophesied kingdom and to rule over it with a rod of iron (19:11-16).[66]

Shortly after His arrival, the Lord Jesus Christ will attack, judge and punish His enemies. He will throw the beast and false prophet into the lake of fire and destroy the armies of the world arrayed against Him

(19:17-21). Then Satan will be bound in the Abyss which will be locked and sealed, making escape impossible (20:1-3). Satan's incarceration will prevent his deceiving the nations any more for 1,000 years, thereby terminating satanic opposition.[67]

These actions against His enemies will set the stage for the Lord Jesus Christ's millennial reign. Although the Bible as a whole contains much evidence supporting a Messianic kingdom preceded by the second coming of the Messianic King who will set it up, it is only in Revelation 20 that the duration of that kingdom is specified as 1,000 years.[68]

At the beginning of the millennial kingdom certain people, seated on thrones, will be given the authority to judge and will reign with Christ for 1,000 years (20:4, 6).[69] These people will evidently be participants of the first resurrection, consisting of all the just.[70] Although including members of the body of Christ (1 Thessalonians 4:16), the people specifically mentioned here are believers who will be strongly committed to Jesus Christ and the Word of God during the tribulation preceding the millennium (Revelation 20:4). Many of these people will be martyred when they refuse to worship the beast or receive his mark (20:4).[71] Blessed and holy, these believers will have both a priestly and governing role with Christ during the millennial kingdom.

3. *The Universal Kingdom of God (20:7-22:5)*

After the millennium the following events will occur: (1) God will terminate a massive Satan-led revolt (20:7-9); (2) there will be the final judgment of the resurrected wicked on the basis of their works, which will occur before the Great White Throne (20:11-15); (3) God will throw Satan and the wicked into the lake of fire, where they will suffer eternal torment (20:10, 15).

Then the Lord will destroy the old heavens and earth and create a new heaven and new earth (21:1). He will also create the new Jerusalem that will descend from heaven (21:2). These events will cause the mediatorial kingdom of God to terminate its existence as a separate entity and merge into the universal eternal kingdom of God.[72]

IV. Conclusion

The issue of premillennialism involves the relationship of the future Messianic King to His future Messianic kingdom.

The theme of the mediatorial kingdom of God runs through the entire Bible. In the Abrahamic Covenant God promised a specific geographical area as Israel's permanent possession. In the Davidic Covenant God promised a permanent Davidic throne, looking toward the future Messianic kingdom. The OT prophets anticipated an earthly Messianic kingdom to be ruled by the Messianic King occupying the Davidic throne. The prophesied qualities of that kingdom will only be possible under the reign of that Messianic King. Thus the coming of the Messianic King must precede His governing of His Messianic kingdom.

The Gospels record Jesus' statement that at His second coming He will sit on His throne and exercise His sovereign authority of judgment at the beginning of His prophesied Messianic kingdom. In Acts Peter described God as restoring everything (including His kingdom) at Christ's second coming. Epistolary references to the future Messianic kingdom of God also picture it as beginning at Christ's second coming. The Apocalypse also declares that kingdom as beginning in connection with Christ's second coming, specifying its duration as a millennium.

The theological view that best fits the biblical data concerning Christ's second coming in relation to His future Messianic millennial kingdom is that it will be premillennial.

Endnotes

1. Alva J. McClain, *The Greatness of the Kingdom* (Grand Rapids: Zondervan, 1959), 6. McCain's excellent book traces the theme of the kingdom of God throughout the entire Bible. The general structure of this essay reflects the influence of McClain's work.

2. William F. Arndt and F. Wilbur Gingrich, *A Greek-English Lexicon of the New Testament and Other Early Christian Literature* (Chicago: University of Chicago Press, 1957), 134.

3. Francis Brown, S.R. Driver and Charles A. Briggs, *A Hebrew and English Lexicon of the Old Testament* (Clarendon Press, 1957 reprint [1907]), 574-5, stated the meanings of *malkut* as "royal power, dominion, reign, kingdom." B. Klappert, "King," *The New International Dictionary of New Testament Theology*, ed. Colin Brown (Grand Rapids: Zondervan, 1976), II, 376, described its focus as on power rather than on location. In the OT it refers mostly to earthly political kingdoms. Although the term "kingdom of God" does not occur in the OT, the concept does (e.g., Psalm 145:11-13). It includes

both God's present rule and His future Messianic earthly kingdom. The parameter of meanings for *malkut* are thus similar to those for *basileia*.

4. J.D. Pentecost, *Thy Kingdom Come* (Wheaton, IL: Victor, 1990), 15.

5. Anthony Tomasino, *"olam,"* *New International Dictionary of Old Testament Theology and Exegesis* (hereafter referred to as *NIDOTTE*), ed. Willem A. Van Gemeren (Grand Rapids: Zondervan, 1997), vol. III, 345-51, points out that although the Hebrew word, *olam* (often rendered "forever" or "everlasting") does not, in itself, necessarily refer to eternity past or eternity future, it can convey that idea, especially when referring to God. See also Allan A. MacRae, *olam, Theological Wordbook of the Old Testament* ed. R.L. Harris, G.L. Archer and B.L. Waltke (Chicago: Moody, 1980), vol. II, 672-3.

6. Pentecost, 18.

7. McClain, 21.

8. Ibid., 41.

9. Exceptions include righteous Abel (Genesis 4:4; Hebrews 11:4), Enoch (Genesis 5:24; Hebrews 11:5-6) and righteous Noah (Genesis 6:8-9; Hebrews 11:7). Yet none of these men was described as a ruler.

10. Robert B. Chisholm, Jr., "Evidence from Genesis," *The Coming Millennial Kingdom: A Case for Premillennial Interpretation*, ed. Donald K. Campbell and Jeffrey L. Townsend (Grand Rapids: Kregel, 1997), 40-2.

11. Ibid.

12. Ibid., 40. That only God, represented by the lights, moved between the pieces of the animals (while Abram slept), meant that only God was obligated to grant the promised land to Abraham's descendants.

13. Ibid., 46-50.

14. This discussion reflects some of McClain's treatment on pp. 52-94.

15. To do this, he was aided by judges and other officials who were to be men of integrity (Deuteronomy 16:18). He was not authorized to produce any legislation. Apart from God's strong influence upon the policies of a government and the character of its leaders, there will inevitably be tension between personal liberty and governmental policies designed to increase governmental authority in ways that restrict or eliminate that freedom.

16. This included the Levitical priesthood, priestly rituals and the tabernacle (later the temple).

17. There were charismatic leaders in Israel both before and after this period (e.g., Moses, David). Nevertheless, to characterize the period from Joshua to Samuel as charismatic seems appropriate, for the Hebrew leaders as a whole during this period were charismatic.

18. McClain, 91-4. Since the leadership was charismatic, there was no provision for succession that would have provided continuous leadership. Thus there were gaps between charismatic leaders.

19. Ibid., 100.

20. Ibid., 110-3.

21. Ibid., 107.

22. Ibid., 126 (cf. Ezekiel 8:3-4; 10:4, 18; 11:22-23).

23. Ibid., 125.

24. Jeremiah prophesied that no descendant of Jehoiachin (the last Davidic king of Judah) would ever rule over Judah (Jeremiah 22:24-30). Nevertheless, McClain (125-6)

perceptively observed that this prophecy did not affect Jesus, who as a result of His virgin conception, was physically unrelated to Joseph, a descendant of Jehoiachin.

25. Pentecost, 142; Ronald B. Allen, "Evidence from Psalm 89," *The Coming Millennial Kingdom*, 70; Gerald H. Wilson, *bayith, NIDOTTE*, vol. I, 656.

26. Pentecost, 142; Allen, "Evidence from Psalm 89," 70-1; I. Cornelius, *kissay, NIDOTTE*, vol. II, 672-4.

27. Pentecost, 142.

28. Ibid., 143-4 (see also Isaiah 9:6-7; Ezekiel 37:24-25; Hosea 3:4-5).

29. Ibid., 146-7.

30. Ibid., 147 (see Amos 9:11).

31. Allen, "Evidence from Psalm 89," 72.

32. Ibid. (This entire paragraph follows Allen's helpful discussion.)

33. Ibid., 76; Pentecost, 148.

34. McClain, 174.

35. Ibid., 209-13.

36. Ibid., 216.

37. Some of these blessings will fulfill God's promises made in the New Covenant (Jeremiah 31:31-34; Ezekiel 36:24-38).

38. McClain, 228.

39. For the difficult problems of the future temple and its animal sacrifices, see McClain, 247-51; Mark F. Rooker, "Evidence from Ezekiel," *The Coming Millennial Kingdom*, 128-34.

40. The Gospel of Matthew refers almost exclusively to the kingdom of heaven. Since in the Jewish usage of that period, "heaven" was a circumlocution for God (Yahweh), the terms "kingdom of heaven" and "kingdom of God" are functionally equivalent and refer to the same entity. See Klappert, 376-7.

41. McClain, 272, points out that the Greek adverb *entos* is best rendered "among" in the sense of "in the midst of." It does not mean "within." It was clearly not "within" the Pharisees whom He was addressing. See Klappert, 382-3.

42. McClain, 275.

43. Ibid., 304-5.

44. Jesus rebuked the Jewish leaders for this explanation of His miracles, calling it "blasphemy against the Holy Spirit," which was unforgivable.

45. It is worth noting that Jesus' disciples at this time were Jews.

46. McClain, 321.

47. The tree described greatly exceeds the normal height of a mustard plant which grows to about twelve feet. The birds pictured the evil one in an earlier parable (Matthew 13:4, 19) and probably have the same significance here. The yeast often refers figuratively to something evil (e.g., Luke 12:1).

48. L. Coenen, "Church," *The New International Dictionary of New Testament Theology*, vol. I, 291-305; McClain, 327.

49. Craig S. Keener, *A Commentary on the Gospel of Matthew* (Grand Rapids: Eerdmans, 1999), 429-30. McClain (329-30) suggests that this authority applied to the future eschatological Messianic kingdom and not to the kingdom during the interregnum.

50. They expressed their rejection in several ways, including their arrest and attempted suppression of certain apostles (Acts 4:1-3, 18; 5:17-40), the martyrdoms of Stephen and the Apostle James (Acts 7:57-58; 12:1-3), the persecution of and efforts to kill Paul

(Acts 13-28). King Agrippa I initiated the action against James, but his motive was primarily to please the Jews.

51. McClain, 424-5.
52. Stanley D. Toussaint, "Acts," *The Bible Knowledge Commentary*, ed. John F. Walvoord and Roy B. Zuck (Wheaton, IL: Victor, 1983), vol. II, 372-3; 410; 413-4; 430-1.
53. McClain, 425.
54. In four texts Paul described the present aspect of the mediatorial kingdom of God without necessarily excluding its future aspect (Romans 14:17; 1 Corinthians 4:20; Colossians 1:13; 4:11). The other epistolary kingdom texts refer to the future.
55. In contrast, the wicked will not inherit it (1 Corinthians 6:9-10; Galatians 5:19-21; Ephesians 5:5).
56. McClain, 435; W. Howard Mare, "1 Corinthians," *The Expositor's Bible Commentary*, ed. Frank E. Gaebelein, et al. (Grand Rapids: Zondervan, 1976), vol. X, 285.
57. Earl Radmacher, *What the Church is All About: A Biblical and Historical Study* (Chicago: Moody, 1972), 168-74, provides several reasons for supporting this conclusion.
58. Coenen, 291.
59. Radmacher, 174-6; McClain, 439-41.
60. Erich Sauer, *From Eternity to Eternity*, 92-3, cited by Radmacher, 176.
61. Elliott E. Johnson, "Premillennialism Introduced: Hermeneutics," *The Coming Millennial Kingdom*, 33.
62. In the NT Asia was a Roman province located in the western part of what is now Turkey.
63. The phrase "kingdom and priests" may be a hendiadys, i.e., two words joined by *and* to convey one idea; if so, this phrase would essentially mean "priestly kingdom." See *NET Bible* (Dallas, TX: Biblical Studies Press, 1998), 777, footnote 7.
64. Robert Thomas, *Revelation 1-7, an Exegetical Commentary* (Moody, 1992), 402.
65. Robert Thomas, *Revelation 8-22, an Exegetical Commentary* (Moody, 1995), 106.
66. That this passage describes Jesus Christ is clear from the distinctive titles ascribed to Him: the Word of God (Revelation 19:13); King of kings and Lord of lords (Revelation 19:16).
67. Thomas, *Revelation 8-22*, 410.
68. For effective arguments that the 1,000 years in Revelation 20 is to be understood literally, see Walvoord, *Revelation*, 294-5; Thomas, *Revelation 8-22*, 407-9.
69. Thomas, *Revelation 8-22*, 413-4.
70. Ibid., 420-1.
71. Ibid., 415-7.
72. The conditions and qualities of that kingdom are vividly portrayed in Revelation 21:1-22:5.

8

Premillennialism

and the Alliance Distinctives

• Joel Van Hoogen •

What relevancy does premillennialism hold for modern evangelicalism? In particular, how relevant is it in giving focus and direction to The Christian and Missionary Alliance? What bearing does premillennialism have on Alliance distinctives? Is ownership of this doctrine really that essential to the future effectiveness of the ministry of the Alliance? In seeking to give answer to these questions it would be wise to set forward some of the distinctives within the Alliance that have uniquely shaped it, distinctives it would affirm as essential components for the future. Five such distinctives are suggested for consideration:

First, The Christian and Missionary Alliance is a missionary denomination. It exists as a denomination primarily to reach the world for Christ. It is foremost an alliance of Christian and missionary churches. It was such an alliance long before it was ever a denomination.

Second, the Alliance has a deeper life message with a strong emphasis on the life of Christ within the believer. There is an expectation of holiness in the child of God because of the wonderful mystery revealed which makes this possible. The mystery is that by faith through death to self, the life of Christ is imparted with power to God's children so that they may live whole and holy lives.

Third, the Alliance has offered to evangelicalism a unique insight into Christology. This is possibly its most significantly distinct contribution to the modern-day Church. This Christology focuses upon the centrality of Christ in everything. Christ is more than the Giver, He is the Gift. With Him the Christian has everything, for in Him are all things. Without Him, one has nothing. The Alliance does say that Jesus is Savior, but would add that He is Salvation. It would affirm that Jesus is Sanctifier, but would add that He is Sanctification. He is Healer, and yet He is more. It is His life, He Himself, that brings health. Over and over it may be emphasized that Jesus is central and all in all. This is the meaning of the fourfold gospel.

Fourth, the Alliance holds to the infallible Word of God. This is not a unique distinctive of the Alliance, but it certainly is a distinctive emphasis which it would affirm as an essential component for its future.

Fifth, the Alliance has a high view of the transcendent integrity of God. This too is not a distinctive unique to The Christian and Missionary Alliance, but it is an emphasis that has found a vital expression in its folds. Dr. A.W. Tozer, for one, was used wonderfully of God to encourage and champion this high and lofty focus upon God in the churches of the Alliance.

As the premillennial position of the Alliance is considered, it should be weighed in the light of these five distinctives. Conversely, these five distinctives can be understood more fully in the light of this position on premillennial doctrine. To develop this understanding, the following outline will be followed:

1. Summary of the three basic positions on the millennium.
2. The Statement of Faith of The Christian and Missionary Alliance and the corresponding views of Dr. A.B. Simpson, its founder.
3. The historical development of millennialism.
4. Interpretations of Revelation 20:1-6.
5. The relevance of premillennialism for the future of The Christian and Missionary Alliance.

1. Summary of the Three Basic Millennial Positions

It is not possible without some significant generalizing to discuss the various eschatological positions on the millennium. There is a wide range of interpretive variance in each of the three positions outlined.

Postmillennialism

Postmillennialism is a theological position that affirms the second coming of Jesus Christ at the end of the millennial period.

The millennium is to be a literal period of 1,000 years of peace and righteousness in the age preceding the return of Jesus Christ. During this time the gospel will be universally preached and broadly received. Postmillennialists generally hold to a spiritual interpretation which states, "the kingdom of God is a state of society in which the will of God is done in the hearts of 'born again' believers."[1] Thus the kingdom will grow until the world is Christianized. At the end of the millennium an outbreak of wickedness will occur, identified as the Great Tribulation. Then Christ shall return, bringing a general resurrection of the dead and ushering in the eternal state with a new heaven and earth.

Amillennialism

Amillennialism is a theological position which affirms the second coming of Christ after a millennial period. Amillennialists are not truly "a" (no) "millennial," since they do believe in a spiritualized millennium. The 1,000 years are to be understood as figurative of the completed present period from the resurrection of Christ to His second coming. Christ's reign in this millennium is spiritual in the lives of those newborn and occurs simultaneously as this evil age progresses, becoming worse and worse. At the same time it is acknowledged that Satan is, in this time, uniquely bound so that he may not deceive the nations, guaranteeing that some from every tribe and tongue will believe in Christ. This age will end in the climax of a great tribulation, after which Christ shall return and usher in the eternal state with a new heaven and earth.

Premillennialism

Premillennialism is the belief that Christ's second coming precedes His earthly rule and the visible implementation of His kingdom of peace and righteousness. He shall personally reign upon the earth with His saints.

The 1,000 years will be literal. Christ's reign upon the earth will be literal. Satan will be bound so that he cannot promote evil in man's fallen nature and in the social order. During this time God will bring into one both the natural and the spiritual Israel and provide the literal fulfillment of His promises to Abraham, Isaac, Jacob and their seed. This age will commence after the Great Tribulation and will conclude with one final outbreak of evil, at which point Christ will put down all evil and usher in the eternal state with a new heaven and earth.

2. *The Statement of Faith of the Alliance and the Corresponding Views of Dr. A.B. Simpson*

Article 11 of the Statement of Faith of the Alliance reads, "The second coming of the Lord Jesus Christ is imminent and will be personal, visible, and premillennial. This is the believer's blessed hope and is a vital truth which is an incentive to holy living and faithful service."

As the Alliance moved toward a more formal denominational structure, they adopted a formal Statement of Faith at their annual Council in 1965, which was derived from long-held beliefs within the movement. As such there was little debate and disagreement on the positions brought forward. In the discussion from the floor on Article 11 the term "imminent" was opposed by a small contingent, but it was defeated soundly. A few also voiced opposition to the term "premillennial." They were, according to Dr. Keith Bailey, a witness to the debate, "stomped" by the affirmative voters. Such a unified embrace of this doctrine was to be expected, when the strong premillennial sentiment of the founder of the Alliance is taken into consideration.

Any casual reading of the poetry of Dr. Simpson will reveal a common theme celebrating the premillennial return of Christ. In A.B. Simpson's book, *The Coming One*, his view of the millennium and his perspective on the importance of the doctrine in the life of the Church are stated. Dr. Simpson states the belief that Christ is yet to come to earth to complete His glorious redemptive plan. He rejected any notion that the promises regarding Christ's millennial coming were fulfilled in the death of the saints, the destruction of Jerusalem, a spiritual indwelling or in any spiritual application through the Church. He spoke against a spiritualizing interpretation of Old Testament prophetic passages. He spoke against the blotting out of the literal Israel from God's future plans. He wrote, "There is a double thread running through the warp and woof of ancient prophecy. There is the crimson line of the cross, but there is the golden thread of the coming glory. . . . It was necessary that He should fulfill the vision of the cross and it is just as necessary that He shall fulfill the vision of the King." [2]

The rejection of a material, terrestrial millennium for a higher spiritual one of heart or heaven (such as amillennialism may design) was to Dr. Simpson compatible with spiritualizing the creation account or the liberalizing of Jesus into an idea with no historical reality. "Such a rejection," he wrote, "takes out of God's Book all reality and makes everything merely a dream as vague as the fooleries of Christian Science. Thank God He is real and we are real and Christ is real and the coming glory is real." [3]

With similar vibrato, Dr. Simpson reacted against the more commonly held postmillennial views of the day, calling them counterfeit millenniums:

> Man has tried to make his own millennium. Poetry has dreamed of it, and degraded it into a sensuous paradise. Patriots and optimists have drawn the vision of a golden age of liberty, equality, peace, and plenty, and have seen only anarchy, license, and misery arise at the touch of their deceptive wand. Moralists have toiled for purity, temperance, and virtue, and dreamed of a day when social reform will have blotted out the last plague spot from our cities, only to see wickedness, crime, and the curse of alcohol, and woman's shame increase with increasing civilization. And Christian reformers have expected a spiritual millennium, in which the Gospel shall cover the myriad populations of earth, and make every land a holy, happy paradise of love and purity; but alas! the lands that are the most evangelized are sometimes the farthest from millennial piety or purity; and were all the world to reach tomorrow the condition to which Christian lands have attained in the three centuries since the Reformation, earth would still be a sight to break the heart of Him who died for us. Nay, God has something better for His weary, hungry children than any of man's counterfeit millenniums.[4]

3. The Historical Development of Millennialism

It should be noted that the doctrinal thought of Dr. A.B. Simpson—and The Christian and Missionary Alliance, for that matter—are products of their times. The Alliance was born during a period of time when premillennial thought and its attendant biblicism were being renewed in church history. To help contextualize the premillennial thought of Dr. Simpson's day, the historical flow of millennial thought from the apostles down to the present follows.

The Premillennial Early Church

The observation shared by the vast majority of historians is that the early Church was premillennial. George N.H. Peters chronicles in proposition 72 of his voluminous work, *The Theocratic Kingdom*, a compelling historical argument demonstrating that the premillennial doctrine of the kingdom, as preached by the apostles, was taught by the early churches.[5]

The following is a sampling of a few of the church and secular historians whose studies have concurred with George N.H. Peters' basic proposition: Edward Gibbon, author of the classic work, *The History of the Decline and Fall of the Roman Empire*; J.C.I. Gieseler, Professor of Theology and highly acclaimed church historian in his day, who himself was not a premillennialist; Henry Sheldon, Professor of Historical Theology at Boston University; Philip Schaff, prominent German Reformed theologian, church historian and author of the monumental eight-volume, *History of the Christian Church*; Adolf Harnack, Lutheran theologian and church historian; Will Durant, author of the multi-volume work, *The Story of Civilization*; Paul Boyer, Professor of History at the University of Wisconsin, Madison, and author of *When Time Shall Be No More: Prophecy Belief in Modern American Culture*.

Many of the early Church Fathers revealed a premillennial indoctrination. *The Epistle of Barnabas* (ca. A.D. 70) was written only a little after the martyrdom of the Apostle Paul. On the creation week, it says:

> Consider what this signifies, He finished them in six days. The meaning of it is this; that in six thousand years the Lord God will bring all things to an end. For with Him one day is as a thousand years. . . . [T]herefore . . . in six days (i.e., 6,000 years) shall all things be accomplished. . . . [W]hen His Son shall come and abolish the wicked one, and judge the ungodly; and shall change the sun, and moon and stars; then He shall gloriously rest on that 'seventh day,' i.e., millennium.[6]

Papias (ca. A.D. 60-130) was reputed to have been taught by John the apostle. Fanciful images of a millennial period are attributed to him.

Justin Martyr (A.D. 100-165) wrote, "I and others who are right-minded Christians on all points, are assured that there will be a resurrection of the dead and a thousand years in Jerusalem, which will then be built, adorned, and enlarged, as the prophets Ezekiel and Isaiah and others declare."[7] Martyr's clear premillennialism prompted Harnack to observe, "That a philosopher like Justin, with a bias towards an Hellenic construction of the Christian religion, should nevertheless have accepted its chiliastic elements is the strongest proof that these enthusiastic expectations were inseparably bound up with the Christian faith down to the middle of the second century."[8]

Irenaeus (A.D. 140-203) was the disciple of Polycarp, the disciple of John the apostle. He affirmed the millennium and two distinct resurrections.

Tertullian (A.D. 170-220) believed in the primacy of the literal sense of Scripture and that a literal millennium would follow the resurrection of the dead. He went deeply into the book of Daniel and taught that Daniel 9:24-27 predicted both the time of Christ's birth and death. He saw the millennium as an interim kingdom before the final translation of the saints into heaven. Tertullian fascinatingly observed, "At His last coming He will favor with His acceptance and blessing the circumcision also, even the race of Abraham, which by and by is to acknowledge Him."[9]

Hippolytus (A.D. 170-236) was a presbyter of the church of Rome. He set out the most complete source of the customs of the ante-Nicene church in his *Commentary on the Book of Daniel*, a premillennial eschatology.

Nephos of Egypt (first half of the third century) wrote a tract entitled *Against the Allegorist* in which he defended the literal, traditional interpretation of the millenarian promises in Revelation 20 and 21.[10]

Sextus Julius Africanus (died A.D. 240) was a friend of the anti-millennialist Origen; in spite of this, he ". . . adopted the familiar apocalyptic notion of a 'world week' of seven thousand years. . . . According to the usual form of this scheme, history will come to an end six thousand years after creation and will usher in a 'Sabbath' of a thousand years."[11]

Methodius (died A.D. 311) spoke of two resurrections and the seventh millennium of the creation.

Victorinus (died A.D. 304) held to two distinct resurrections as taken from Revelation 20, separated by 1,000 years. He expresses the seventh day as an eschatological image of the millennium.

Lactantius (died after A.D. 317) was a confessor to Constantine. He was premillenarian and also interpreted the three-and-one-half years of the last half of the tribulation to be a three-and-one-half year reign of terror by a Syrian king, the real Anti-Christ who will be defeated prior to the millennium by the Great King from heaven, who will then set up a 1,000-year reign with the just, over the remnants of earth. During this time, the "Prince of Demons" will be chained in prison and freed at the end to lead an unsuccessful assault against God's people. God will then bring about a total transformation of this natural order. The second resurrection will then take place in which the unbelieving dead will rise to eternal punishment.[12]

Peters concluded that the premillennial return of Christ and subsequent kingdom rule were taught by the early disciples and received by the young Church and that amillennial teaching was not clearly evidenced in Church history until the time of Augustine.

Development of Amillennialism

Amillennialism first appeared in the negative sense with no positive proposition regarding the millennium. Thus, the first expressions of amillennialism were a reaction against the gross sensual extremes that characterized some expressions of the dominant literal view of the millennium. It was also trying to put distance between the Christian doctrine of the end times and what was considered Jewish sensualism.

Origen (A.D. 185-253) was the most prominent of the negative amillennialists. It was he who popularized the allegorical method of biblical interpretation which provided a means by which Greek philosophical thought could be wed to Old and New Testament passages. With this view he maintained that there were three levels of interpretation for every passage of Scripture: the literal, the moral and the allegorical. He affirmed that the literal interpretation was not essentially the correct one. Such a hermeneutic enabled him to distance himself from the literal and "sensual" sense found in much of the prophetic passages of Scripture.

A positive amillennialism did not appear until the writings of Augustine (A.D. 354-430). Augustine was the chief architect of Catholic theology up to the time of Thomas Aquinas. His amillennial scheme is still the foundational thought behind Catholic and Reformed eschatology and millenarianism to this day. So strongly were his views adopted that church authorities went so far as to expurgate from the works of Irenaeus and Victorinus all millennial taint.[13]

Augustine was highly influenced by the Neoplatonism of Plotinus (A.D. 205-270) and the allegorical method of Philo, which Origen developed for Christian thought. This influence was profoundly dualistic. "Plato believed that the ultimate goal of a human being was to arrive at a disembodied state of pure spirit. . . . The material, and especially the body . . . was looked upon as evil and to be loathed."[14]

This dualism is seen in Augustine's writings on the afterlife and influenced his development of purgatory as a place to " . . . cleanse them from the remnants that are owing to this cement of flesh."[15]

The influence of Platonic thought is also revealed in the expressive monastic forms of Augustine's day, forms that he, in some degree, followed. Refusing to marry his common-law wife and the mother of his son, he became a celibate monk, with a monastic order following after his example.

This dualism ultimately resulted in Augustine's development of a new concept of the kingdom and the millennium. It is important when considering the history of this doctrine to note that Augustine's belief in a spiritual millennium was not the recovering of an old truth neglected, but the establishment of a new scheme, not advanced by anyone before him. Historian Christopher Dawson well observes that Augustine is "entirely alienated from the realistic literalism of the old apocalyptic tradition."[16]

As A.E. Pinell lucidly demonstrated, Augustine never attempted to refute millennialism but simply ignored it on the grounds that its materialism was unseemly. Augustine states:

> This opinion would not be objectionable, if it were believed that the joys of the saints in that Sabbath should be spiritual only, and consequent on the presence of God. But as he asserts that those who then rise again shall enjoy the leisure of immoderate carnal banquets, famished with an amount of meat and drink such as not only to shock the feeling of the temperate, but even to surpass the measure of credulity itself, such assertions can be believed only by the carnal. They who do believe them are called by the spiritual "Chiliasts" which literally may be millenarians.[17]

Pinell gives further light on this prejudice Augustine had against millennialism by noting:

> As Platonistically conditioned as he was and given his monastic mentality, it was understandable that Augustine should have reacted as he did to the millennialism of his day. His basic aversion to thinking of any future rest for the saints, as including any kind of material enjoyments, showed heavily in the reason he gave for rejecting millennialism. He said he could believe in millennialism, if it only stated that "the joys of

saints in the Sabbath shall be spiritual." Otherwise, he said, "this opinion would not be objectionable." That is, to please him, an eschatological system had to be free of references to future material enjoyments. Not finding in millennialism the pure spiritual system he sought from the Christian writings of past history or from anything else, the only recourse he had left was his large and resourceful intellect.[18]

It should be noted that with the rise of Constantine and the graduation of Christianity to the official religion of the Roman Empire, there was little need to perpetuate a millennial doctrine of hope for the end of all human government upon the earth and the ushering in of a distinctly divine one. It should also be noted that from this time forward, up through the Reformation period, until the early nineteenth century, the Church was wedded to the leadership of, or allegiance to, earthly powers and rulers. Each of the three main Protestant traditions of the sixteenth century—Lutheranism, Calvinism and Anglicanism—had the support of the state, even as they continued in the same Constantinian (amillennial) approach to theology.[19] It is noteworthy then that with the dawning of the nineteenth century and the increasing separation of church and state, there was also a significant shift in church doctrine toward premillennial thought.

It can be said in review that Origin's attempts to allegorize, Augustine's dualistic Platonism[20] and Constantine's Christianization of human government effectively killed a vigilant spirit of defense for and development of premillennial theology. Amillennialism was not the primary historical testimony of the Church; rather, it was premillennialism that expressed the hopes of the early Church. Amillennialism did not rise out of a rediscovery of biblical truth, but out of reaction to a "Jewish sensualism" that was incompatible with the "Hellenistic dualism" of the day. Amillennialism was born out of the convergence of spiritualizing interpretation, dualistic philosophy that disparaged the physical, and realized social triumphalism. These three are generally recognized in evangelical thought as negative developments in the Church.

Yet, in spite of this suspicious genesis, today's amillennialists are satisfied to identify their position and, in particular, their reading of Revelation 20:1-6, as defensible through their allegiance to the teaching of Augustine. Anthony Hoekema, for example, states in defense of an amillennial interpretation, "The amillennial understanding of Revelation 20:1-6 as describing the reigning souls of deceased believers with Christ in heaven has had good standing in the church since the days of Augustine."[21]

Development of Postmillennialism

Postmillennialism appeared on the historical scene in the seventeenth century with the Age of Enlightenment. Augustine's antimaterialism was increasingly incompatible with a budding age of science and a focus upon a material universe. Literal measurements and calculations conflicted with the allegorical method of interpreting nature and God's Word.

With Daniel Whitby (1683-1726), a Unitarian, postmillennialism was introduced. Eventually there came about two kinds of postmillennialism. One was liberal and secular, with adherents like John Locke and Thomas Paine, and later liberals such as Shirley Jackson Case, author of *Christianizing the Social Order*. Over time there appeared many other books trumpeting the social triumph of Christianity. The other was a conservative postmillennialism represented in a chain of succession by Jonathan Edwards, Charles Hodge, B.B. Warfield and Loraine Boettner. The succession of two world wars dealt a deathblow to the optimism of postmillennialism. Today the new Reconstructionism has arisen, which makes a curious blend of the two, at times militantly combining a conservative view of Scripture and the gospel with the law and its social demands and political mandates.

The Renewal of the Premillennial Doctrine

One should be aware that there is not a century from the time of the early Church where there is not some record of premillennial teaching and thought. Paul Boyer's book, *When Time Shall Be No More*, demonstrates that even during the Middle Ages the religion of the populace had strong material, premillennial hopes.[22] *The Evangelical Dictionary of Theology* confirms this point, stating that the allegorical interpretation of Augustine became the official doctrine of the Church during the medieval period. In defiance of the main teaching of the Church, however, the earlier apocalyptic premillennialism continued to be held by certain counterculture groups.[23]

Long before John Darby (1800-1882) was sketching his first dispensational charts, Joachim of Fiore (1135-1202) had sketched his three ages of law, grace and the Spirit, and was publishing his *Book of Figures* charting out these ages. Out of an inductive study of the book of Revelation he concluded that the chiliasts were right.[24]

John Wycliffe and John Hus, morning stars of the Reformation, were avowed millennialists. Premillennialists in the Reformation period also existed with more and more frequency, e.g., Joseph Mede, Isaac Watts, Hugh Latimer and Puritan John Bunyan, all argued for the literal interpretation of all the prophetic passages of Scripture. Bunyan, for example, wrote on Zechariah 14:4, "His feet shall stand in that day upon the mount of Olives" (KJV), arguing against the spiritualizers of God's Word. He says, "This is the day of His second coming," and then asks, "Where is the Mount of Olives? Not within thee! But that which is without Jerusalem." On the millennium, Bunyan further writes:

> God's blessing the Sabbath day, and resting on it from all His works, was a type of that glorious rest that saints shall have when the six days of this world are totally ended. . . . This day is called a great day . . . which shall end in the eternal judgment of the world. God hath held this forth by several other shadows, such as the Sabbath of weeks, the Sabbath of years, and the great Jubilee. . . . In the seventh thousand years of the world will be that Sabbath when Christ shall set up His kingdom on earth: according to that which is written, "They lived and reigned with Christ a thousand years."[25]

David Larsen in his book *Jews, Gentiles and the Church* makes note that Martin Bucer, successor to Zwingli, and Theodore Beza, Calvin's successor, started a small but growing trend returning to chiliasm.[26] Robert Baillie in 1645 claimed that most of the divines in London were chiliasts. By 1649 Grotius had counted eighty books published in England expounding the millennium.[27] Larsen also demonstrates a growing trend among theologians, church leaders and political leaders, such as Oliver Cromwell, to reevaluate the role of Israel in the plans of God. There was an ever-increasing embrace of the thought that Israel would have a part in the glorious plans of God and that Old Testament prophecy contained not only the glory of the New Testament Church but also a literal promise for the glory of Israel. Among those who held to an eschatological belief in the restoration of Israel were such Puritans as John Cotton, Thomas Shepherd, John Eliot, the American Mathers and John Owen.

Owen wrote, "The Jews shall be gathered from all parts of the earth where they are now scattered, and brought home into their 'homeland' before the 'end of all things' prophesied by St. Peter can occur."[28] It would be stretching it to say that these individuals were premillennialists. What would be a safe statement is that such a growing sentiment added to the ultimate climate in which premillennialism was widely embraced.

The new rise of premillennial thought, though strongly initiated by John Darby, was not the sole domain of one version of dispensational thought. There were those like Anglican Bishop of Liverpool, John Charles Ryle, who wrote the *Premillennial Creed*, and those who would now likely be called progressive dispensationalists, such as George N.H. Peters, author of the three-volume *The Theocratic Kingdom*; Nathaniel West, author of *One Thousand Years in Both Testaments*; and W.C. Stevens, a teacher at Nyack College and author of *Revelation, the Crown Jewel of Biblical Prophecy*.

According to secular historian Boyer,

> Dispensationalism arrived at a time of mounting evangelical concern over challenges to the Bible's divinely inspired status by liberal theologians in the United States and by historical-critical scholars in Germany. The formation of the Evangelical Alliance in England in 1846 and of an American branch in 1867 signaled the rising uneasiness. At the founding convention in London, the eight hundred delegates adopted a creedal statement explicitly affirming the Bible's inspiration and authority. Many embattled evangelicals thus welcomed Darby's strong emphasis on Biblical authority and his literal reading of the prophetic texts.[29]

The dispensational premillennial movement corresponded to, and further encouraged, a growing confidence among the everyday Christian that he or she could readily understand the clear teaching of Scripture. Thus premillennial teaching and thought was a strong influence in the rise of Bible institutes throughout North America, as well as in the Bible conference movement. Premillennialism was strongly wed to a confidence in the verbally inspired, inerrant Word of God and gave impetus to the development of early twentieth-century fundamentalism.

This new movement also gave strength to a strong missions movement and evangelical thrust which ran counter to the progressive or postmillennial hopes for an advancing humanity. Premillennialism gave an answer to the false evolutionary hopes of Darwinism for the human race. "Far from paralyzing . . . missionary effort," wrote Nathaniel West in 1879, "premillennial belief was . . . one of the mightiest incentives to earnestness in preaching the Gospel to every creature, until He comes, not to make the world better, but to save people out of the world."[30] Dr. A.B. Simpson saw a twofold incentive arising from what he called the blessed hope: encouraging a missionary message of warning, and also awakening and issuing a call to the practice of holiness in preparation for Christ's coming.[31] It was this renewed premillennialism, with its inclination for the clear, literal teaching of the Bible and a refocused mission to the world, that swept up new church movements in the late 1800s—including that movement which would become The Christian and Missionary Alliance.

4. Interpretations of Revelation 20:1-6

And I saw an angel coming down out of heaven, having the key to the Abyss and holding in his hand a great chain. He seized the dragon, that ancient serpent, who is the devil, or Satan, and bound him for a thousand years. He threw him into the Abyss, and locked and sealed it over him, to keep him from deceiving the nations anymore until the thousand years were ended. After that, he must be set free for a short time.

I saw thrones on which were seated those who had been given authority to judge. And I saw the souls of those who had been beheaded because of their testimony for Jesus and because of the word of God. They had not worshiped the beast or his image and had not received his mark on their foreheads or their hands. They came to life and reigned with Christ a thousand years. (The rest of the dead did not come to life until the thousand years were ended.) This is the first resurrection. Blessed and holy are those who have part in the first resurrection. The second death has no power over them, but they will be priests of God and of Christ and will reign with him for a thousand years. (Revelation 20:1-6)

Dr. Simpson's and the Alliance's belief in the millennium does not rest on Revelation 20 alone, but on the numerous prophecies of the Old Testament that herald the coming Messiah who will reign on David's throne and rule over a peaceful kingdom. The truth of the Messianic age rests on the literal interpretation of these many Old Testament passages. The primary contribution that Revelation 20:1-6 makes regarding the Messianic Kingdom is to disclose its duration of 1,000 years. It should be considered significant that this duration is mentioned six times within this brief passage.

However, because the amillennial/postmillennial advocates deny the relevance of Old Testament passages and promises (conceiving all these promises either to be spiritually transferred to the Church where possible, or made null and void on account of Israel's unbelief), the scriptural ground for the debate between them and premillennialists has been generally narrowed down to Revelation 20:1-6. Therefore, a brief overview of the respective competing interpretations of this passage is in order. This will be followed by a framing of the historic expectation for a millennium that qualifies how the audience was likely to read the author's intent.

Premillennial View

Chapter 19 is the key passage in Revelation describing the second coming of Christ to earth. This second coming is a key theme of the book according to Revelation 1:7, "Look, he is coming. . . ." Chapter 20 follows in clear chronological order and describes two bodily resurrections separated by a period of 1,000 years. In between them, Satan shall be bound, and those first raised shall reign with Christ upon the earth. At the end of this time there shall be a brief release of Satan followed by his being cast into the lake of fire, the second resurrection and the final judgment. Then the eternal state shall be established.

Amillennial/Postmillennial View

As has already been observed, this interpretation of Revelation 20:1-6 finds its historical roots in the novel thinking of Augustine on the passage. The interpretation is figurative and not literal.

Chapter 20 is not viewed chronologically by the amillennialist nor by the postmillennialist as following chapter 19, but rather as a return to the time of the present period of the Church.

This would not be the natural rendering when considering the succession of *kai eidon* ("And I saw") in Revelation 19:11, 17; 20:1, 4, 11; 21:1. This repeated phrase seems to introduce an unfolding series of interrelated visions which moves progressively forward, not retrogressively. With this understanding, the progressive sequence would then be obvious: the second coming, the judgment of the armies, the judgment of the Beast and the False Prophet in the lake of fire, the binding of Satan in the Abyss for 1,000 years, the reign of those participating in the first resurrection, the final judgment and the new heavens and new earth.

The 1,000 years are taken symbolically to mean the complete and full present state of the Church. Verses 1-3 would then refer to the present age here on earth with Satan bound from deceiving the nations and stopping the spread of the gospel. Verses 4-6 would refer to this same period in heaven with the departed souls of the redeemed with God.

The first resurrection is said to be a spiritual resurrection of souls into the presence of God. (Augustine added to this the spiritual resurrection of the redeemed on earth according to Ephesians 2:1.) The second resurrection is the one general physical resurrection at the end of the age.

In response to this interpretation Henry Alford gave the well-known quote:

> If, in a passage where two resurrections are mentioned, where certain *psychai ezaesan* at the first, and the rest of the *nekoi ezesan* only at the end of a specified period after the first; if in such a passage the first resurrection may be understood to mean spiritual rising with Christ, while the second means literal rising from the grave, then there is an end of all significance in language, and Scripture is wiped out as a definite testimony to anything.[32]

Millennial Expectation and John's Intent in Revelation 20

There was a well established belief in the ancient world that there was to be a literal 1,000-year millennium of peace and righteousness upon the earth.

Bishop Russell of Scotland, an anti-millenarian, says:

> With respect to the millennium it must be acknowledged that the doctrine concerning it stretches back into antiquity so remote and obscure, that it is impossible to fix its origin. The tradition that the earth, as well as the moral and religious state of its inhabitants, were to undergo a great change at the end of 6,000 years, has been detected in the writing of Pagans, Jews and Christians. It is found in the most ancient of those commentaries of the Old Testament, which we owe to the learning of the Rabbinical school.[33]

Zoroaster, an ancient Persian philosopher, taught "in the end Sosioch [a name resembling in sound the Hebrew Messiah] makes his appearance, under whose reign the dead are raised, the judgment takes place, and the earth is renovated and glorified. . . . He also taught the six-millennial duration of the world."[34]

Theopompus, who flourished in 340 B.C., relates that the Persian Magi taught the present state of things would continue 6,000 years, after which Hades, or death, would be destroyed, and men would live happily. Bishop Russell, from whom we extract, adds that the opinion of the ancient Jews on this point may be gathered from the statement of a Rabbi who said, "The world endures 6000 years, and in the 1000, or millennium that follows, the enemies of God will be destroyed."[35]

The ancient Etruscans taught, "The world was formed in the course of six periods; each period comprehending a millenary; while 6000 years are allotted for a seventh period, viz, that of its duration."[36]

Rabbi Elias, a Jewish doctor of high antiquity, lived, says Bishop Russell, about 200 years before Christ. His opinion is called by the Jews, "A tradition of the house of Elias." He taught that the world would be "2,000 years void of the law; 2,000 years under the law, and 2,000 years under the Messiah." He limited the duration of the world to 6,000 years and held that in the seventh millenary, "The earth would be renewed and the righteous dead raised; that these should not again be turned to dust, and that the just then alive should mount up with wings as the eagle: so that in that day they would not fear though the mountains be cast into the midst of the sea. Psalms 46:3."[37]

There was also a contemporary millennial expectation in John's day. Rabbi Gamaliel, the teacher of Paul, used the phrase "in the land that the

LORD swore to give your forefathers" from Deuteronomy 11:21, to demonstrate the resurrection of the dead to silence the Sadducees. He said, "as Abraham, Isaac, and Jacob had it not; and God cannot lie; therefore, they must be raised from the dead to inherit it." The importance of this quotation proves that there was a real, literal—not figurative—anticipation of an earthly millennial reign in John's day.

Acts 1:6 is the last of many dialogues of expectation that the disciples had with Jesus on the subject. In each case Jesus never speaks to correct their core conviction of an expected physical kingdom but by implication or limited qualification seems to encourage it.

The Sibylline Oracles are frequently quoted by the early Church Fathers. They are a rare and ancient writing of Greek verse comprising fourteen books by various authors, some written before Christ and some after. These oracles, as well, taught of a coming millennium. This millennium with surrounding judgments is one of the strong themes of the oracles. (Paul quoted from these writings in Acts 17:28 and Titus 1:12.)

Finally, it is well known that John's nemesis and Gnostic contemporary, Cerinthus (A.D. 100), taught of the coming of Jesus before 1,000 years of sensuous pleasure, after which there would be a consummation of this age.

In John's day there is little or no evidence that this period of 1,000 years of bliss was ever understood in any other way than the literal. The evidence abounds that such an interpretation and expectation was strongly set in the minds of his contemporaries. The weight of both the ancient expectation and the contemporary expectations makes it highly unlikely that John would have chosen to use such a culturally overloaded language unless he had intended not a figurative understanding, but a literal one. In the same way the audience that heard and read John would have been so primed by the contemporary expectation that they certainly would have received the millennial language in the framework of the popular literal expectation.

5. *The Relevance of Premillennialism for the Future of The Christian and Missionary Alliance*

A final consideration must be given to the value of this doctrine as it applies to The Christian and Missionary Alliance. Many of the views of

Dr. A.B. Simpson on this topic and its relationship to the early Alliance were presented in response to the postmillennialism that was around at the end of the last century. This concept of postmillennialism was largely humanistic and promoted a social gospel ministry for the Church. Its confidence in the growth of the human spirit left one unguarded against the darkness of his own nature, and unimpressed with his need for the abundant life of Jesus within him which would enable him to please God. Here was an optimistic view of history that set, accidentally or not, man at its center. Dr. Simpson's view of history and what the future would eventually comprise, however, required the active intervention and revelation of Jesus Christ.

Dr. Simpson was not so pessimistic that he saw the earth passing away without a golden age of historical peace and a reign of righteousness. He was not so optimistic that he saw that age coming by any other means than the intervention of the Son of God as King of the earth. In all this he looked beyond to the great and final glory of the eternal state, where God, having brought in the ultimate expression of glory in history, would climax His display of glory throughout all eternity.

The Alliance teaching on the centrality of Christ in the history of the world is evidenced by its unwillingness to be sidetracked into focusing upon God's dealing with the nation Israel as the primary key for understanding eschatology. Rather, the focus remained on Christ, the blessed Olive Root of the people of God and the basis of blessing for Jew and Gentile in every age and in the age to come. Together there would be one fold, regardless of the administration, in the millennium. This truth is expressed in the structure of the New Jerusalem where on the gates of the city are engraved the names of the twelve tribes of the sons of Israel and on the foundation stones are the names of the twelve apostles of the Lamb. In the city of God it is Jew and Gentile who will, when grafted into Christ, live as the people of God.[38]

Alliance Distinctives in Review

Now consider again the five distinctives introduced at the beginning of this paper in order to help answer the question, "How relevant is this doctrine in giving focus and direction to The Christian and Missionary Alliance?" Consider the following questions.

Is it possible to be motivated for missions and be either amillennial or postmillennial? Is it possible to issue a call for holiness through the abiding life of Christ and be either amillennial or postmillennial? Is it possible to develop a Christocentric view of history and be either amillennial or postmillennial? Is it possible to believe in the inerrant Word of God and be either amillennial or postmillennial? Is it possible to affirm the integrity of God and be either amillennial or postmillennial?

To all of these questions, in deference to both the amillennialist and the postmillennialist, we must give a resounding "Yes."

The Transcendent Integrity of God

One should remember, however, that the early conviction of the Alliance was that the overriding purpose of human history was the glory of God, a public display of His integrity. This glory manifested in the Church, manifested in the Son and manifested in God's faithfulness to Israel was reflected in the premillennialism of the Alliance. Dr. Simpson wept when he read the Balfour Declaration to his congregation, following Allenby's taking of Jerusalem. That declaration stated, "His Majesty's Government views with favor the establishment in Palestine of a national home for the Jewish people. . . ."[39] Dr. Simpson later wrote, "Israel is going home and Christ is coming back again!"[40]

This same premillennial sentiment for God's glory and integrity is expressed by Marv Rosenthal when he writes,

> If God does not keep His word to Israel, He is not true. If God does not have power to fulfill His purposes, He is not omnipotent. If God does not know that certain things are going to occur and gets caught off guard, He is not omniscient. If God has wearied of Israel, He is not long-suffering. If God has changed His mind, He is not immutable. And in this we must be clear—if God has changed His mind in relation to His purpose for Israel, perhaps He will change His mind concerning His purposes for the Church. Perhaps we do not have a home in glory land. Perhaps He is going to rescind His grace toward us. Enough! God is holy, just, true, loving, good, long-suffering, faithful, omnipotent, immutable, and infinitely more. In the first instance, the

millennial issue is not prophetical, it is theological. It is not so much a consideration of what will happen tomorrow, it deals with what God's character is like today. Because He is a faithful God, He will keep His promises to Israel—that requires a literal, Millennial Kingdom established by the Lord Jesus Christ. God will keep His promises to the believer—that requires a home in glory in His presence forevermore.[41]

The Infallible Word of God

It must be recognized again that it was the belief of the founders of the Alliance that this teaching was true to the testimony of Scripture.[42] Among every other perceived advantage, it kept the Old Testament from becoming a deserted city, left only for Bible scholars and archaeologists to rummage through for relics of abandoned and voided hopes. Instead, the Old Testament remained a living testament to the sufficient and assured grace of Christ for every age and for the ages to come. As such, the whole of the Word of God is understood to be living and powerful and sharper than any two-edged sword and fit for every man and woman of God (see Hebrews 4:12).

Although Dr. Simpson was committed to the study of types within the Scripture, he held to the literal and historical nature of the Bible.[43] The great danger introduced by the combination of Darwinism, liberal theology, the Social Gospel and liberal biased critical Bible scholarship in Dr. Simpson's day was the erosion of long-held beliefs. Along with this erosion, modernism effectively removed the Word from the rank and file of Christianity and placed it in the hands of an elite "scholarship." Against this tide, premillennialism supported a countermovement of growing confidence in Scripture expressed in the belief that every part of the Bible could be understood in its literal and normal sense; that, excepting the cases of resulting absurdities, it should be taken literally. This confidence turned common people boldly back to the Word, and as they applied this principle of understanding the Scripture to both Old and New Testament prophecy, they saw written there the secrets of a coming millennial kingdom over which Christ would reign as King upon the earth.

Loraine Boettner, postmillennialist, recognizes this point of a literal, not letter-al, interpretation of prophecy when he admits that, "It is generally agreed that if the prophecies are taken literally, they do foretell a restoration of the nation of Israel in the land of Palestine with the Jews having a prominent place in that kingdom and ruling over the other nations."[44] This was a part of what the early Alliance saw in the millennium and what they invited its rank and file membership to see in their private and public study of the Bible.

The Centrality of Christ

The centrality of Christ was seen in His progressive goal for history climaxing in a reign of glory in which all the nations are subject to His rule of peace for 1,000 years. Today Christ's rule in history is the invisible reign within the hearts of God's children. This rule is hidden from the world's view. The rule of the eternal state shall be outside of history. But in history there shall be the final phase of time in which Christ shall rule from an earthly throne and display His glory over time, in time. Thus, nothing of the created order shall escape the full manifestation and reign of Christ's glory in it, not even time.

The millennium, ending in a final rebellion, will also serve to commend the justice of God on that last day of judgment. Man will have demonstrated, in that day, that his sin is due to nothing else than the depravity of his own heart. This fixed and progressive goal of history, that Christ shall be glorified and demonstrated as triumphant in time and place, was the hope of the early Church and the source of their encouragement in the face of a corrupt age. It was a hope renewed in the movement of the early Alliance.

The Christ Life

It is not the threat of judgment alone but the hopeful prospect of a historical holiness, a Christ-in-us-ness that should ultimately inspire God's children. Holiness in Jesus is not only a taste of finding heaven today, of living in the glory; it is the foreshadowing of a real and earthly reign of glory that we shall enjoy with Christ in time, on earth. Dr. Simpson wrote, "Because we are going to be like Him, then, we wear His image now. We anticipate our coming glory . . . so we try on even here the robes of our approaching coronation."[45]

Dr. Simpson pushed this application home strongly in his exposition of Isaiah 11: "We have no right to be looking for the millennium unless we have the millennium in our own hearts. We have no business to expect an eternity of peace if we are living in strife and envy now. Let us begin the millennial life here if we expect to enjoy it by and by."[46]

A Missionary Alliance

It is true that premillennialism teaches that the only hope for the future of the world is Christ, not Christianization. Therefore, people need to be saved out of the world. Yet there is as well the hopeful incentive that one day Christ will rule the nations and gather from them the fruit of worship from upon this earth, in time and as a goal of history. For the early Alliance each victory won overseas, and here, was a small foreshadowing of the triumph Jesus was bringing to earth and to eternity. Dr. Simpson's call to bring back the King was less the cry of desperation as it was a call to join in Christ's ultimate triumph.

It is possible to hold to these five passions for the integrity of God, the inerrancy of His Word, the centrality of His Son, the prospects of His sanctification and the supremacy of His mission apart from one's view of the millennium. Still, for the Alliance these passions have risen historically, not in spite of its eschatology, but in some ways uniquely because of it. These things are more closely related than we can appreciate at first or second glance. They are intertwined in a delicate cause and effect. We should devote ourselves to fully understand the role this position had in shaping our denominational distinctives and emphases. As the Alliance moves into a new century, in a check against historical drift, care must be taken not to cut the cords which bind us to the moorings of our movement even as we hold fast to that which is good.

> O Christ, my Lord and King, This is the prayer I bring,
> This is the song I sing: Thy Kingdom come.
> Help me to work and pray, help me to live each day,
> That all I do may say, Thy kingdom come, Thy kingdom come.
>
> Upon my heart's high throne, Rule Thou, and Thou
> alone;
> Let me be all Thine own! Thy kingdom come, Thy kingdom come.

Through all the earth abroad, Wherever man has trod,
Send forth Thy Word, O God—Thy kingdom come, Thy kingdom come.

Soon may our King appear! Haste bright millennial
    year!
We live to bring it near. Thy kingdom come, Thy kingdom come.[47]

Endnotes

1. Raymond Ludwigson, *A Survey of Bible Prophecy* (Grand Rapids: Zondervan, 1978), 96.
2. A.B. Simpson, *The Coming One* (New York: Christian Alliance Publishing, 1912), 7-18.
3. Ibid., 16.
4. Ibid., 152-3.
5. George N.H. Peters, *The Theocratic Kingdom*, 3 vols. (Grand Rapids: Kregel Publications, 1988), 449.
6. D.T. Taylor, *The Voice of the Church on the Coming and Kingdom of the Redeemer or A History of the Doctrine of the Reign of Christ on the Earth* (Boston: H.L. Hastings, 1861), 52.
7. Ludwigson, *A Survey of Bible Prophecy*, 127.
8. Dr. Renald Showers, "A Description and Early History of Millennial Views," *Israel My Glory* (June 1986): 25.
9. David Larsen, *Jews, Gentiles and the Church* (Grand Rapids: Discovery House Publishing, 1995), 120, citing Tertullian, *Against Marcion*, 7.5.9.
10. Brian E. Daley, *The Hope of the Early Church: A Handbook of Patristic Eschatology* (Cambridge: Cambridge University Press, 1992), 61.
11. Ibid.
12. Ibid., 68.
13. Paul Boyer, *When Time Shall Be No More* (Cambridge, MA: The Belknap Press of Harvard University Press, 1992), 49.
14. E.A. Pinell, *Christian League Newsletter on the Millennial vs. Amillennial Debate*, 1980, 9.
15. Ibid.
16. Larsen, *Jews, Gentiles and the Church*, 122.
17. Augustine, *The City of God*, in *The Nicene and Post-Nicene Fathers*, Philip Schaff, ed. (Grand Rapids: Eerdmans, 1979), series I, vol. II. ed., 426.
18. E.A. Pinell, *Christian League Newsletter*, 10.
19. Walter Elwell, *The Concise Evangelical Dictionary of Theology*, 314.
20. A revealing study of Augustine's Neoplatonism is found in Robert J. O'Connell, *St. Augustine's Early Theory of Man*.
21. Anthony Hoekema, *The Bible and the Future* (Grand Rapids: Eerdmans, 1979), 183.
22. Boyer, *When Time Shall Be No More*, 50.
23. Elwell, *The Concise Evangelical Dictionary of Theology*, 314.
24. Larsen, *Jews, Gentiles and the Church*, 123.
25. Taylor, *The Voice of the Church on the Coming and Kingdom of the Redeemer*, 200-1.
26. Larsen, *Jews, Gentiles and the Church*, 124.

27. Ibid., 127.

28. Ibid., 126.

29. Boyer, *When Time Shall Be No More*, 89.

30. Ibid., 97, quoting *Premillennial Essays* by West.

31. Simpson, *The Coming One*, 201.

32. Robert G. Clouse, *The Meaning of the Millennium: Four Views* (Downers Grove, IL: InterVarsity, 1977), 37-8. The quote of Henry Alford is cited by George Eldon Ladd.

33. D.T. Taylor, *The Voice of the Church on the Coming and Kingdom of the Redeemer*, 25, citing Bishop Russell from *Discourse on the Millennium*, 39.

34. Ibid., 28, citing Dr. Hengstenberg in *Christology*, vol. 1, 16. Dr. Hengstenberg thinks Zoroaster stole and adulterated the truths of Revelation.

35. Ibid., 27.

36. Ibid., 28.

37. Ibid., 25-6.

38. Keith Bailey, *Christ's Coming and His Kingdom* (Camp Hill, PA: Christian Publications, 1981). Chapter 6, entitled "The Rich Root of the Olive Tree," is a wonderfully sweet discussion on this matter and resounds with a feel of the central glory of Alliance Christology applied to eschatology.

39. Abba Eban, *Heritage: Civilization and the Jews* (New York: Summit Books, 1984), 256.

40. Simpson, *The Coming One*, 192.

41. Marv Rosenthal, "The Importance of a Premillennial Theology," *Israel My Glory* (October 1986): 7.

42. The hermeneutical assessment of the basis of premillennialism is bound up in an understanding that the 1,000 years referenced in Revelation 20:1-7 is a literal period of 1,000 years. For a thorough presentation of the literal interpretation of these passages see Robert L. Thomas, *Revelation, An Exegetical Commentary* (Chicago: Moody Press, 1995), vol. 2, 403-23 and also Excursus 4 at the end of volume 2. The author states

> Chronological sequence is the natural understanding of the visions. Also the Old Testament framework that supplies the foundation for this book requires a future period on earth to fulfill the promises of a Messianic age. It is a structural necessity of Revelation that this 1000 years lies in the future too. . . . If the writer (John) wanted a symbolic number why did he not use 144,000 (cf. 7:1; 14:1), 200,000,000 (9:16), "ten thousand times ten thousand, and thousands of thousands" (5:11) or an incalculably large number (7:9)? The fact is that no number in Revelation is verifiably a symbolic number. On the other hand, nonsymbolic usage of numbers is the rule."

For a concise summary of the genre and hermeneutic of Revelation and further study for the compelling case of a literal interpretation see *Revelation, An Exegetical Commentary*, vol. 1, 23-39.

43. A.B. Simpson, *Divine Emblems* (Camp Hill, PA: Christian Publications, 1995), 9.

44. Clouse, *The Meaning of the Millennium: Four Views*, 95.

45. Simpson, *The Coming One*, 203.

46. A.B. Simpson, *Christ in the Bible Series—Isaiah* (Harrisburg, PA: Christian Publications, n.d.), 146.

47. A.B. Simpson, *Hymns of the Christian Life* (Camp Hill, PA: Christian Publications, 1978), 472.

Future Considerations

9

Premillennialism

Imminence, the Tribulation
and Prophetic Preaching

• William R. Goetz •

It was a bright Sunday morning in Pennsylvania. As a guest speaker, I had just concluded a prophetic message entitled, "Is That Wedding Music I Hear?" I had presented a number of scriptural reasons for believing that we should be looking for our Lord in the Rapture, to be followed by the Judgment Seat of Christ and the Wedding Supper of the Lamb.

As I greeted people at the door, an attractive middle-aged woman said to me, "I can't remember the last time that I heard a message on prophecy. Thank you so much. We need to be reminded of such truths!" Hers was the first of several similar comments that morning.

I have found that sort of response from congregations to be typical—all over North America.

As a non-itinerant minister I was surprised to realize, upon reflection, that I have preached in nearly a dozen states, every Canadian province west of Quebec, Puerto Rico, the Philippines and Korea. For most of these ministries I was asked to give a prophetic message, probably because I have written books on prophecy. And almost without exception someone, or a number of people, spoke to me afterward in the manner described above. What is even more interesting is the fact that nearly all of my guest preaching has been in churches that profess the "Fourfold Gospel," which includes belief in Christ as Coming King!

If my experience is any indicator, prophetic preaching is not currently in vogue, even in circles that claim to hold to the doctrine of the return of Christ.

To me this is little short of tragic. For one thing, it represents a failure to declare the whole counsel of God, since almost twenty-five percent of Scripture is prophetic. And equally unfortunate is the loss of the spiritual impact, both evangelistic and edifying, which the "blessed hope" (Titus 2:11-14) affords. Believing that the Rapture could occur at any moment can have a wonderfully positive effect on a believer's lifestyle and certainly provides powerful motivation for evangelism.

Why the Dearth?

There are several possible reasons for the apparent widespread failure to preach prophecy.

The recent proliferation of highly publicized false dates for the Rapture and other unfulfilled predictions from prophetic writers may be one. People become weary and wary of such ill-advised and unscriptural pronouncements and so tune out *all* prophetic topics. Such skepticism or even opposition from his people may well impact a pastor's choice of sermon subjects.

A second possible reason for the neglect of prophetic preaching may be the affluence of our age. Christians have it so good, here and now, that going to heaven doesn't have too great an appeal. A cartoon I saw recently summarized such an attitude: a woman says to her husband, "Now that the kids are through college and we have the mortgage paid off, wouldn't it just be our luck for the Lord to return?"

The shift away from expository to topical—especially "felt needs"— preaching, which has affected many pulpits, is another possible explanation for the lack of preaching on prophecy. In light of the current affluence, desiring or preparing to leave it all is not a widespread "felt need" of our generation.

Perhaps a major reason for the dearth, however, is that many pastors are not certain of what they believe on eschatological issues. I have had more than one young pastor confide that he was not sure where he stood on the subject of the millennium, the tribulation, imminence and so on. Some have indicated that in their theological training they were given little or no direction—at best a cursory smorgasbord of positions, with the choice of what to believe left to the individual. The revival of amillennialism, as promoted by the reconstructionist movement, may also have a role in the ambivalence on prophecy which many feel.

Thus, unsure of their position and consequently lacking passion for the truth of the "blessed hope," many pastors choose not to preach on the subject. Or, sensing that—for a variety of reasons—the return of Christ is not a popular topic, some pragmatic preachers leave it unaddressed. Yet others, aware that differing viewpoints are held by segments of their church family, decide not to raise a matter which has the potential of polarizing the congregation.

And there may be other reasons, as well, to explain the lack of prophecy proclamation. None, however, compare in weight or importance with the reasons *for* such preaching.

Reasons to Preach on Prophecy

As the first of several reasons to preach on prophecy, I want to express—by way of personal testimony—the great joy of seeing people's lives touched by the message of the return of Christ. It has been my unspeakable privilege to know of well over 3,000 salvation decisions which have come through the spoken and printed proclamation of this truth—all praise to the Lord!

The imminence of Christ's coming for His Bride (which we'll consider shortly) adds great impetus for people to respond to the evangelistic message, particularly when it is pointed out that they may not have another chance. According to Second Thessalonians 2:10-11, those who have heard the gospel and refused it will not have opportunity to repent after the Rapture, but will be confirmed in their unbelief by God Himself.

A second reason to preach the prophetic Scriptures relates to the edification of believers. The appeal to the child of God to live a self-controlled, upright and godly life in the light of the "blessed hope" is a powerful message to all believers, since it covers every possible relationship of life: to one's self, all others and God. Thus it illustrates how the anticipation of being caught up at any moment to be with the Lord, as described in First Thessalonians 4:13-18, is a marvelously motivating force for godliness in every area of life. First John 3:3 underscores this by pointing out that the hope of seeing Christ and being like Him will cause everyone who possesses such a hope to purify himself, even as He is pure.

A third major reason for prophecy preaching, which has great bearing on the reasons listed above, is one to which we have already alluded: Failure to do so is failure to proclaim the whole counsel of God, since prophecy comprises such a large part of God's Word, with such potent application for evangelism and edification.

To declare the full counsel of the Lord in these matters is, I believe, to preach the premillennial appearing of the Lord Jesus Christ, which, as I understand the prophetic Scriptures, is preceded by the imminent Rapture of His Bride, the Church, and by the resultant Great Tribulation, in which God pours out His wrath upon a world controlled by the counterfeit trinity: Satan, the Antichrist and the False Prophet.

The Imminence of the Rapture

So far as the Rapture is concerned, imminence ("ready to take place"— Merriam Webster) means simply that there is no need for intervening events prior to the return of Christ to take the Church in the Rapture. The promise of the Lord in John 14:3, 28 quite apparently does not require that there be any signs or prerequisite events in order for it to be fulfilled, for clearly the Lord indicated none.

A number of Scripture portions unmistakably indicate that the early Church held the view that Christ could return at any moment, and that no signs had to precede the Rapture.

In Philippians 3:20 Paul declares, "we eagerly await a Savior from [heaven], the Lord Jesus Christ." The Thessalonian believers are described in First Thessalonians 1:10 as those who "wait for his Son from heaven." Timothy is charged to keep "this command . . . until the appearing of our Lord Jesus Christ" (1 Timothy 6:14). James assures his readers that "the Lord's coming is near" (James 5:8), while in Second Peter 3:3-4 the apostle plainly indicates, in his reference to scoffers who were mocking because the Coming had not occurred, that the Lord's return was expected by the Church at any moment. There is no reference to preliminary signs in any of these passages cited above.

Further, Scriptures such as First Thessalonians 5:6, Titus 2:13 and Revelation 3:3 all encourage the believer to be watching for the Lord

Himself, not for any signs which would precede His coming for His Bride.

In the light of the above it is difficult to understand how the charge can be made that the doctrine of imminence is of recent origin. Henry C. Thiessen writes:

> [The early church fathers as well as the writers of the New Testament] held not only the premillennial view of Christ's coming, but also regarded that coming as imminent. The Lord had taught them to expect His return at any moment, and so they looked for Him to come in their day. Not only so, but they also taught His personal return as being immediately. Only the Alexandrians opposed this truth; but these Fathers also rejected other fundamental doctrines. We may say, therefore, that the early Church lived in the constant expectation of their Lord, and hence was not interested in the possibility of a Tribulation period in the future.[1]

Lewis Sperry Chafer quotes a number of reformers—Luther, Calvin, Knox, Latimer—to show that they, too, believed in the imminency of the return of Christ.[2] J. Barton Payne states, "[The Church] expected that the Lord could appear in the clouds in immediate connection with any day of contemporary life. The ante-Nicene fathers, in other words, were committed to the concept of the imminence of their Lord's return."[3]

Indeed, the scriptural exhortations indicated above are realistic and sensible only if the imminent premillennial coming of the Lord for His Church is understood. "Eagerly waiting," "being alert and self-controlled," "purifying oneself" and directives to the believer make sense only in view of the possibility of an imminent translation.

The Rapture and the Appearing are Different

But while there are no signs indicated as preceding the translation of the Church in the Rapture, the opposite is true concerning those living before the appearing of Christ when He comes to establish His millennial kingdom. The exhortation to those living in the Tribulation period is to look for signs, and after the signs, to look for Christ to appear.

This is the force of our Lord's Olivet discourse, recorded in Matthew 24, Mark 13 and Luke 21. In Mark 13:8 Jesus called the signs, which He indicated would precede His coming in power and great glory, "birth pangs" or "the beginning of birth pains." Birth pangs begin at a point in time and then increase in both frequency and intensity up to the moment of birth. In this case, the "birth" represents the appearing of Christ as He comes with His saints to deal with the false trinity and their followers, and to establish His millennial reign.

Thus the list of signs which Christ gave, as recorded in the Gospels, correspond very definitely in many instances with the judgments detailed in Revelation. In these, the "birth pang" concept of a steady increase in the intensity and frequency of the signs is also clearly present. It is very instructive to compare the signs which Christ listed—war, pestilence, famine, great earthquakes, persecution of Israel, false Christs, global proclamation of the gospel,[4] fearful signs in the heavens, great fear—with the description of the three intensifying phases of God's wrath poured out on the earth during the seal, trumpet and bowl judgments, as recorded in Revelation 6-16. It is very apparent that Christ, in the Olivet discourse, and John, in Revelation, are describing the same signs.

And even though the imminence of the Rapture requires no signs, the relationship between the Olivet discourse signs and those in Revelation, along with the "birth pang" factor, gives validity to prophetic preaching which considers the presence of such signs in the world today. The appearance of what are believed to be either similar signs or the beginning of the actual indicators which precede Christ's return—in steadily increasing frequency and intensity—surely suggests that the Rapture must be that much nearer.

Israel and the Church Are Different

Prophetic preaching which is truly evangelistic and edifying must address not only the difference between an imminent Rapture and the appearing of Christ, but also the difference between Israel and the Church. Two major facts stand out in this regard.

The first is that Daniel's prophecy concerning Israel's future, outlined in Daniel 9:24-27 as seventy weeks, or "sevens," of years, has seen the fulfilment of events predicted for sixty-nine of the "sevens," leaving one seven-year period of prophetic fulfillment for Israel still to come. Solid documentation for the sixty-nine-week precise fulfilment and the fact of a gap between the sixty-ninth and the seventieth week is beyond the scope of this writing, but has been painstakingly accomplished by Sir Robert Anderson in his classic volume, *The Coming Prince*.[5] Thus, God's dealing with the world in relationship to His chosen people, the nation of Israel, has yet another chapter to come. This setting aside and later reinstatement of Israel, as seen in Daniel's prophecy and reinforced by the Apostle Paul in Romans 9-11, has made possible the age of the Church, which leads to the second major fact.

The Church, the Body and Bride of Christ, is a unique entity in God's dealings with the world, completely distinct from Israel. The Church, which is comprised of regenerated individuals, both Jewish and Gentile, was born at Pentecost, when the Holy Spirit came as promised by Jesus in Acts 1:4-11, and will be taken from the world when the Lord Jesus Christ comes for her in the Rapture, as foretold in First Thessalonians 4:13-16. Thus, the Holy Spirit, as the One who regenerates individuals and baptizes them into the Body of Christ (Acts 2, 10, 19; 1 Corinthians 12:12-13), is intimately and inseparably linked with the Church.

Because this is so, many (though certainly not all) students of prophecy believe that the Holy Spirit is the restrainer referred to in Second Thessalonians 2:1-11. In this portion the Apostle Paul writes that the lawless one, the Antichrist, is held back from taking control in the world until the One who restrains is taken out of the way. The Holy Spirit, in the sense of His indwelling a Body, the Church, is seen as that Restraining One who is taken away when the Church is raptured. John F. Walvoord, acknowledging numerous differing interpretations of the restrainer's identity, writes,

> The ultimate decision on [the identity of] the restrainer goes back to the larger question of who, after all, is capable of restraining sin to such an extent that the man of sin cannot be revealed until the restraint is removed. The doctrine of divine providence, the evidence of Scripture that the Spirit characteristically restrains and strives against sin (Gen. 6:3, John 18:8), and the teaching of Scripture that the Spirit is resident in the world and indwelling the church in a special sense in

> this age combine to point to the Spirit of God as the only adequate an-
> swer to the problem of the identification of the restrainer.... It should
> be evident that [since] the Spirit of God characteristically indwells the
> church as well as the individual saint in this age, the removal of the
> Spirit would involve ... the removal of the church as well.[6]

Of course, this does not mean that the Holy Spirit will be absent from the earth following the Rapture. As the omnipresent Spirit of God, He will be here and will be active as He was prior to Pentecost, but in His ministry of indwelling and empowering the Church, His work will be completed.

For all who are committed to the literal interpretation of Scripture, there can be no question: the nation of Israel and the Church are two different entities in God's economy. Failure to understand that fact will unquestionably dampen enthusiasm for prophetic preaching, since it will prove difficult to chart the future without a great deal of spiritualizing of the Scriptures.

In particular an understanding of the difference between the two entities is essential to an understanding of the Tribulation. Walvoord's comment on this is interesting:

> While it is difficult to make an accurate generalization, usually
> those who sharply distinguish Israel and the church are both
> premillennial and pretribulational, while those who consider Israel
> and the church more or less the same concept, even if premillennial,
> tend to be posttribulational. The concept of the church as a distinct
> entity, peculiar to the present age since the day of Pentecost, usually
> goes along with the idea that the church will be translated before the
> Tribulation.[7]

Certainly the extensive description of the Tribulation period in Revelation 4-18 frequently mentions "Israel" and "saints," but contains no reference to the Church. In fact, following the exhortations to the seven churches in chapters 2 and 3, there is, in chapter 4:1, the command from heaven to "Come up here," after which there is no mention of the Church until Revelation 19, when she is described in connection with the appearing of Christ.

The Olivet discourse descriptions, parallel to the Revelation prophecy as suggested earlier, clearly have reference to Israel, as may be seen from the use of terms like "the Sabbath" and "synagogue," which have no significance for the church. Consequently it is believed that the purpose of the Tribulation is not that of purging the Church in preparation for her translation to heaven, but rather relates to Israel, as a prelude to her restoration and exaltation in the millennial kingdom. The final throes of Gentile world dominion, ending with its complete destruction at the appearing of Christ, are also part of the Tribulation purpose.

It is my conviction that an understanding of the above distinction is a vital aspect in the degree of motivation one will have to preach on prophecy. To be able to proclaim the "blessed hope" of being translated, of seeing and being like Christ our Redeemer (1 John 3:3), is far more motivational than announcing the fearful prospect of enduring God's awesome Tribulation judgments.

While some who believe that the Church experiences the Tribulation hold that believers will be protected from the judgments, many of these predicted events, by their very nature, could not distinguish the saved from the ungodly. Famine, earthquakes, stars falling from heaven, darkness for a third of the days, water turned to blood—such judgments would necessarily fall on the just and unjust alike.

Tribulation and the Great Tribulation are Different

The Word of God makes it clear that the Church should not expect to be free of trial and tribulation (Note Matthew 13:21; John 16:33; Acts 14:22; Romans 2:9; Revelation 2:10). Our Lord plainly said, in John 16:33, "In this world you will have trouble" ("tribulation," KJV). But there is a vast difference between tribulation which is the result of the hatred and opposition of ungodly and wicked men[8] toward all who confess Jesus as Lord, and the Tribulation wrath of God, which is poured out on a godless world during the period immediately preceding the appearing of Christ. This distinction is a vital one to understand.

Dwight Pentecost, in *Things to Come*, shows that the Old and New Testament description of the Tribulation period (Daniel's seventieth week) uses the words "wrath," "judgment," "indignation," "punishment," "hour of trial," "hour of trouble," "destruction" and "darkness"—all of which proceed from God.[9] He quotes author Norman Harrison:

> Let us get clearly in mind the nature of the [Great] Tribulation, that it is divine "wrath" (Revelation 11:18; 14:8, 10, 19; 15:1, 7; 16:1, 19) and divine "judgment" (14:7; 15:4; 16:7; 17:1; 18:10; 19:2). We know that our blessed Lord bore for us the wrath of God and His judgment; therefore we who are in Him "shall not come into judgment." The antithesis of 1 Thessalonians 5:9 is conclusive evidence: "For God appointed us not unto wrath, but unto the obtaining of salvation through our Lord Jesus Christ."[10]

Walvoord questions the belief that "saints of the present age who are perfectly justified by faith, given a perfect position of sanctification, and declared to be in Christ, have to suffer the 'great day of [God's] wrath' in the Tribulation." He concludes that while "Christians can be disciplined and chastened, they cannot justly be exposed to the wrath of God."[11]

Even posttribulationist Harold J. Ockenga distinguished between the two kinds of wrath:

> The church will endure the wrath of men, but will not suffer the wrath of God. . . . If [the identification of the tribulation with the wrath of God] can be proved, we must believe that the church will be taken out of the world before the tribulation, for there is no condemnation to them which are in Christ Jesus.[12]

Motivation for Proclamation

In summary, I believe that being convinced of the imminent Rapture of the Church—an entity distinct from Israel—which will occur before the outpouring of God's wrath during the seventieth-week Great Tribulation, is powerful motivation for preaching on prophecy. Its appeal is for people to love His appearing and to live in the light of the fact that He could come at any moment. Such motivation seems to me to be far superior to that of proclaiming the alternative message of expecting first the reign of the Antichrist and the awesome judgments of God, with its application to "bulk up spiritually, because otherwise you'll not be prepared to stand during the Tribulation."

While I do not deny that overt persecution may well be the future lot of the North American church, as it already is in many parts of the world, I believe that it will come from the enemies of Christ, not as part of God's judgment. And in any case, the best preparation for whatever difficult days may come is to focus on the kind of a relationship with the Lord Jesus Christ that longs for Him as a prospective bride longs for her bridegroom.

Perhaps a failure to hold such a perspective is another reason for the decline in the frequency of preaching on prophecy.

Endnotes

1. Henry C. Thiessen, *Will the Church Pass Through the Tribulation?* (New York: Loizeaux Brothers, 1941), 13, as quoted in J. Dwight Pentecost, *Things to Come: A Study in Biblical Eschatology* (Grand Rapids: Zondervan, 1972), 203.
2. Lewis Sperry Chafer, *Systematic Theology IV* (Dallas: Dallas Seminary Press, 1947), 278-9.
3. Robert Anderson, *The Coming Prince* (London: Hodder and Stoughton, 1909).
4. The concept that the gospel must be preached in all the world for a witness before the Lord will come for His Church has been, during the past century and more, a powerful motivation for missionary ministry—particularly to unreached people groups. It unquestionably has validity. The complete fulfillment of this sign will come, however, during the Tribulation through the activity of the 144,000 sealed servants of God (Revelation 7:3-8), the Two Witnesses (Revelation 11) and the preaching of the angel described in Revelation 14:6, who will "proclaim [the everlasting gospel] to those who live on the earth—to every nation, tribe, language and people." Obviously, people who have never heard the gospel before will be born again throughout the Tribulation, for though many will be martyred (13:5-7), only through conversions which occur *after* the Rapture will there be righteous human beings left upon the earth capable of repopulating the planet during the Millennium, since those who have been translated will be as the angels of heaven, who, as our Lord declared in Mark 12:25, "will neither marry nor be given in marriage."
5. J. Barton Payne, *The Imminent Appearing of Christ* (Grand Rapids: Eerdmans, 1962), 14-5.
6. John F. Walvoord, *The Rapture Question* (Grand Rapids: Zondervan, 1979), 78-81.
7. Ibid., 62-3.
8. *Foxe's Book of Martyrs* and *On This Day* are but two of many volumes which describe in graphic detail some of this extreme hatred and persecution throughout history, which continues today.
9. Pentecost, *Things to Come*, 194.
10. Norman B. Harrison, *The End* (Minneapolis: Harrison Service, 1941), 120, as quoted in Pentecost, *Things to Come*, 195.
11. Walvoord, 159.
12. Harold J. Ockenga, "Will the Church Go Through the Tribulation? Yes." *Bibliotheca Sacra* 92 (April-June 1935), 22, as quoted in Walvoord, *The Rapture Question*, 159.

10

Premillennialism

Armageddon and Judgment

• Robert Wetmore •

Premillennialism's greatest strength is its hermeneutic. Premillennialists insist that we must interpret the Scriptures according to their most natural sense within their grammatical, literary and historical context. By "natural" sense, we mean what the original author intended his original audience to understand naturally as they read the passage, without any "secret" meanings.

When Genesis 15 tells us that God spoke to Abraham, we accept this as a true event because the grammatical, literary and historical context most naturally point to this. When God tells Abraham that his descendants will be numerous as the stars of heaven, we recognize that the most natural way to understand the comparison is to see God's statement as hyperbole. The original readers of Genesis would know that God was using hyperbole when He said, " 'Look up at the heavens, and count the stars—*if indeed you can count them.*' Then he said to him, 'So shall your offspring be' " (15:5, emphasis added). The original readers would have known that there were simply too many stars for anyone to count and in the same way, if all of Abraham's descendants stood before him, he would likewise be unable to count them.

The interpreter's task is to determine what would have been the most natural way for the original readers to understand the statement. Because premillennialists are committed to this hermeneutical principle, they interpret Old Testament prophecies according to their most natural sense within their historical, literary and grammatical contexts. This is the real reason that premillennialists believe in the 1,000-year reign of Christ. The most natural interpretations of dozens of Old Testament prophecies undeniably describe a Davidic king who is divine and reigns in Jerusalem over the nations.

On occasion, New Testament writers seem to undermine this rule by interpreting Old Testament prophecies according to a different principle. Sometimes they apparently ignore the most natural single meaning of a prophecy and apply it instead to several very different fulfillments. For example, the Old Testament generally describes the "Day of the LORD" as a time of judgment, doom and destruction for Israel and the nations (Ezekiel 13:5; 30:3; Joel 1:15; 2:1, 11, 31; 3:14; Amos 5:18-20; Obadiah 1:15; Zephaniah 1:7, 17; Malachi 4:5, etc.). But in the New Testament, Acts sees the "Day of the Lord" fulfilled in the outpouring of the Holy Spirit on Pentecost (Acts 2:16-21). Paul describes it as the return of Christ (1 Corinthians 1:8). John describes the battle of Armageddon as "the battle on the great day of God Almighty" (Revelation 16:14). Peter places it as that time when the elements will be destroyed by fire (2 Peter 3:10). From a casual reading, anyway, the New Testament does not always seem to agree with the premillennialists' conviction that we should always look for the natural single sense of a prophecy. It is small wonder that amillennialists would prefer to interpret Old Testament prophecy spiritually. For them, the battle of Armageddon, for example, refers to the battle which Christ and His Church wage against Satan and his demonic hordes. They do not look for this battle to take place in a particular time and place in the future. What is the correct way to interpret end-time prophecies about the "Day of the Lord"?

This essay approaches the "Day of the Lord," the battle of Armageddon and the coming judgment as literal events, and argues that the single natural sense of the passages describing these events includes prophetic progression. This article will show that often the Old Testament prophecies about Armageddon, Gog and Magog, and the final judgment describe stages of fulfillment, leading up to the final culmination in the destruction of the earth and heavens and re-creation of the new heavens and new earth.

Progressive Prophetic Fulfillment

God often fulfills both His promises and warnings progressively. In other words, He brings about the completion of His promises in stages, where the early phases prepare the way for those which follow. Willis J.

Beecher describes the way God fulfills His promises as cumulative. "Throughout the Old Testament, as we have seen, the prophets give us the conception of a promise that is eternally operative. This necessarily implies a cumulative fulfillment, and certain culminating periods of fulfillment."[1] Each fulfillment builds upon the previous one, bringing us closer and closer to the ultimate fulfillment. One of many examples would be Isaiah 9:6-7: "For to us a child is born, to us a son is given, and the government will be on His shoulders. . . ." God fulfilled some of Isaiah's prophecy at Christ's birth, but Christ's rule as the Prince of Peace was impossible until He reconciled us to God through His cross and resurrection. In addition, Christ's ascension paved the way to a further stage of prophetic fulfillment, Jesus Christ's present reign at God's right hand. Christ's future millennial reign also *necessarily* fulfills the prophetic word, for Isaiah promises that He will reign on the throne of David and his kingdom. Thus God has been progressively fulfilling Isaiah 9:6-7 over the past 2,000 years and will continue to fulfill it until He has accomplished all of His purposes in Christ.

This is a natural way for humans to communicate and we do so on a daily basis. When a mother tells her child that soon they are going to buy sundaes at the ice cream parlor, the child knows that this "prophecy" will be fulfilled in stages. At a particular point in time, the mother may say, "OK, dear, clean up your room so we can leave." If the little girl keeps on playing with her toys, the mother will warn her, "If you do not clean up your room, we will not be going anywhere." Cleaning the room is a necessary stage in fulfilling the prophecy. Getting into the car, fastening the seat belt, stopping at the gas station and ATM are all necessary steps toward buying ice cream sundaes. Even a child understands that many statements concerning the future take successive steps to fulfill. The big difference with biblical prophecies is that the steps take place over centuries and the scope of biblical prophecy is often "biblical" in proportion.

It would be irresponsible to argue that Isaiah had only one prophetic fulfillment in mind when he wrote his prophecy about the birth of a child.[2] Just as the mother's promise of an ice cream sundae carries in it implicit stages, so also Isaiah's prophecy condenses those stages into a few key elements. Jesus had to be born to a mother and in the future He will reign as King. The fact that the prophecy comes in stages does not force us to treat the prophecy as if it were five different prophecies squeezed into two verses. Rather, the natural way to understand statements about the future would recognize that this message describes the progression which the Lord fulfilled at Christ's birth, life, death, resurrection and ascension, is fulfilling now through His reign, will continue to fulfill in the millennium and will finish completely at the judgment and creation of the new heavens and new earth.

What is true for Christ's advent is true as well for many other prophecies in Scripture, including those which deal with the great battles at the end of history. God accomplishes many of these prophecies through a progression of events, often separated by hundreds and even thousands of years. Nevertheless, each progressive fulfillment builds upon those previous realizations, paving the way for future stages.

The Progress of the Great End-Time Battles

This approach to premillennialism and the battles of Armageddon and Gog and Magog solves several problems which cause non-premillennialists to stumble along the way. Rather than attempting to limit the passages to a single stage of fulfillment, we should see if the passages actually describe several stages which culminate in the climax at the destruction and re-creation of the heavens and earth.

The three most familiar descriptions of end-time battles are Armageddon (Revelation 16:16), Gog/Magog (Ezekiel 38; Revelation 20:8) and the "Day of the LORD" (Ezekiel 30; Joel 3:14; Zephaniah 1). What do the Scriptures mean by these descriptions?

Armageddon. The book of Revelation presents Armageddon as God's judgment upon sinful humanity. The battle flows immediately out of the sixth bowl of judgment in Revelation 16 and demonic spirits inspire the encounter, going out to assemble the nations for the battle. "Then I saw three evil spirits that looked like frogs; they came out of the mouth of the dragon, out of the mouth of the beast and out of the mouth of the false prophet. They are spirits of demons performing miraculous signs, and they go out to the kings of the whole world, to gather them for the battle on the great day of God Almighty" (Revelation 16:13-14). The battle is *worldwide* in scope and is related to the "great day of God."

John's divine viewpoint shows us that the battle is initiated as God's bowl of judgment and is energized by demonic inspiration.

From the viewpoint of those who are participating, it will seem like the "great day of mankind" rather than the "great day of God." Humans will feel as if they are at the pinnacle of their power. Their hearts will overflow with confidence and rebellion and will lead them to attack the city of Jerusalem. Yet ultimately God Himself is the one who originated this judgment, and He will use it to bring a devastating sentence upon the rebellious nations of the world.

The focal point of the judgment itself concentrates on unbridled human depravity in rebellion against God's rule. This becomes clear when one observes the way John introduces Armageddon and then immediately turns to God's judgment of the city of Babylon (16:17-19:10). This "digression" is not accidental to the plot, but forms the heart of the story concerning Armageddon. The city of Babylon, described as "BABYLON THE GREAT, THE MOTHER OF HARLOTS AND ABOMINATIONS OF THE EARTH" (17:5, KJV), epitomizes the rebellious heart of humanity against God. When God hurls His wrath most intensely at Babylon, He is judging iniquity's core for the entire planet, this city of apostasy and whoredom. Once God judges the symbolic source of human defiance, He is ready to deal with the vast armies which surge against His chosen people, Israel.

Ironically, the nations' rebellious act becomes their destruction, for it drives them into a hopeless direct confrontation with the Lamb of God. God uses their malice against Him to bring them to destroy themselves. The wrath of mankind against God becomes the wrath of God against human rebellion as He turns the battle of Armageddon into a judgment every bit as poignant as the devastation He pours upon Babylon. God is executing His fury upon those who have dared to touch the apple of His eye.[3]

When he describes the actual battle, John never focuses on strategies or heroism, almost as if the battle's events themselves hold little importance in the overall scale of history. Instead he draws our attention to the preeminence of Jesus Christ (19:19-20). If the battle of Armageddon is a battle of judgment, then it is even more so the battle of the Lamb who judges those who challenge Him.

God Judges Israel. All premillennialists agree that Abraham's physical descendants continue to be God's special people among all of the families of earth. Why would God allow Israel to become the object of humanity's rebellion against God? The answer is that Armageddon not only judges mankind, but also brings judgment upon God's chosen people, Israel. Armageddon is God's final cleansing of the covenant people, the Jews.

Many Old Testament prophecies make it clear that God will cleanse Israel in the end times by judging her. Amos tells us that even though Israel longs for the day of the Lord, it will not be a time of rejoicing but sorrow. "Will not the day of the LORD be darkness, not light—pitch-dark, without a ray of brightness?" (Amos 5:20; see also Isaiah 9:19; 24:11 and many other passages). God will use these end-time battles to cleanse Israel and return her to follow Him and David's descendant.

> How awful that day will be!
>> None will be like it.
> It will be a time of trouble for Jacob,
>> but he will be saved out of it.
> "In that day," declares the LORD Almighty,
>> "I will break the yoke off their necks
>>> and will tear off their bonds;
>>> no longer will foreigners enslave them.
> Instead, they will serve the LORD their God
>> and David their king,
>> whom I will raise up for them." (Jeremiah 30:7-9)

God will judge Israel for her sin, but the judgment will one day end in restoration. Zechariah describes this end-time event as the point in future history when all Jerusalem will repent of sin and return finally to the Lord. As all of the nations of the earth surround Jerusalem, God promises that He will change Israel's hearts. "And I will pour out on the house of David and the inhabitants of Jerusalem a spirit of grace and supplication. They will look on me, the one they have pierced, and they will mourn for him as one mourns for an only child, and grieve bitterly for him as one grieves for a firstborn son" (Zechariah 12:10).

As we study these Old Testament prophecies, we might wonder why they should be applied to the battle of Armageddon. After all, God has progressively fulfilled the prophecies that He will judge Israel, first in 587 B.C., then at Christ's cross, at Pentecost (Acts 2:14-21) and A.D. 70. Even the horrors of the dispersion over the past two millennia are in some manner a form of judgment. Thus many Old Testament prophecies can easily be applied to other events which have already occurred.

Nevertheless, many of these prophecies have not come to their final culminations. All of Jerusalem has not yet looked upon Christ and mourned His death on their behalf (Zechariah 12:10-14). During the past 2,000 years, no more than just a small remnant of the Jews has actually turned to serve the Lord and David's Son, His anointed King. Since the first fall of Jerusalem, there has been no time when God has rendered judgment upon all of the nations of the earth, gathered to war against Jerusalem.

> In those days and at that time,
>> when I restore the fortunes of Judah and Jerusalem,
> I will gather all nations
>> and bring them down to the Valley of Jehoshaphat.
> There I will enter into judgment against them
>> concerning my inheritance, my people Israel,
> for they scattered my people among the nations
>> and divided up my land. (Joel 3:1-2)

Paul tells us that "all Israel will be saved" (Romans 11:25-26) when the fullness of the Gentiles has come in. When will that be? Apparently when God judges Israel at the battle of Armageddon, when the kings of all of the earth assemble to attack Israel, then all Israel will be saved (Zechariah 12). And that will happen at the battle of Armageddon.

Where will this battle of Armageddon take place? Revelation 16:16 tells us: "Then they gathered the kings together to the place that in Hebrew is called Armageddon." We cannot be sure what the word "Armageddon" means. The most common description is the mountain or hill ("*har*") of Meggido, which is a geographical location where many battles have occurred.[4] Alan Johnson's commentary on Revelation argues that the word is built out of the Hebrew *gadad*, whose secondary meaning is "to gather troops."[5] It is very difficult to discern whether the word itself describes a location or has a symbolic meaning.[6] In some ways, it really matters little. With the complexities of modern warfare, we hardly need to pin down the exact meaning of the word or its geographical location in the land of Israel. The battle will most certainly point toward Jerusalem (Zechariah 12) and will probably fill the entire land. Since John does not tell us the outcome of the battle in Revelation 16:16, but stops his narrative in order to describe God's judgment of Babylon, we can safely assume that he is referring to the same battle in 19:19. This is also suggested by the fact that John describes the "kings of the earth and their armies" as "gathered together" (*sunago*, same word as he uses in 16:16 to describe them) without feeling a need to explain why they are there and how they got there.

The Last Battle. John describes the second great battle in Revelation as the battle of Gog and Magog, the final chapter in humanity's rebellion against God. Many have argued that this battle is actually simply a prophetic recapitulation of Armageddon. "Names and places are different, but there can only ever be one battle which is both so universal and so final as this one. It must be the same as the Armageddon of Scene 5, where 'the kings of the whole world' are assembled for 'the great day of God the Almighty. . . .' "[7]

Of course, amillennialists simply deny that such a battle will ever take place in time and space history. Kuyper states categorically, "Thus also here an actual period of time is not to be thought of."[8] Alan Johnson wonders how such a massive host could be found after the disastrous destruction of earth's forces at Armageddon, but admits the possibility that these simply could be marshalled from "other people who during the millennial reign defected in their hearts from the Messiah."[9] One can only imagine that these two passages describe the same battle by ignoring the clear differences between the two. Gog and Magog do not appear to fit the context of those terrifying days of God's wrath in the book of Revelation.[10] Of course, the actual context clearly places the battle *after* the millennium (20:7-8).

Even the Ezekiel 38-39 description of Gog and Magog sounds much different from Armageddon. Gog and Magog happen during a time of peace and prosperity.[11] Armageddon happens in the midst of a war which is destructive to the forces of Israel, assuming that Zechariah 13:8-9 was written to describe that day:

> "In the whole land," declares the LORD,
> "two-thirds will be struck down and perish;

yet one-third will be left in it.
This third I will bring into the fire;
   I will refine them like silver
   and test them like gold.
They will call on my name
   and I will answer them;
I will say, 'They are my people,'
   and they will say, 'The LORD is our God.' "

This destruction contrasts significantly from the battles described by both Ezekiel and Revelation, which do not even hint that the saints suffer any loss at all at the hands of Gog and Magog. Indeed, Ezekiel tells us that Israel will be living securely (Ezekiel 38:8, 14). While Israel suffers horribly from the terrors which lead up to Armageddon, Israel is enjoying peace when God and Magog come against it. Furthermore, there is no hint that Gog/Magog consists of a progressive battle which brings enemy forces closer and closer to the holy city. Instead, Revelation pictures the battle as a singularly lopsided event, where the nations come to Jerusalem and Christ completely annihilates the forces with a single stroke. Also, Ezekiel never indicates that the Gog/Magog wars are judgments against Israel. The only purpose of the battle is to judge those who oppose God's chosen people (38:10-13; 38:16).[12] The differences between Armageddon and Gog/Magog are strong enough to cast serious doubt if Armageddon and Gog/Magog are actually the same battle.

Yet there are definite similarities between the two battles. Both battles are on the surface fought against Israel, although both really are attacks against the Lamb. Both battles gather all of the nations of the earth. Both battles are inspired by demonic forces. In addition, these two battles seem to overlap in Old Testament prophecy, a fact that confuses interpreters who attempt to assign particular Old Testament prophecies to one or the other battle. One can even find in Ezekiel 38-39 some references which might be describing Armageddon instead of the battle of Gog and Magog in Revelation 20:8.[13] How do we resolve these apparent conflicts?

The Day of the Lord. We cannot resolve the apparent overlap of Armageddon with Gog and Magog until we examine what Old Testament prophets and New Testament writers often describe as the "Day of the Lord." These prophecies sometimes seem to refer to much more than simply the battles of Armageddon and Gog/Magog.[14] They can depict Jerusalem's destruction in 587 B.C. (see, for example, Jeremiah 17:17; 18:17; 46:21). Malachi 4:5 seems to be describing a day which includes Christ's cross, resurrection and ascension. Jesus describes Jerusalem's destruction in A.D. 70 as "days of vengeance" (a term which Old Testament prophets use synonymously with the "Day of the Lord" in Isaiah 34:8; 61:2; 63:4; Jeremiah 46:10). These "days of vengeance" are happening in order "that all things which are written may be fulfilled" (Luke 21:22, KJV). That suggests that some aspects of Old Testament prophecies concerning the "Day of the Lord" can refer to Rome's annihilation of Jerusalem in A.D. 70. Certainly many aspects of these "Day of the Lord" prophecies actually point to a great future conflict, such as the battle of Armageddon or perhaps to Gog and Magog.

With such "looseness" in the "Day of the Lord" prophecies, perhaps we can understand why amillennialists simply give up trying to interpret them according to their natural meaning within their historical context. It is much easier just to spiritualize their meaning and apply them to the cross or the church age as Christ's victory over Satan or the church's victory over the powers of darkness.[15]

There is, however, a better approach. We find our answers to our problems concerning the prophetic overlaps of these end-time judgment prophecies by realizing that all are a part of the much larger "Day of the Lord." The "Day of the LORD" is a time of destruction (Isaiah 13:6-9); Israel's judgment (Ezekiel 13:5); universal judgment (Obadiah 1:15); anguish for the nations (Ezekiel 30:3); deliverance (Joel 2:28-32, which really includes the outpouring of the Holy Spirit at Pentecost); darkness (Amos 5:18); and restoration (Malachi 4:4-6). The theme is familiar in the Old Testament and is also important to New Testament writers (Acts 2:20; 1 Corinthians 5:5; 1 Thessalonians 5:2; 2 Thessalonians 2:2; 2 Peter 3:10).

When we attempt to pin down the timing of this "Day of the Lord," we discover that God fulfilled it throughout Israel's history. Indeed, the "Day of the Lord" began when God brought Babylon to destroy Jerusalem, although in a real sense we can say that the eschatological "Day of the Lord" commenced at Pentecost. When God poured out His Holy

Spirit upon the church, the very end of human history began. Peter certainly understood this in his Pentecost message.

> Then Peter stood up with the Eleven, raised his voice and addressed the crowd: "Fellow Jews and all of you who live in Jerusalem, let me explain this to you; listen carefully to what I say. These men are not drunk, as you suppose. It's only nine in the morning! No, this is what was spoken by the prophet Joel:
>
> "In the last days, God says,
> I will pour out my Spirit on all people. . . ." (Acts 2:14-17)

Yet the "Day of the Lord" prophecies are not so loose that we can apply them to anything we please. Instead, we must recognize that God fulfills these "Day of the Lord" prophecies progressively, starting with 597 B.C. and ending with Gog and Magog. Just as God fulfilled the prophecies concerning Christ's coming in progressive stages, so also is He bringing about His final judgment and vindication in progressive stages. There are overlaps within many prophecies concerning Christ's first and second coming so that events separated by at least 2,000 years stand side by side in the same paragraph.

These examples remind us that we should expect overlaps as well concerning God's wrath upon sin. God has been bringing the Day of the Lord to this planet since Jesus Christ judged the ruler of the world through His cross (John 12:31-32). At Pentecost, Peter told the crowds that the outpouring of God's Spirit fulfilled Joel's prophecy concerning the Day of the Lord, because God's judgment of the world includes the outpouring of the Holy Spirit upon all of those who are redeemed. Peter was not spiritualizing Joel at all, but recognized that the Day of the Lord would come to the earth in progressive stages. Thus Old Testament prophecies which seem to mix up the two falls of Jerusalem, Armageddon, Gog and Magog, and the Great White Throne are describing the whole of God's eschatological work which began with the fall of Jerusalem and will not be completely satisfied until all things are made new. All of those elements are steps along the way to the final culmination.

There will be a consummation, however, to this progressive Day of the Lord. The last battle, finally once and for all, will reveal the heart of human rebellion. The millennium will be a marvelous physical environment, with an absolutely perfect Ruler, with the help of hundreds of millions of resurrected saints, and with prosperity and safety on all sides. Nevertheless, human beings will end up rebelling against God. When given an opportunity, humans will still defy their Creator.

Because the various "Day of the Lord" prophecies contain progressive stages of fulfillment, we can far too easily confuse or mistake various prophetic elements. Thus for the past 2,000 years Christians have fallen prey to various last-days schemes and panics. There is nothing wrong with the prophecies. The problem lies with missing the fact that many prophecies unfold over hundreds and even thousands of years. Thus, in the end, all of the prophecies will be fulfilled according to their most natural sense within their grammatical, literary and historical context. As long as we recognize that progressive stages are a part of that natural sense, we will much more be able to interpret their true meaning.

The Final Judgment

Prophetically, the final judgment of humanity in Revelation 20:11-15 is simply the culmination of God's work of judgment going on since the fall of Jerusalem. God has been preparing the human race for the Great White Throne judgment since the beginning. The prophets who warn that God will judge the earth (Isaiah 11:4, etc.) were pointing to both aspects—the progressive steps of God's wrath in history and the final Great White Throne judgment.

There are no surprises in the terrifying Great White Throne judgment. God's mercy, which He has richly expressed in a variety of ways, has been satisfied in the cross of His Son, the Lamb of God (Romans 5:17; Hebrews 2:9; 2 Timothy 1:9-10). Now, one must come to the Lamb to find God's mercy. Thus only those who reject the Lamb miss out on the rich and infinite mercy which God offers to every human. "The Spirit and the bride say, 'Come!' And let him who hears say, 'Come!' Whoever is thirsty, let him come; and whoever wishes, let him take the free gift of the water of life" (Revelation 22:17). The judgment is the last stage. Unless their names are written in the Lamb's book of life (21:27), humans now will eternally experience the incomprehensible horrors of unending punishment. God's process will be complete on that day, that final "Day of the Lord."

Endnotes

1. Willis J. Beecher, *The Prophets and the Promise* (Grand Rapids: Baker Books, 1975 reprint [1907]), 376.
2. Keil and Delitzsch list several Jewish commentators who interpret it this way, as well as Grotius and Gesenius. F. Delitzsch, "Isaiah," *Commentary on the Old Testament in Ten Volumes* (Grand Rapids: Eerdmans, 1975), vol. 7, 251.
3. R.J.A. Sheriffs, "Armageddon," *New Bible Dictionary* (Wheaton, IL: Tyndale, 1962), 83.
4. Ibid.
5. Alan Johnson, "Revelation," *The Expositor's Bible Commentary* (Grand Rapids: Zondervan, 1981), vol. 12, 552.
6. This does not suggest that the battle itself is symbolic, but only that the name God chose for the battle gives us no clues concerning its geographical reference. The battle of Britain does not describe a specific geographical location as much as it describes the air battles which stopped Nazi Germany from destroying Great Britain in World War II. In contrast, the battle of Gettysburg describes a specific geographical location in Pennsylvania. I am suggesting that Armageddon is akin to the former rather than the latter example.
7. Michael Wilcock, *The Message of Revelation*, The Bible Speaks Today Commentary Series (Downers Grove, IL: InterVarsity, 1975), 193.
8. Abraham Kuyper, *The Revelation of St. John* (Grand Rapids: Eerdmans, 1963), 292.
9. Alan Johnson, *Revelation*, 587.
10. Daniel Block describes Ezekiel's approach to Israel's last days as "(1) a change in disposition of the deity; (2) the appointment of a new ruler; (3) the reconstruction of the temple; (4) the return of the deity; (5) the regathering of the scattered population; (6) the establishment of peace and prosperity" (p. 90). I would suggest that the battle of Gog and Magog in Ezekiel 38-39 requires that all of these have already occurred, which could be possible only after the millennial period.
11. For example, Israel is living securely (Ezekiel 38:14); the Jews have been restored to their land in peace (38:25-28); God has poured His Spirit out upon them (38:29); etc.
12. Daniel I. Block, "Gog and Magog in Ezekiel's Eschatological Vision," *Eschatology in Bible and Theology: Evangelical Essays at the Dawn of a New Millennium* (Downers Grove, IL: InterVarsity, 1997), 115-6.
13. The most obvious is Ezekiel's reference to the cleanup from the great battle, which will last seven months (Ezekiel 39:9-10).
14. See, for example, Isaiah 13:6-9; Ezekiel 13:5; Joel 1:15; Amos 15:18, 20; Obadiah 1:15; Zephaniah 1:7, 14; Malachi 4:5.
15. There is certainly some validity to this approach. Peter himself applies Joel's "Day of the LORD" (Joel 2) prophecies to the day of Pentecost (Acts 2:17-21). That sounds much like an amillennial interpretation of Old Testament prophecy. Does that suggest that: a) we are to spiritualize all of these "Day of the LORD" prophecies; b) apply them solely to previous historical events; or c) apply them to the last judgment?

11

Premillennialism
the Tribulation and the Millennium

• Donald A. Wiggins •

The distinctive feature of the premillennial position is its expectation that Jesus Christ will return personally and visibly to the earth, defeat the Antichrist and his forces, bind Satan and establish the 1,000-year reign referred to in Revelation 20. This "earthly kingdom will not come into reality through a gradual process of progressive growth or development. Rather it will be dramatically and cataclysmically inaugurated by [His] second coming."[1]

Premillennialists agree that immediately prior to Christ's return the earth will experience unparalleled anguish. That time period is referred to as the tribulation. This chapter summarizes the biblical teaching on the tribulation and explains the major premillennial positions on its relationship to the millennium. Such a subject is of interest largely to premillennialists. Though other millennial viewpoints might develop an emphasis on the tribulation, premillennialism is the only one that devotes significant attention to it.[2] Not surprisingly, proponents engage from time to time in vigorous intramural debate regarding the particulars of their views. This chapter acknowledges the divergent positions, but it shows that premillennialists have more positions of agreement than differences.

Defining Tribulation

The Greek word for tribulation is *thlipsis*. In its few occurrences outside of the Septuagint and the New Testament, *thlipsis* meant literal pressure upon an object. However, almost all of its forty-five occurrences within the New Testament connote the more figurative sense of "opposition, affliction" or "tribulation." At least eight times in the New Testament its cognate verb form, *thlibo*, takes the same sense.[3] Most frequently, the term refers to the tribulation that the followers of Christ may encounter. Jesus warned His disciples, "In this world you will have trouble [*thlipsis*]" (John 16:33). His Olivet discourse specifically alerts the Twelve to expect severe opposition and persecution, even to the point of death (Matthew 24:9; cf. Mark 13:9). Intense tribulation weeds out the pseudo-disciple from the true. Jesus warned that "when trouble [*thlipsis*] or persecution comes" upon the follower who sinks no permanent root into His Word "he quickly falls away" (Matthew 13:21; cf. Mark 4:17).

Other than the Lord Himself, no one encountered more personal tribulation than the Apostle Paul did. On account of the gospel and for the sake of the churches he planted, Paul passed through severe suffering and persecution (Ephesians 3:13; 1 Thessalonians 3:7). Yet he gloried in such things because they produced within him godly character (Romans 5:3) and enhanced his ministry to those who were similarly troubled (1 Corinthians 1:4). Paul's experiences more than fulfilled what Jesus predicted would come upon His true followers. The apostle went so far as to say, "I fill up in my flesh what is still lacking in regard to Christ's afflictions [*thlipsis*], for the sake of his body, which is the church" (Colossians 1:24).

Is this a wildly boastful statement or a denial of the sufficiency of Christ's atonement? Not at all, for Paul boasted only in the cross as the basis of redemption (Galatians 6:14). It is more accurately understood as a statement of his unique call to extend the gospel with great sufferings to the Gentiles. In that sense, he completed in Christ's stead what the Lord suffered on behalf of the church. The role of suffering was not his alone, however. The young congregations he planted also endured much tribulation at the hands of their persecutors for the name of Christ (Romans 12:12; 2 Thessalonians 1:4, 6).

Taking into account the cluster of closely allied nouns (persecution, suffering, affliction, trouble), the New Testament contains more than 100 references to what might be called *general* tribulation. This kind of anguish does not appear limited to one period of time, or to one segment of the church. The sobering reality presented by the Lord Himself and affirmed by the Apostle Paul is that through this age Christians should expect tribulation (John 16:33; Romans 5:3; 1 Thessalonians 3:3-4). In fact, as the church's history reveals, the absence of tribulation is unusual for the saints of God. General suffering and persecution is the norm. That the modern Western church has been spared much tribulation up to this point should be considered an exception to the rule.

Identifying and Understanding the Great Tribulation

However severe general tribulation might be, it pales in comparison to that which is yet to come. Scripture prophesies a great and final tribulation at the end of the age that will exceed anything before it, both in the Old Testament and the New Testament. This is what premillennialists typically call the "Great Tribulation." The Old Testament shows glimpses of this great tribulation, while the New Testament provides additional revelation of this period.

The Great Tribulation in the Old Testament

The primary Old Testament evidence for the Great Tribulation is in the Book of Daniel. Premillennialists commonly see four passages "that must refer to the Great Tribulation":[4]

7:7-8, 23-25	"another king" arises, opposes God, oppresses the saints
8:9-12, 23-25	little horn arises to oppose the Prince of princes
9:26-27	ruler to come sets up abomination of desolation
11:26-12:1	great king (Antichrist) conquers many nations, sets up the abomination of desolation

Daniel's "seventieth seven" (9:27) is frequently interpreted as a seven-year period corresponding to the great tribulation.[5] The significance of the midpoint in the seventieth week is impossible to overlook. Daniel referred to it in 9:27, 7:25, and 12:7, 11. In the middle of the week, the three-and-one-half year mark, the "ruler to come" breaks his covenant and sets up an abomination of desolation that lasts until he meets his end (9:27). The Book of Daniel provides sufficient evidence to explain the further specifics given by our Lord Himself and by John in the Revelation. Some premillennialists turn to passages such as Isaiah 26, Jeremiah 30 and Joel 2 as further evidence for the great tribulation.[6] Since none of them can be connected with absolute certainty, they are better taken as related descriptions of the kind of distress that will befall the earth during the great tribulation.[7]

The Great Tribulation in the New Testament

In Matthew 24:21-29 Jesus told His followers about a future period of "great distress [*thlipsis*], unequaled from the beginning of the world until now—and never to be equaled again." He gives few particulars, but the warning is foreboding enough. Mounce comments on Jesus' words: "Persecution has always been the lot of those who follow the Lamb (Jn. 16:33; II Tim. 3:12). The intensity of the final conflict of righteousness and evil will rise to such a pitch as to become *the great tribulation* [emphasis his]."[8] Jesus Himself referred to the abomination of desolation of Daniel in Matthew 24:15. That is the signal for those living in Judea to flee to the mountains, for it ushers in the unparalleled *thlipsis* before His return (Matthew 24:21, 29; Mark 13:19, 24).

The Apostle John in Revelation 7:9-17 received further revelation of this "Great Tribulation." In his vision he surveyed a vast, uncountable multitude from all the peoples of the earth, dressed in white robes and gathered around the throne of God to worship Him and the Lamb. One of the elders nearest the throne inquired of John, "who are they, and where did they come from?" (7:13), perhaps anticipating the apostle's very question. John asserted that the elder himself knew the answer, and indeed, he answered his own question: "These are they who have come out of *the great tribulation*; they have washed their robes and made them white in the blood of the Lamb" (7:14, emphasis added). This is the same Greek phrase, *thlipsis megalee*, as Jesus used in Matthew 24:21.

The elder spoke of "*the* great tribulation." Mounce points out that the definite article in front of *thlipsis* denotes with emphasis "that final series of woes which will immediately precede the end."[9] When the elder uses this term, it appears as though he expects John to understand its meaning, recalling the words of Jesus in Matthew 24 and making the connection.

The preceding parts of the vision provided John with a fuller understanding of the elder's use of *thlipsis*. In Revelation 5:1, God held a sealed scroll in his right hand. After a search, only the Lamb was found worthy to take a scroll from God's hand, break the seven seals and unroll it (5:1-5). From the center of heaven's throne he successively opened the first five seals (6:1, 3, 5, 7, 9, 12), unleashing a series of powerful judgments upon the earth. The sixth seal (6:12) released a great earthquake and falling stars that darkened the sun and moon. Earth's inhabitants, aware finally of God's judgment in these intensifying phenomena, called for the rocks and mountains to fall and hide them from His wrath (6:15-17).

In a dramatic interlude before the Lamb opened the seventh and final seal, John witnessed the protective sealing of 144,000 from the tribes of Israel (7:1-8) and saw before him an even greater multitude of worshipers surrounding the throne (7:9-12). In distinction from the 144,000, some "from every nation, tribe, [tongue], people and language" made up this latter group whose number "no one could count." They had either escaped catastrophic judgment at some previous point or, more likely, had just been rescued.[10] The most natural understanding within the context is that "the great tribulation" in 7:14 finds its reference point in the catastrophes culminating in the sixth seal.

John also foresaw the significance of Daniel's midpoint in the seventieth week. The Gentiles trample the holy city for forty-two months, and two empowered witnesses prophesy for 1,260 days (Revelation 11:2-3). In 12:14 he observed a woman who is taken care of in the desert for "a time, times and half a time, out of the serpent's reach" (cf. Daniel 7:25). John later saw a beast from the sea that gains authority over earth's inhabitants and wages war against the saints for forty-two months (Revelation 13:1-8).

Revelation 6-18 presents John's entire vision of the tribulation. He saw three series of sevens—opened seals, blowing trumpets and outpoured bowls—which describe the progress of divine world judgment. The precise relationship of each seven to the others is difficult. Merrill Tenney describes the problem:

> Are the series of sevens . . . successive in the sense that each is an enlargement of the seventh item in the preceding series? Are they partially concurrent, each having a narrower scope than the one preceding? Are they simultaneous, being different aspects of the same judgments or of the same period?[11]

Tenney himself prefers to see them as "three differing but partly synchronous periods."[12] However, given the apocalyptic language, he wisely urges interpreters to avoid dogmatic conclusions as to the chronology.[13]

Interpretative Approaches

Students of this section have taken widely different approaches. Futurist premillennialists conclude that the judgments describe the horrors of an end-time tribulation.[14] This point of view, usually connected with dispensationalism, has predominated among many conservative, evangelical Christians since the late nineteenth century. At the other end of the spectrum, historicists see this section as a series of symbols presenting the entire history of the Church from the close of the first century until the return of Christ. One survey lists as advocates of this view Luther, Zwingli, Isaac Newton and the nineteenth-century leaders A.J. Gordon and A.B. Simpson.[15]

Still another group of premillennial interpreters draws together elements of the futurist and preterist viewpoints. Preterists assert that the Revelation has no future prophetic aspect, but was composed as a tract to encourage early Christians to expect divine deliverance from their Roman persecutors.[16] The combination point of view put forth by Ladd and Mounce applies the book *both* to John's first readers as well as to later believers through the centuries who would long for the blessed hope.[17] They conclude that John envisioned an impending tribulation in the near future that foreshadowed an intense and climactic tribulation at the end of the age. A growing number of advocates contend that this viewpoint is truly "classical" or "historic" premillennialism.[18]

If in his early days Simpson adhered to the historicist approach, he later considerably modified his views. For example, he rejected the dispensational interpretation of Matthew 24, which locates the rapture of the Church sometime before verse 14. Instead, Simpson taught that Jesus lays out the details of both an earlier Roman persecution *and* an end-time distress. In this his view bears greater resemblance to historic premillennialism than to the strictly futurist position so popular in the prophecy conferences of the late nineteenth century. Simpson held that a Gentile parenthesis (24:14) punctuates the interim before the final tribulation, during which the gospel of the kingdom must be preached to the whole world. When that mission is accomplished, then the end will come.[19] Not surprisingly, Ladd commends Simpson for his interpretation of Matthew 24:14 in regard to its implications for world missions.[20]

Areas of Disagreement

Premillennialism asserts that in fulfillment of His promise (John 14:1-6), Jesus Christ will return bodily to earth before His reign as King for 1,000 years (Revelation 20:1-6). By now it should be clear that premillennialism is anything but monolithic. The most obvious indication is in the names attributed to the major premillennial views. The pretribulationist position holds that the Church will be taken off the earth, or raptured, before the tribulation begins. The posttribulationist view locates the church's deliverance at the end of the tribulation. In addition, several mediating positions locate the rapture halfway through the tribulation (midtribulationist) or immediately before the final outpouring of divine wrath (pre-wrath).[21] In addition, some evangelical writers such as Hudson Taylor, Watchman Nee and, for a time, A.B. Simpson and other leaders of The Christian and Missionary Alliance, held to a partial rapture position in which those spiritually prepared and holy are raptured earlier, while those less mature are raptured later after refinement.[22] While these views capture the significance of the biblical emphasis on the midpoint and resolve some of the knottier interpretive issues, none of them has elicited enough support to mount a convincing challenge to the two prevailing viewpoints.

The fundamental divergence between pre- and posttribulationists is their theological/hermeneutical approaches to scriptural teaching on Israel and the Church. Most of the remaining differences between their respective systems flow from that watershed issue. Most pretribulationists follow the sharp distinction dispensationalism makes between Israel and the Church in the economy of God.[23] He has exclusive programs for each entity. For Israel, it is the restored kingdom during the millennium. For the Church, it is to be the Gentile instrument of spreading the gospel until its rapture into heaven. The tribulation has nothing to do with the Church and everything to do with Israel; in fact, it is the time of *Jacob's* trouble (Jeremiah 30:7). Thus the Church must be removed, so that God may turn His attention to the salvation of Israel and the restoration of His long-promised kingdom.

Posttribulationists find such a distinction dubious at best, finding instead a fundamental continuity between God's Old Testament people and

New Testament people. The Church is not a parenthesis in His program for Israel, but a foreordained body of the redeemed from all nations incorporated into the people of God. Many of the promises to Israel were fulfilled in the Church, the spiritual Israel. Therefore, posttribulationists are inclined to interpret eschatological sections of the Old and New Testament as pertaining to the Church, not to a restored nation of Israel. Typically, advocates apply the tribulation passages such as Daniel 9, Matthew 24 and Revelation 7 without chronological precision to the New Testament saints, who are spared from the wrath of God but not from the Antichrist's persecution.[24]

Though it is argued that one's conclusion on the relationship of Israel and the Church does not lead necessarily to opposite conclusions on the tribulation,[25] in actuality there is very little crossover. Many have accepted the conclusions of their respective viewpoints without having examined the hermeneutical/theological assumptions from which they came. This reality begs for greater diligent study of Scripture and more charity toward those of other views.

Areas of Agreement

To most observers, the array of different viewpoints among premillennialists on the tribulation is confusing, and may give the impression that it is a divided camp. Confusion is heightened by the popularized versions of the apocalypse in books and movies. The more spectacular ones dramatize eschatological conjecture without adequate biblical support. Controversial (and so far, inaccurate!) predictions about the date of the rapture and the Antichrist's identity may sell, but they also divert believers' attention from the central truth that Jesus Christ is returning as triumphant Lord. Believers who otherwise might unite for the cause of Christ have needlessly separated over such things. Reacting understandably to the embarrassment over such spectacles, some Christians resort to what one friend calls "pan-millennialism." Throwing up his hands in frustration, he says: "I believe it will all pan out in the end." This conclusion generally precludes any further interest in studying the subject.

But frustration is not the only option. A more helpful approach is to consider the substantial common ground shared by virtually all premillennialists. The heat of debate highlights their differences and exaggerates small matters beyond their importance. The fact is, however, that premillennialists of all stripes and persuasions have more agreement than they may realize. Consider the following:

1. The Reality of the Great Tribulation

As a whole, premillennialists hold that the great tribulation is a special period of anguish upon the earth that immediately precedes Christ's second coming.[26] This is explicit in Jesus' own teaching concerning a future tribulation (Matthew 24:15-28). John's account of tribulation in Revelation, though given in figurative language, describes literal events. The catastrophic phenomena, persecution and judgments he foresaw stand in stark contrast to the authority and justice that Christ will establish in His millennial reign (Revelation 20:1-6). As a rule, pretribulationists interpret the relevant passages in a more literal sense than do posttribulationists, and they find a more elaborate chronology of events. However, even John Walvoord, the ardent dispensationalist who critiques posttribulationists for spiritualizing away many of the details, nevertheless recognizes that they share his belief in a future, actual tribulation.[27]

There is less consensus about the length of the tribulation. Pretribulationists see Daniel's seventieth week fulfilled in a seven-year tribulation described in Revelation. Not all posttribulationists make that connection, but even if they do, it is without insistence on precisely seven years.[28] Nevertheless, proponents of either view readily acknowledge that God may mercifully shorten those days, as Jesus said, "for the sake of the elect" (Matthew 24:22).

2. Uniqueness of the Great Tribulation

As seen earlier, premillennialists agree that general tribulation falls widely, though unevenly, on the disciples of Jesus throughout this age. They also concur that that the great tribulation is a period of accelerated persecution and anguish. Those saints present on the earth will bear the brunt of the Antichrist's furious opposition. And God will pour out His wrath on rebellious human beings with increasing severity. Tenney points out that the judgments (seals, trumpets and bowls), if not strictly consecutive, nevertheless grow progressively intense.[29] Nothing like it

175

has ever been seen before. On this point, pretribulationists[30] and post-tribulationists[31] agree.

3. Responsibility for the Tribulation

Those responsible for tribulation from Jesus' day until now have been the unbelieving opponents of the gospel. Yet in the great tribulation there is a new element. Human initiative alone does not bring it on. God Himself acts in judgment on the earth. Revelation portrays a sovereign God preparing the sealed scroll of seven judgments (5:1), sending His angels to trumpet the arrival of seven greater calamities (8:2) and pouring out deadly plagues upon the earth from seven bowls (16:1). Tenney's summation expresses a consensus on this point:

> Behind all the action of the Apocalypse, planning, regulating, and directing toward the ultimate goal is the person of the Eternal God. The forces of evil in this tremendous drama are not illusory, nor are they merely the puppets with which he plays. Nevertheless, he controls them, and in final victory brings the triumph of the good.[32]

4. God's Purpose

Through the centuries the gospel's opponents have set about to silence or even eliminate the witness of the Church. While in the gracious providence of God tribulation has purified the saints, the human intent was to destroy them. But in the great tribulation God acts to fulfill His own purposes. All positions acknowledge that *one* purpose is to mete out a full measure of His wrath against sin (6:17; 15:1). Pretrib- ulationists hold that the Church will be taken out of the world before that happens. The unbelieving population that is left will experience the brunt of God's wrath against sin.[33] Posttribulationists agree that God will pour out His wrath, but they hold that the Church will remain on the earth though it all, protected and purged. In accordance with First Thessalonians 5:9, the Church will be spared the effects of His wrath.[34] While differing on that point, the various proponents acknowledge that God will accomplish His righteous purposes leading to the arrival of the King.

5. Urgency of the Church's Mission

Ladd proposes that pretribulationism weakens the missions impetus of the Church by relegating the fulfillment of Matthew 24:14 to Jewish evangelists during the tribulation. He cites a roster of missionary statesmen, including A.B. Simpson, who he believes rightly rejected the dispensational interpretation and applied Jesus' words directly to the Church's mission in this age.[35] Ladd concludes that posttribulationism appeals to the strongest motive for world evangelization, hastening the blessed hope by proclaiming the gospel to all peoples.[36] Walvoord strongly objects to Ladd's claim to a superior motive for missions. He insists that an equal commitment to world evangelization can be found among many mission groups that hold to a pretribulationist position.[37]

The most charitable observation, Ladd's comments notwithstanding, is that premillennialists with widely divergent views on the tribulation share a common commitment to fulfill the Great Commission of Christ. The prospect of a glorious eternal heaven and the awful final judgment of hell prompts an urgent effort to reach all peoples of the earth with His gospel.[38] With substantial agreement on many of the most important points, premillennialists share a rich heritage of expectancy for the blessed hope of Christ's return.

Conclusion

In the end, the vital point is not which current position on the tribulation proves accurate. Of far greater importance is to keep before God's people now the glory of the victorious, reigning Christ. The prospect of witnessing His inestimable worth and joining with all true worshipers throughout history for all of eternity outweighs the fact that at present we see through a glass darkly. Knowing the final outcome, the Spirit and the bride say, "Come, Lord Jesus!" Until that day, may we be charitable toward one another and united in the mission of Christ on earth.

Endnotes

1. Millard J. Erickson, *A Basic Guide to Eschatology* (Grand Rapids: Baker, 1998), 92.
2. Ibid., 125, 145.

3. William F. Arndt and F. Wilbur Gingrich, *A Greek-English Lexicon of the New Testament* (Chicago: University of Chicago Press, 1957), 362-3.

4. Douglas J. Moo, "The Case for the Posttribulation Rapture Position" in Richard R. Reiter, et al., *The Rapture: Pre-, Mid-, or Post-tribulational?* (Grand Rapids: Zondervan, 1984), 173.

5. See Robert D. Culver, *Daniel and the Latter Days* (New York: Revell, 1954), 138-160, for an elaboration of the argument.

6. John F. Walvoord, *The Blessed Hope and the Tribulation* (Grand Rapids: Zondervan, 1976), 77, 114; see also Leon Wood, *Is the Rapture Next?* (Grand Rapids: Zondervan, 1956), 15-9.

7. Moo, 173-4.

8. Robert Mounce, *The New International Commentary on the New Testament: The Book of Revelation* (Grand Rapids: Eerdmans, 1977), 173.

9. Ibid.

10. Ibid., see footnote 22; see also David E. Aune, *Word Biblical Commentary: Revelation 6-16* (Nashville: Thomas Nelson, 1998), vol. 52b, 473.

11. Merrill Tenney, *Interpreting Revelation* (Grand Rapids: Eerdmans, 1957), 71.

12. Ibid., 81.

13. Ibid., 135.

14. Renee Pache, *The Return of Jesus Christ* (Chicago: Moody, 1955), 251-61.

15. Ibid., 138.

16. See R.C. Sproul, *The Last Days According to Jesus* (Grand Rapids: Baker, 1998), 153-9, for a description of preterism. Sproul himself favors a partial preterist position, which allows for an ultimate *parousia* at the end of human history.

17. George Eldon Ladd, *A Commentary on the Revelation of John* (Grand Rapids: Eerdmans, 1972), 12-4; Mounce, 44-5.

18. See Stanley Grenz, *The Millennial Maze* (Grand Rapids: Zondervan, 1992), 127-47, for a helpful account of the resurgence of classical premillennialism since the 1950s.

19. Albert B. Simpson, *The Christ in the Bible Commentary* (Camp Hill, PA: Christian Publications, 1993), vol. 4, 126-7.

20. George Eldon Ladd, *The Blessed Hope* (Grand Rapids: Eerdmans, 1956), 152.

21. Gleason Archer, "The Case for the Mid-Seventieth-Week Rapture Position," *The Rapture*, 115-45.

22. H. Wayne House, *Charts of Christian Theology and Doctrine* (Grand Rapids: Zondervan, 1992), 130; J. Dwight Pentecost, *Things to Come* (Grand Rapids: Zondervan, 1958), 158; J. Hudson Taylor, *Union and Communion with Christ* (Minneapolis: Bethany House, n.d.), 94; Watchman Nee, *God's Plan and the Overcomers* (New York: Christian Fellowship Publishers, 1977), 77-83.

23. The classic text is Charles Ryrie, *Dispensationalism Today* (Chicago: Moody, 1965). Some modification of the strict distinction is suggested by Craig A. Blaising and Darrell L. Bock, eds., *Dispensationalism, Israel and the Church* (Grand Rapids: Zondervan, 1992) and in their second work, *Progressive Dispensationalism* (Wheaton, IL: Victor, 1993).

24. See Grenz, 91-125, for a helpful summary of the respective arguments for and against dispensationalism and posttribulationism.

25. Both Charles Feinberg, "The Case for the Pretribulation Rapture of the Church," *The Rapture*, 48-9, and Moo, *The Rapture*, 177-8, make this assertion.

26. Erickson, 92.
27. Walvoord, 148.
28. Erickson, 146.
29. Tenney, 80, 165.
30. Walvoord, 77.
31. Robert H. Gundry, *The Church and the Tribulation* (Grand Rapids: Zondervan, 1973, 1977), 76-7.
32. Tenney, 76.
33. Walvoord, 54-55.
34. Ladd, *The Blessed Hope*, 122, 129; Gundry, 50; Moo, 174-176.
35. Ladd, *The Blessed Hope*, 146-52.
36. Ibid., 148-9.
37. Walvoord, 57.
38. Richard R. Reiter, "A History of the Development of the Rapture Positions," *The Rapture*, 43; see also J. Barton Payne, *The Imminent Appearing of Christ* (Grand Rapids: Eerdmans, 1962), 107-8.

12

Premillennialism

and Worship in the Millennium

• Matthew A. Cook •

A small church in rural Oklahoma was making preparations. Sunday was their 100th anniversary and they were having many special guests attend the worship celebration that day. They painted the walls; they prepared special music; they got the piano tuned; they ordered worship banners; the pastor prepared a special sermon; and they waxed the hallway floors. The anticipated day finally arrived with all of the musicians and expected guests in place. Everyone noticed one guest was oddly dressed. He wore a glowing, flowing robe. His face shone. His presence evoked adoration in some and rage in others. Jesus had arrived. The pastor and leaders didn't know what to do. "Can we continue with our planned service now that Jesus Himself has come to our church?"

The return of Christ is hailed in songs and creeds[1] old and new:

> When Christ shall come with shout of acclamation
> And take me home, what joys shall fill my heart!
> Then I shall bow in humble adoration
> And there proclaim, my God, how great Thou art.[2]

This is just one of numerous hymns and songs which depict worship in the Millennium. While many songs in this genre may actually refer to the eternal state, the Millennium is the "foretaste of the eternal estate itself. The world will be restored. The judgment of the nations will assure that only those who are the Lord's sheep will be allowed to enter."[3]

Worshipers of Jesus will experience no pain, suffering, separation or hardship when Jesus returns. There will be joy, fellowship and access to God. When Christ returns He will reign for 1,000 years. Theologically, we call that time the Millennium.[4] Our anticipation of the Millennium is based on the "blessed hope" of the Christian life, the Lord's own return (Titus 2:13). In fact, it may well be argued that much of the Bible and the

Christian life is eschatologically oriented.[5] Our present obedience, worship and service should be carried out in the light of the return of Christ.

But what will these things look like once we have arrived in the Millennium? Specifically, what will worship be like for followers of Jesus once He has returned and we are living in His very presence? To some, this allows the most obvious answer possible: We will be reigning with Christ for 1,000 years (Revelation 20:4). Surely our worship will be pure and good. I agree, but what are the details? What will Sunday morning be like when Jesus physically joins you for worship?

If we can catch a glimpse of what worship will be like in such a good place, under ideal circumstances, then that comprehension may shape our worship today. I would like my worship to be more like millennial worship, when I shall be reigning with the King of Glory, sitting on a throne near His very own, participating with Him as He makes His kingdom come on this earth. The motivation for understanding worship in the Millennium is not merely a theological curiosity. That high form of worship should invade our daily worship even as that kingdom obedience should invade our present world.

Unfortunately, there is not much direct biblical data that address worship in the Millennium. Many of the conclusions others have made were done through theological inference (which is, admittedly, an important task in systematic theology). Besides the scarcity of biblical data, theologians have not written much about worship under the heading of eschatology,[6] much less the Millennium. One might think that the two topics don't have a relationship. That is certainly not the case. Every part of theology is connected with every other part.[7] In the same way, worship in the Millennium depends on several other parts of theology. To help us understand worship in the Millennium, I need to refocus several theological vectors so that we will see more sharply their impact on our understanding of worship in the Millennium.

Before I begin, allow me to offer a preliminary definition of worship.[8] The *Anchor Bible Dictionary* includes the following section in its article, "Early Christian Worship":

> Christian worship functioned in two primary ways: (1) it was not only
> a model and celebration of the distinctive religious and moral ideals of
> Christians, but (2) it also had an anticipatory function in that it pro-

vided a vehicle for actualizing the perfect future realization of these religious ideals in the present.[9]

When Christians worship they are participating in a relational activity[10] in which they intend to express (to self, others and God) the superiority of God;[11] inspire awe for the unseen but all-powerful and present God;[12] offer praise or commendation to God;[13] refocus all of life from the perspective of the final triumph of God through Christ;[14] and finally elicit a life of commitment by each worshiper for obedience to God.[15] Although this is not a very compact nor complete definition of worship, it will offer us further fodder for reflection on worship in the Millennium.

As I mentioned previously, before we can actually arrive at the discussion of worship in the Millennium, we have to refocus our thinking on three theological issues. This won't take a great deal of space, but is crucial for understanding the final section.

Three Theological Vectors

1. The church is an eschatological community.

While the Greek word for church, *ekklesia*, denoted "a 'meeting' or an 'assembly,' rather than an 'organization' or a 'society' "[16] in its pre-Christian uses (and even in some NT passages, such as Colossians 4:16, Romans 16:5 and 1 Corinthians 16:19), there exists a more important use: each of the many local churches that exist today "are manifestations of that heavenly church, tangible expressions in time and space of what is heavenly and eternal."[17] The eschatological nature of the Church not only points to the location of the true Church (with Christ, in heaven), but also to the function for which that Church exists. The Church exists—at the very least—to serve Christ, its Head, to follow Him in resurrection and to gather those redeemed through the shed blood of Christ for worship.[18]

The Church, once partial, segmented and splintered, will be complete in the Millennium. I have to deal with two thorny theological issues before I can proceed (although I will do so with excessive brevity): When is the Wedding Supper of the Lamb (Revelation 19:7, 9)? Will the Church really be on earth in the Millennium? The Wedding Supper seems to be toward the climax of the cosmic battle raging throughout the latter half of the book of Revelation. The Millennium is at the climax. Therefore, the Wedding Supper is around the threshold of the Millennium. If that is the case, then the Church will not be separated from Christ during the Millennium. Further evidence for this is that believers reign with Christ (20:4) and will never be separated from Christ from the time of their resurrection (1 Thessalonians 4:17). If Christ reigns on the earth then believers—the Church—are on the earth with Him.[19]

If the Body of Christ finally and fully resides with the Head, Christ; if the Bride of Christ, the Church, is married to her Groom, then we have entered into a glorious age when the Church fulfills her purposes. Finally, the Church, the divine community of God's people, the eschatological gathering of worshipers, is complete and fulfilled to worship as it was intended to do.

2. Satan is bound during the Millennium.

Satan is pictured at various places throughout the Bible as interrupting the purposes of God and His people.[20] We rarely see him interrupting or disturbing the worship of God in the Bible. Although we rarely see him doing this explicitly, his purpose is to distract, deceive and dissuade followers of Christ from hotly pursuing obedience to the true King. It seems likely, or at least possible, that Satan was behind the confusion in the Corinthian worship; that the useless philosophies mentioned in Colossians were motivated by unholy means; that the false teachers Peter argued against do not receive their teaching from God. When the Millennium approaches, Satan will attempt to disrupt worship through overt means. Humans will be made to worship Satan's emissary, the beast (13-14). If one is forced to worship that beast, one is prohibited from worshiping Christ. They are mutually exclusive. Satan's presence inhibits (and if acceded to, prohibits) appropriate worship of God. But Satan will be bound during the majority of the Millennium (20:1-3). With Satan bound, and his power confined to the Abyss, there are finally no supernatural hindrances to worship. The Millennium is better than a spiritually neutral context. We can worship in a spiritually positive environment.

3. Many inhabitants of the millennial kingdom—perhaps all of the inhabitants—will have their glorified bodies.

Those who have participated in the first resurrection will be given glorified bodies. That first resurrection occurred at the dawn of the Millennium (20:4-6). This first resurrection included at least the believers who were martyred during the tribulation. If one postulates a premillennial return of Christ,[21] then all who were Christians at the time of their death or subsequent return of Christ have also been caught up in the air—thus receiving their glorified bodies (1 Thessalonians 4:16-17). If those persons all come to earth with Christ during His millennial reign (as I suggested above because they are part of the eschatological Church), then there will be a great quantity of individuals who have received their glorified bodies and will be living on earth during the millennial reign.

However, not all the inhabitants of the earth will have glorified bodies. This statement, although somewhat speculative, is based on the position that there will be individuals who may yet be deceived by Satan when he is released at the end of the Millennium (Revelation 20:8). It seems highly unlikely that an individual with an imperishable and spiritual body, made for glory and power, bearing similarity to Jesus, the Man from heaven (1 Corinthians 15:42-49), could be deceived by Satan. We, in our glorified bodies, will not be like the angels in their gullibility,[22] but like the angels in glory and imperishability (Luke 20:36). Therefore, my statement about the glorified saints worshiping God does not apply universally to millennial kingdom inhabitants.[23]

The crucial point here is that all those who have received their glorified bodies have been freed from their sinful nature. This may seem an obvious point, but let me offer some scriptural support anyway. I'll offer four brief points: First, our glorified state[24] will reverse the effects of the Fall for us (Romans 8:18-25). Second, we will be transformed to be like Jesus at the very sight of Him because we are already His children[25] (1 John 3:2). Third, at the glorification we will finally fulfill our creation intention: to be like Jesus (2 Peter 1:4; Ephesians 4:24). And fourth (1 Corinthians 15:55-56), sin has brought about death, but our glorified bodies have escaped death and, therefore, sin.[26] In sum, we who have glorified bodies can finally obtain perfect submission of our intellect, emotion and will to God—and thus worship fully. We will no longer have rebellion in our hearts as we approach God. We will be able to worship with a pure heart.

Characteristics of Millennial Worship

There are six characteristics of millennial worship that I wish to address:

1. Some things will not change. Jesus will be the focus of our worship. Note that Jesus is the focus in the courts of heaven even before the Millennium begins (Revelation 4-5). Not only will Jesus be the focus, but there will also remain no blood sacrifices (contrary to many scholars' reading of Ezekiel 40-46). The reasons why there will be no sacrifices in the Millennium are very similar to why there are no sacrifices necessary in our day: There were four functions of the Old Testament sacrificial system:[27] 1) offering was a means to restore one's relationship to God and insure right standing within the theocracy; 2) Old Testament sacrifices were a type of what was to come in Christ's sacrifice; 3) the believer was performing an act that brought glory to God (sacrifice as worship); 4) sacrifices were an expression of commitment and obedience to God who said that He would cleanse the believer of sin when the believer brought such sacrifices. Mere sacrifices never saved anyone, but performing those sacrifices was the means of expressing faith, whereby God would cleanse one from sin and restore one to fellowship with God. This aspect of sacrifices falls under the category of sanctification rather than justification. It strikes the believer, not the unbeliever. "Before Christ's sacrifice, the public offering had to accompany the repentance of the believer," notes John Feinberg. "Once the all-sufficient sacrifice of Christ had been made, the repentant believer need not give another sacrifice in order to have cleansing."[28] Feinberg goes on to say,

> First, Scripture is very clear that the system of the law, including the sacrifices, is superseded and done away with by the sacrifice of Christ (cf. Gal 3:24-25; the book of Hebrews). Second . . . Old Testament sacrifices actually covered sin and assured the believer of cleansing and forgiveness. However, it was the sacrifice of Christ that actually once and for all removed the sin (Heb. 9:13; 10:4, 11-14).[29]

Third, each sacrifice is for a specific sin. Only that sin is covered by the sacrifice. But Christ's sacrifice is all-inclusive, once for all, never to be repeated, in order to forgive all sins for all time.

Dispensationalists, among others, hold that the temple will be rebuilt at the dawn of the Millennium and that a sacrificial system will be initiated in order to celebrate Christ's death.[30] This sacrificial system would be analogous to the practice of the Lord's Supper during the Church age. Pentecost argues that the sacrifices will not remove sin, because the blood of animals can never remove sin (Hebrews 10:4). Nonetheless, Feinberg has shown that sacrifices serve an important function in the removal of sins through faith. They did not remove the sins themselves, but pointed to the death of Christ as the thing which would ultimately remove those sins. To return to sacrifices in the millennial kingdom would be like returning to sacrifices today. Once the death of Christ—the reality—has occurred, there can be no more typological foreshadowing practiced.[31] Pentecost argues that these sacrifices in the Millennium are not intended to cover sin; they are a memorial of Christ's death.[32] It is my understanding that Pentecost makes that statement because he, too, understands that there can be no more sacrifices as a means of expressing faith in God who will remove our sin. Yet that is the precise assertion of Ezekiel, who writes of sin offerings in many places (40:39; 43:19, 21, 25; 44:27, etc.) and guilt offerings in other places (40:39; 46:20) in his discussion of the millennial kingdom.[33] The sacrifices mentioned by Ezekiel are specifically for atonement (43:20; 45:17). Dispensationalists have utilized one means of interpreting Ezekiel (memorial sacrifices) because the Old Testament sacrificial system has been replaced, but they have contrived the wrong interpretive scheme. I suggest that Ezekiel's apocalyptic vision should be interpreted as any other text in the genre: understanding reality from the connotation of the symbols used in the text. If that is done, then we would understand the temple, sacrifice and river to generally refer to the immanence and intimacy of God. The text in Ezekiel is worth studying to understand worship in the Millennium, but there will not be animal sacrifice in the Millennium.

There is not space here to discuss all of Ezekiel's vision; let us just focus on some ideas taken from the temple. Ralph H. Alexander writes,

Old Testament apocalyptic literature, as found in these chapters, was to be a source of hope and encouragement in a time of discouragement. Revelation that a temple would be rebuilt in the messianic kingdom to which God's glory would return and in which the nation would worship the Lord as he had commanded would surely be an encouragement of hope. Should not the description of worship in the messianic kingdom be in terms both understandable to Israel as well as in keeping with the covenant worship of her God? . . . The holiness of the Lord's temple and the worship of him are contrasted with the profaning of his name and his temple in Israel's past worship. Israel would have a final opportunity to worship God correctly—in the purity of holiness. Such worship would demonstrate that Israel had truly been redeemed and cleansed.[34]

The mention of the temple and sacrifices is necessary in this Old Testament apocalypse because the original readers could not have conceived of true worship of God without such accouterments. Alexander continues:

Ezekiel sets forth two major purposes for the millennial temple. First, the temple will provide a throne for God among his people (43:6-7), the residency of his glory (43:1-12) from which he will rule over his people. Second, the temple complex will reflect God's holiness by its walls of separation, various courts, and temple divisions (40:5; 42:14-20).[35]

Are we to believe that the priesthood of believers has been abrogated in the Millennium, that the high-priesthood of Christ has been replaced by a descendant of Zadok,[36] that the temple will be able to hold God, that the Bride of Christ—finally assembled—will be snubbed? Rather, Ezekiel's apocalyptic vision of worship in the Millennium provides crucial teaching, but does not provide the literal format for worship. One would not expect it to do so, just as one does not expect the book of Revelation (written in the same literary genre) to provide a literal format for the final conflict. These passages contain symbols to be interpreted and understood. There is a divine message in this revelation. Let us understand it correctly.

Worship in the Millennium will be characterized, then, by a focus and access to Christ, the One who effectively removed the penalty, power and now presence of sin. In His presence, the presence of sin will be removed.

His demand for holiness and obedience will be evident. He will be the focus of our worship.

2. Worship in the Millennium will reflect great joy. This is true if for no other reason than the fact that we will no longer argue over hymns versus choruses (since we will sing a new song) and John doesn't mention drums in the accompaniment!

On a more serious note, Isaiah 35:10 says the redeemed will "enter Zion with singing; everlasting joy will crown their heads. Gladness and joy will overtake them, and sorrow and sighing will flee away." Think of the reason for this joy, for the creation of new songs (Revelation 5:9; 14:3): We will finally reap the reward Jesus purchased for us on the cross. We will be in the very presence of the King because it is He who will reign over the nations; He will judge the nations—and we will judge the world with Him (1 Corinthians 6:2-3). Many churches today exude a modicum of joy during worship, but the millennial gathering will be effusive with joy.

If we could transport that kind of unrestrained outpouring of joy to our day, our culture, our churches, something would seem wrong. We do not yet see Jesus face-to-face. We are not yet unconcerned about the impression made on others. We do not yet realize the incredible work Jesus did on the cross. Some Christians are brought to tears when they think of the change Jesus has wrought at their salvation. But none of us have experienced the transformation from perpetually fighting our sinful nature to the freedom of the glorified body. Worship will be genuinely joyful.

We will not need a charismatic song leader to "whip up" the crowd. We will not have to urge people to sing loudly ("with all your heart") or softly ("meditating on the work of Christ"). We will not have social expectations on worship. It will be a genuine expression of joy. This expression may include dancing, singing, shouting, crying, etc. The actual expression of that joy is irrelevant. We will not even find the form relevant in the Millennium, because we will be freed from our present carnal self-consciousness that either prohibits "dignified" worshipers from shouting, clapping, etc., or impels "exhibitionists" toward such acts.

3. Similar to the joy that comes from knowing the fullness of the work of Christ (not just understanding it, but experiencing it), there will be a sense of awe that comes from our new ability to comprehend God's magnitude. This is the same magnitude that emits flashes of

lightning and peals of thunder from His throne (Revelation 4:5), even when there is no hint of rain. This same magnitude defies explanation by John (and certainly by me). John abandons literal description and resorts to describing God as one having the appearance of jasper and carnelian with a rainbow, resembling an emerald, encircling the throne (4:4). Can there be such a thing in "real life"? No. Our current understanding of substance, color and movement cannot describe the magnitude and majesty of God. Our language is incapable of circumscribing it, and our intellect of comprehending it.

When we receive our glorified bodies (see the preceding discussion), we will see God as He is. Does God veil Himself from us because He is secretive? No. We are neither able to ingest the view of God, nor fit to sustain His immanence. It is no wonder that Old Testament saints assumed it meant death to see God (Exodus 20:19; Judges 13:22). Surely, a full-face view of God by a mortal would be mortal. But we will eventually see God (Job 19:26; Matthew 5:8) and know Him as He knows us (1 Corinthians 13:12; 1 John 3:2).

The worship that will flow from this knowledge will be reverent, sometimes silent, always laudatory and exclusively focused on God. When we see God in this fullness, we have no image to protect, no idols to worship, no ideologies to defend, no mask to wear. We are awestruck by the One who created all things and who will sustain our lives for all eternity. What a blessing it would be (for us and for God) if our worship these days would attain this level of awe for the Creator of the universe.

I recently sat through a series of helpful Bible studies on the *eschaton*. The teacher,[37] as part of his presentation, listed the various kinds of crowns the Bible mentions.[38] There may be some debate whether these are real crowns, a symbol of some reward, or merely a commendation. The descriptions differ so widely, these substances may not even be of one cloth. Regardless, when we see God with our own eyes we will—with the twenty-four elders (Revelation 4:10)—gladly abrogate all reward or commendation to the One who deserves far more attention, praise and honor. At that time, we will no longer seek for others to see our accomplishments. We would not even think of it. We will be too overwhelmed with the weight of God's glory.[39]

4. It has been said that imitation is the sincerest form of flattery. Similarly, holiness seems to be a significant form of worship toward the holy God. Note the description of the millennial temple: Through figurative language, this description points toward the dominant motif of holiness in worship. Since the majority of worshipers will exist in their glorified state, the imitation of God will be natural. In other words, worship in the Millennium will be characterized by holiness in everyday life. Of course, that is the goal today, but we have sinful natures, carnal desires that war against the Spirit at every turn. Worship is limited by our sinfulness. God is not glorified by every activity in life when we are not wholly holy. Worship, today and in the Millennium, is not restricted to a gathering of believers. Worship can exude from every part of life: a father worships God as he nurtures his children with the love and care of God; a construction worker worships God as she displays the attitude of Christ; a lawyer worships God as he strives for divine justice. That will take place in the Millennium. Worship will characterize every part of life, because holiness will reign in the millennial kingdom through our glorified bodies.

5. Because the Church will be complete and its members will be holy, the Church will effectively utilize its complementary gifts (Ephesians 4:11-13) without backbiting, envy, etc. (Galatians 5:25-6:4). Admittedly, this topic belongs more to ecclesiology than to eschatology, but it is worth noting that the Church will finally function as it was intended. Spiritual gifts are intended for bringing the Body of Christ into a state of perfection. Why do I assert that gifts will still be utilized in the Millennium when the Church has reached such a state? Because the millennial kingdom is still a real community.[40] Real life is going on with social interaction between individuals. Since the Church finally will function as it was intended, then worship in that community of believers will be undergirded by solid relationships, clear communication and love. Worship today would be better if we did not have power struggles, personality conflicts and personal agendas. Sometimes the church functions as Satan's ally in creating divisions and factions that inhibit worship. With Satan bound, there will be neither denominations nor theological divisions, neither personal conflicts nor church splits. We

will not be distracted from Christ in our worship by any of these plagues.

6. Finally, I need to mop up several more differences in worship from our age to the millennial age. For one thing, worship will no longer include a sermon. No instruction will be necessary (Jeremiah 31:34). Also, suffering will not be part of our worship there.[41] The sufferings of Jesus will be completed by then (Colossians 1:24). That is why the prophet speaks of a time (properly interpreted as a millennial prophecy) when God will come and save us: "Strengthen the feeble hands, steady the knees that give way; say to those with fearful hearts, 'Be strong, do not fear; your God will come, he will come with vengeance; with divine retribution he will come to save you' " (Isaiah 35:3-4).

Furthermore, there will not be intercessional or confessional worship for all trouble and all sin have been removed. Our worship will focus exclusively on adoration and thanksgiving.

Conclusion

The Millennium will be a time of great worship—worship like we have never seen nor comprehended before. The Bible does not complete the picture of worship, because we are not capable of understanding nor responding to God as we will in the Millennium. It will be a glorious time; we pray for it now ("thy kingdom come"); we long for it now (especially during difficulty). Let us follow the ways of the millennial kingdom: in justice, in obedience, in holiness, in the church, at work and especially in worship.

"Even so, Lord Jesus, come quickly" (Revelation 22:20, author paraphrase).

Endnotes

1. "And he shall come again to judge both the living and the dead" is from the Nicene Creed, A.D. 325.
2. Stuart K. Hine, "How Great Thou Art," copyright 1955 by Manna Music, Inc., Burbank, CA.
3. Jeffrey J. Richards, *The Promise of Dawn: The Eschatology of Lewis Sperry Chafer* (New York: University Press of America, 1991), 186.
4. Note well that I am not referring to the year 2000. I am addressing the period of time when Christ shall return to the earth to establish His kingdom reign.

5. For example, the completion of the Great Commission is partially motivated by the return of Jesus and the inauguration of the Millennium (cf. Matthew 24:14). Additional support for this suggestion is added by the repeated admonitions to "watch," "be alert," "wake up," etc. Although these don't focus on the Millennium, per se, they do focus on the return of the Lord Jesus.

6. I looked in the index of every book in the Wheaton College library in the "Eschatology" section. Precious few of them included any citation pointing to a discussion of worship or sacrifice in the entire work.

7. For example, it has been said by various people in my hearing that "Eschatology is formative for our ecclesiology"; "Ecclesiology is formative for our missiology"; "Our idea of God is crucial for our view of Scripture"; "Our epistemology is foundational for our hermeneutic"; etc. I'm not going to try to demonstrate the truth of any of these assertions here.

8. Bruce Leafblad, associate professor of church music and worship, Bethel College and Seminary (now at Southwestern Seminary), offered this definition at one time: "Worship is communion with God in which believers, by grace, center their mind's attention and their heart's affection on the Lord Himself, humbly glorifying God for who he is and what he does." As adapted by Don Wyrtzen the definition goes like this: "Worship means 'putting the Lord first in your values, your affections and your commitments.' Values have to do with the objective truth (so we preach); Affections deal with emotions (so we have music); Commitments have to do with priorities and convictions (so we live). We worship when we put the Lord first in all these." (parenthetical comments mine; information from "Wyrtzen: Kindred Spirit," by Dallas Theological Seminary, Aut. 1996. Vol. 20, No. 3, p. 8-A through C).

9. D.E. Aune, "Worship, Early Christian," *The Anchor Bible Dictionary*, ed. David Noel Freedman (New York: Doubleday, 1992, 1997).

10. Many of the ideas of this paragraph are condensed from other parts of D.E. Aune's article, "Early Christian Worship."

11. "Worship at his footstool" (Psalm 99:5; 132:7).

12. Cf. the retelling of the story of creation, exodus and redemption that have been historically important for Christian worship.

13. Consider the following choruses: "You are worthy to receive our praise"; "We exalt you"; "We place you on the highest place." There are many other choruses and hymns that reflect this element of worship.

14. Many of the worship passages in the New Testament refer to the triumph won through the death of Christ on the cross, e.g., Colossians 1:20; the Lord's Supper (Luke 22;17-20; 1 Corinthians 11:23-26, etc.); First Corinthians 15:55-57, etc.

15. There can be no more famous example of this than the call to commitment after a sermon and the response song, "Just As I Am." Cf. also such passages as First Corinthians 15:58; First Thessalonians 5:11, etc.

16. Peter T. O'Brien, *Colossians, Philemon*, vol. 44, Word Biblical Commentary (Waco, TX: Word Books, 1982), 58.

17. O'Brien, 61. Notice that I am not utilizing M. Luther's expression of the local vs. the universal church. O'Brien's synthesis of the data makes good use of the Bible and squares with the rest of theology. With him, I refer to the eschatological church and each local gathering of believers as a manifestation of that church. Each church is THE church without excluding any other church as being THE church.

18. Colossians 1:18-20 "serve" from "head of the body" (Christ = head; Church = body); "follow" from "firstborn" (implying there will be many more who will rise from the dead as Christ did); and "gather" from the mention of Christ's redemption in this context.

19. Of course, dispensationalists see the Millennium as the time of sociopolitical salvation to other peoples that is uniquely mediated through national Israel. Cf. Robert Saucy, *The Case for Progressive Dispensationalism: The Interface Between Dispensational & Non-Dispensational Theology* (Grand Rapids: Zondervan, 1993), 321; and J. Dwight Pentecost, *Things to Come: A Study in Biblical Eschatology* (Findley, OH: Dunham, 1958), 519. Further support for the presence of the Church could be garnered by understanding the nature of the Church as the collection of those baptized by the Spirit of Christ. Saucy realizes this is an important issue (although we disagree on the conclusions). He addresses it in pp. 174-86 of his 1993 work.

20. Cf. Job 1; Zechariah 3; Matthew 4; Second Corinthians 2:11; 11:14; 12:7; First Thessalonians 2:18; First Peter 5:8, among others.

21. If one is a premillennialist, then one believes that Christ will return before the Millennium. For the matter at hand, it doesn't matter whether one advocates a pre-, mid-, or posttribulational position for the return of Christ.

22. This gullibility refers to the fall of the angels who rebelled against God (Jude 6; Isaiah 14:12 may refer to Satan; Luke 10:18; Revelation 12:7-9; 2 Peter 2:4). I assert we will not be like them in their gullibility because we have already made the choice to follow Christ. Some of us will have endured great suffering for that decision, but remained faithful to the end—even while struggling with our sinful nature—and so have received our reward. At our glorification, the sinful nature is removed. (Romans 8:30 delineates a progression from God foreknowing the individual, to predestining, calling, justifying and glorifying that individual. This progression is stated in anticipation of its final actualization, but indicates the incomprehensibility of one rebelling against Christ once one has reached the stage of glorification.)

23. The question of how non-glorified individuals got into the millennial kingdom is also part of speculative theology. If one advocates a pre- or midtribulational return of Christ, then these are the ones who have converted to Christ after the Rapture, but before the Millennium and somehow survived the cosmic war (as difficult as that may be). If one advocates a posttribulational return of Christ, then these individuals may be ones who have called out for mercy after the Rapture and before their own destruction. The text specifically mentions that all the armies of the beast will be killed (Revelation 19:19, 21), but others may have remained alive if they submit to the reigning King of the earth, Christ. Of course, this is highly speculative and not worthy of great confidence.

24. In the context, this text primarily refers to the transformations that come in the eternal state (of humans and nature alike), but our glorified bodies will already have realized the objectives of this transformation by the millennial kingdom.

25. Of course, those who are not already God's children will not be transformed to be like Jesus. Each person will become more like he already is: those who follow, like Christ; those who rebel, like Satan. (C.S. Lewis makes this point in *The Great Divorce*, among other places.)

26. The primary focus of the contrast in First Corinthians 15:44-46 between *psychikos* (physical) and *pneumatikos* (spiritual) is probably just a contrast between a body of

flesh and a body quite different. There doesn't seem to be any or much contrast between the carnal and the spiritual.

27. John S. Feinberg, "Salvation in the Old Testament," in *Tradition and Testament*, ed. John S. Feinberg and Paul D. Feinberg (Chicago: Moody, 1981), 67-9.

28. Ibid., 70.

29. Ibid., 71-2.

30. Pentecost, 525.

31. For the nonbeliever, the specific revealed content of faith finally coincides entirely with the basis, or ground, of faith, namely, the death of Christ for our sins (Feinberg, 60). The point I am making in the text has more to do with the believer: The issue is how the believer can have sins removed. It cannot be through obedience to God in sacrifice. It is through *consciously* trusting in the work of Christ.

32. Pentecost, 525. Note also Pentecost's citation, with affirmation, of the following: "Never again will the Lord's Supper be kept after the Saints of God have left the earth to be with the Lord in glory. The resumed sacrifices will be the memorial of the Cross and the whole wonderful story of the redemption for Israel and the nations of the earth, during the kingdom reign of Christ" (Pentecost, 525-6). From Arno C. Gaebelein, *The Prophet Ezekiel*, 312-3.

33. It is important to observe that millennial sacrifices are discussed elsewhere in the OT prophets (Isaiah 56:5-7; 60:7, 13; 66:20-23; Jeremiah 33:15-22; Zechariah 14:16-21).

34. Ralph H. Alexander, "Is Not the Existence of a Temple, Priests, and a Sacrificial System a Retrogression to OT Modes of Worship?" *Ezekiel*, Expositors Bible Commentary, ed. Frank E. Gaebelein (Grand Rapids: Zondervan, 1989), CD-ROM version.

35. Ibid.

36. Ezekiel 40:46. Adding to the confusion of the dispensational system is how the tribulation martyrs can be called "priests of God and of Christ" (Revelation 20:6) when it is unlikely that these individuals are all descendants of Zadok. Perhaps, one could retort, the martyrs will not minister before the Lord. That is true: they will have a more exalted position, reigning with Christ for 1,000 years.

37. Rev. Mark Rohrer, Millersburg, Ohio.

38. First Corinthians 9:25—the incorruptible crown because of mastery over the old man; First Thessalonians 2:19—the crown of rejoicing because of engaging in evangelism; James 1:12—the crown of life for withstanding persecution and temptation; Second Timothy 4:8—the crown of righteousness because we love God's appearing; First Peter 5:4—the crown of glory because of faithful execution of ministry (particularly elders).

39. Cf. C.S. Lewis, *The Weight of Glory* (Grand Rapids: Eerdmans, 1965).

40. Micah 4 is one of several examples (e.g., Isaiah 11; Ezekiel 36:22ff; Jeremiah 31) where there seem to be promises of life continuing in an ideal state. If there were no plowing, there would be no need for plowshares.

41. The churches that have not installed air-conditioning yet believe fully that the suffering of the saints is part of worship.

About the Authors

Keith M. Bailey, LL.D., is a retired pastor, district superintendent and editor living in Dayton, OH.

Matthew A. Cook, Ph.D., is a missionary in Côte d'Ivoire, West Africa.

K. Neill Foster, Ph.D., is President of Christian Publications, Inc., in Camp Hill, PA, the publishing house of The Christian and Missionary Alliance.

William R. Goetz, D.D., is a retired pastor and author living in Linden, AB.

Paul L. King, D.Min., Th.D., is an editorial adjunct and editor of *Classic-Christianity* for Christian Publications, Inc.

Harold Shelly, Ph.D., is Professor of Church History and Religions at Alliance Theological Seminary, Nyack, NY.

Samuel J. Stoesz, Th.D., is a retired seminary professor, pastor, author and editor.

Joel Van Hoogen, M.Div., is a designated Evangelist in the Rocky Mountain District of The Christian and Missionary Alliance and Executive Director of Church Partnership Evangelism, Boise, ID.

Steven L. Ware, Ph.D., at Nyack College, Nyack, NY.

Robert Wetmore, Th.D., at Toccoa Falls College, Toccoa Falls, GA.

Dr. Donald A. Wiggins, D.Min., is Vice-President for National Church Ministries of the U.S. Christian and Missionary Alliance, Colorado Springs, CO.

Eldon Woodcock, Ph.D., is Professor Emeritus of Bible at Nyack College, Nyack, NY.